Qatar and the 2022 FIFA World Cup

"What is striking about the book is the demonstration of balance and a sense of objectiveness in a discussion that has been sorely missing in many academic articles and journalistic pieces published to date. While Qatar's shortcomings—both past and present—are acknowledged, it is refreshing to see a project of this nature resist the temptation of portraying the Gulf state drenched in orientalist stereotype and examine positive changes that have arisen from hosting the World Cup also."

—Dr Thomas Ross Griffin, Assistant Professor of American Literature, *Qatar University, Qatar*

"This book is well-written and balanced. It shows Qatar's ruling elite's sound vision for preserving its distinction and sovereignty. Qatar is carving out a niche on the world stage by investing in sports to transform itself into a nationalistic community distinct from its neighbours and taking pride in its achievements."

—Professor Hilal Khashan, Professor of Political Studies and Public Administration, *American University of Beirut, Lebanon*

"This first fully dedicated academic book on Qatar and the 2022 World Cup provides essential information on how various global actors respond to, and come to challenge, states' attempts at harnessing globalization. A must-read for those interested in understanding the politics and power of small states on the international stage, and the role played by international sports in this regard."

—Dr Cem Tinaz, Director of the School of Sports Science and Technology, *Istanbul Bilgi University, Turkey*

Paul Michael Brannagan • Danyel Reiche

Qatar and the 2022 FIFA World Cup

Politics, Controversy, Change

palgrave
macmillan

Paul Michael Brannagan
Faculty of Business and Law
Manchester Metropolitan University
Manchester, UK

Danyel Reiche
Georgetown University in Qatar
Doha, Qatar

ISBN 978-3-030-96821-2   ISBN 978-3-030-96822-9   (eBook)
https://doi.org/10.1007/978-3-030-96822-9

Cover pattern © Harvey Loake

This Palgrave Macmillan imprint is published by the registered company Springer Nature Switzerland AG.
The registered company address is: Gewerbestrasse 11, 6330 Cham, Switzerland

ACKNOWLEDGEMENTS

Dr Paul Michael Brannagan: there are a number of people that I would thank for their support in the construction of this text. First, all of my colleagues within the department of Economics, Policy and International Business (EPIB) at Manchester Metropolitan University. Special mention here needs to go to Prof Jonathan Grix, Prof Donna Lee, our senior management team (consisting of Leonie Moore, Dimitrios Syrrakos and Catherine Elliott), and everyone in the Sports Policy Unit (SPU). Second, to Prof Richard Giulianotti of Loughborough University, whose guidance and support greatly added to the successful completion of my PhD in 2018 (a PhD that focused on Qatar, and thus provided much of the underpinnings of this text). Finally, to all my family and friends, and especially to Lucy Burman for all her continued love and care, as well as for her propensity to always make me laugh and smile. This book is part of a continuous dedication to the loving memory of Patricia and Michael Brannagan.

    Dr Danyel Reiche: I am grateful for the opportunity Georgetown University Qatar provided me to work in Doha and lead a research initiative on the FIFA World Cup 2022, a once-in-a-lifetime opportunity for a scholar researching sport. This gave me insights into Qatar that I would have otherwise never got. These insights, in combination with Paul Brannagan's expertise from his dissertation on Qatar, became the perfect combination in accomplishing this book. I want to thank Anjali Singh and Ayesha Iqbal, my research assistants at Georgetown University Qatar, whose support and advice in the research and writing process were tremendously helpful. I am dedicating this book to my children Emma and Johan, who are the joy of my life.

CONTENTS

About the Authors

Paul Michael Brannagan is an international relations scholar specializing in the study of major global events. His research primarily focuses on the role and use of sports mega-events by national governments for achieving specific political, economic, social and cultural objectives. To date, his research has centred most specifically on sport in the Middle East, focusing in particular on the State of Qatar and its forthcoming staging of the 2022 FIFA World Cup. His work has been published in leading political science and sports studies journals, including *Leisure Studies, Global Society, Diplomacy and Statecraft* and *International Affairs*. Paul has also (co-)authored and edited various books on the subject of sport and international relations/politics, including *Entering the Global Arena: Emerging States, Soft Power Strategies and Sports Mega-Events* (2019), *The Routledge Handbook of Sport in the Middle East* (2022) and *Comparative Elite Sport Development* (2nd edition, forthcoming). He has also frequently been interviewed and quoted by major media outlets, such as the *BBC World Service, The Independent, Deutsche Welle, The New York Times* and *Sky Sports News*.

Danyel Reiche is a visiting associate professor at Georgetown University Qatar, where he leads a research initiative on the FIFA World Cup 2022. He is a tenured associate professor of comparative politics at the American University of Beirut (AUB) in Lebanon. His past research has focused on two areas: energy and sport policy and politics, with the latter his current priority. He published *Success and Failure of Countries at the Olympic Games* in 2016 (Routledge) and edited with Tamir Sorek a volume entitled *Sport, Politics and Society in the Middle East* (Hurst/Oxford University Press 2019). His peer-reviewed articles have been published in both area study journals, such as *International Journal of Sport Policy and Politics* and *Journal of Energy Policy*, and broader-oriented journals, such as *Third World Quarterly* and *The Middle East Journal*. Dr Reiche has also been invited to write op-eds for leading international newspapers such as *Washington Post* and *Spiegel Online*, and has been frequently interviewed and quoted by major media outlets such as *Le Monde*, *The New York Times* and *The Wall Street Journal*. Reiche is the co-founder of the Sports Scholars in Lebanon Network (LESSN) and chair of the Political Studies Association's Sport and Politics Study Group.

LIST OF FIGURES

LIST OF TABLES

CHAPTER 1

Introduction

Abstract This chapter provides the reader with a background to the political analysis of Qatar and the 2022 FIFA World Cup and to the text itself. It does so by first offering a succinct account of the motives underpinning Qatar's desire to stage one of the largest events on the planet, as well as various responses to FIFA's decision to award Qatar the games. The chapter then progresses towards providing the reader with the key theoretical framework which the authors use throughout the text: small states and international relations; in doing so, it is made clear in this chapter that the authors look to analyse Qatar from a social constructivist-international relations perspective, one that views 'power' in broader terms, encompassing *both* material and subjective factors. Finally, the chapter sets out the structure of the text, and the remaining chapters.

Keywords Small states • International relations theory • 2022 World Cup • Global sport

On 2 December 2010, football's world governing body, the Fédération Internationale de Football Association (FIFA), awarded the State of Qatar (henceforth 'Qatar') the rights to stage one of the largest events on the planet: the 2022 World Cup finals. To many, FIFA's decision was met with much surprise. After all, Qatar, a country that had never competed in a World Cup, exerted little football pedigree, and who had only ever picked up a handful of medals at the Olympic Games, had managed to beat off competition from the likes of the United States (considered favourites by many observers), Australia, Japan and South Korea. Furthermore, with a population of under three million inhabitants, and covering an area of just 4473 square miles, Qatar would be, by some distance, the smallest state ever to host an event of such magnitude.

For the Qataris, securing the rights to the 2022 World Cup provided the state the opportunity to truly cement its position on the global stage. On the one hand, its success in this regard showed not only that the state could positively compete with its larger peers but also that, as the smallest and first ever Middle Eastern country to be awarded either a World Cup or Summer Olympic Games, it could be entrusted with the huge responsibility that comes with organizing and hosting a major sports event.[1] On the other, and perhaps more significantly, the World Cup would provide Qatar with a 'platform', one that sought to be used in an attempt to positively 'open up the gates of communication' between Qatar and the rest of the world, in order to showcase the former's economic and cultural 'distinctiveness' (Hassan Al-Thawadi, secretary general of the Qatar Supreme Committee for Delivery and Legacy, in *The Guardian*, 3 December 2010). Thus, like so many countries who host sports events, for the Qataris there existed the evidential desire to use the spotlight generated by the tournament to inform and educate onlooking global audiences—on who the small state is and what is has to offer, be that in terms of its tourist attractions, its trade and investment opportunities, or the heritage and hospitality of its peoples (see also: Brannagan & Giulianotti, 2015, 2018; Reiche, 2015).

Nonetheless, for some audiences, FIFA awarding Qatar the hosting rights to the 2022 World Cup provided a different opportunity altogether. While the tournament granted Qatar a unique communications platform, the spotlight brought about by the event also provided others a stage on which to critically highlight many of the state's fallacies. Taken together, such criticisms have (to date) manifested around three areas. The first, led mainly by various sporting officials from across the globe, has centred on Qatar's (un)suitability as a major sports event host. At the centre of this debate has been the claim that Qatar acts as a 'high-risk' World Cup destination for visiting fans and athletes, in large part due to the state's summer climate, which, in the hottest months, can reach highs of over 40 °C. In 2014, for instance, FIFA's own chief medical officer, Professor Jiri Dvorak, proclaimed a July–August World Cup in Qatar would equate to a 'highly critical risk' to those expected to travel to the state in 2022 (*The Guardian*, 3 November 2014). A year later, such concerns resulted in FIFA moving the 2022 World Cup to the cooler months of November and December (*The New York Times*, 18 March 2015). This, in turn, culminated in the European Professional Football Leagues—and in particular the English Premier League—as well as the International Olympic Committee (IOC) publicly criticizing such a move, claiming a winter World Cup would severely disrupt national and international sporting calendars (cf. *The Telegraph*, 19 March 2015a). Such disruption has been compounded by safety and security fears over Qatar's plan to locate eight stadiums within a 55 km radius of one another, which will equate, it has been claimed, to 'major crowd management and traffic problems' during the tournament (*BBC*, 14 June 2014).

Second has been the scrutiny concerning accusations of bribery and corruption surrounding Qatar's successful bid to secure the rights to the 2022 World Cup. Amid substantial discussion in the global media and political and sporting spheres on the reasons for the bid's success, UK-based newspaper, *The Sunday Times*, reported to have received numerous streams of emails and other communications from inside the Qatari sports system, which alleged to reveal that the state had breached FIFA rules by bribing key political and sporting officials in order to win favour (see: *The Sunday Times*, 10 March 2019). At the centre of these allegations has been the Qatari Mohammed bin Hammam, at that time president of the Asian Football Confederation and a member of FIFA's executive committee, who, it was claimed, employed multiple slush funds to pay FIFA officials in order to influence the vote. Although FIFA's own ethics investigation cleared Qatar on the grounds that there was 'very limited scope' that its rules had been breached, allegations of corruption have continued (see: *The New York Times*, 6 April 2020), partly owing to the resignation of FIFA's own ethics committee chairman, Michael Garcia, in 2014, after he himself directly accused the governing body of publishing a summary of his report into the bidding for the 2018 (awarded to Russia) and 2022 World Cup finals which contained 'numerous materially incomplete and erroneous representations of facts' (*The Telegraph*, 17 December 2014).

Finally, and arguably most damming, has been the criticism from various international non-governmental organizations and global media networks in relation to Qatar's human development issues at home, relating, for example, to limitations in civil and political rights. Since being awarded the 2022 World Cup, central here has been the intense global scrutiny the state has faced for its treatment of migrant workers, particularly in the construction sector. Global North media outlets, such as the *BBC*, *CNN*, *Le Monde*, *The Guardian* and *The New York Times*, along with Amnesty International and Human Rights Watch, have criticized Qatar for its reluctance to end *kafala*, a sponsorship system that is a product of British colonial rule. This system binds migrant employees from poor regions to their Qatari employers in legal and social terms (see: Millward, 2017). It has been argued that this system abuses the human rights of workers by curtailing basic freedoms (including the banning of labour unions or civil protests), repeated failure to pay wages and consigning them to substandard living and working conditions, leading to the deaths of 'thousands' of workers on Qatari building sites in recent years (*see*: Human Rights Watch, World Report, 2020). Along similar lines, and contrary to 'universal' human rights standards, Qatar has also been condemned by various international organizations for being one of the countries in the world where homosexuality remains illegal (*BBC*, 21 November 2018).

The resulting outcome of all this (thus far) is consequently one with a great deal of irony. Indeed, whilst Qatar intends to use the 2022 World Cup to promote a positive image of the country abroad, the tournament has, in contrast, come to introduce and educate many global audiences to the state in largely negative terms—how many people outside of the Arabian Gulf, for instance, had ever even heard of the term 'kafala' and its associated human rights abuses prior to Qatar being awarded the World Cup in 2010? In offering up the first, fully dedicated academic book on Qatar and the 2022 World Cup, we seek to make sense of the power politics and controversies surrounding the tournament. At the broadest level, this book is concerned with pinpointing and understanding in what ways small states endeavour to achieve what we may call 'globalization-for-state-purposes', referring to attempts by national leaders to actively harness global processes in the pursuit of higher forms of international competitive advantage and domestic growth. Our focus on Qatar is arguably a well-suited case study in this sense: on the one hand, having only gained its full independence in 1971, Qatar is a relatively young state, and one still very much in the midst of achieving its national developmental agenda. On the other, thanks to its abundance of oil and natural gas reserves, the state nonetheless has the capital to favourably engage with globalization in ways that most other states are unable to do so (through, for instance, contributing to the energy security of major states, including

China and the United Kingdom; via large investments in overseas ventures; or the funding and hosting of multiple prestigious global events).

Furthermore, this book is also concerned with how various global actors respond to and come to challenge states' attempts at harnessing globalization. As we discuss in detail in later chapters, while globalization—and subsequent advances in information technology and global communications—has permitted (small) states with new opportunities for power acquisition, influence and progress, so too has it granted non-state actors with greater means through which to keep checks on states' (in) actions, policies and intentions. In pinpointing and discussing the ways through which various actors seek to counter states' global endeavours, Qatar once again arguably provides an exemplary case study: after all, the level of scrutiny the state has received since acquiring the rights to the 2022 World Cup has led some to label the tournament as 'the most controversial ever' sports event (see: *The Telegraph*, 24 February 2015b; *CNN*, 27 May 2015).

Lastly, this book also falls into the realms of what we might call 'sports politics'—that is, the study of the politics within sport itself, as well as the analysis of how sport is used for achieving non-sporting political objectives. Such an analysis does, of course, go beyond simply the politics of major sports events, and when discussing Qatar in this regard, it would be nearly impossible to ignore the state's plethora of other global sporting ventures that have complemented its acquisition of the 2022 World Cup: take, for instance, the 2010 announcement that the Qatar Foundation, Qatar's central organization for educational and cultural development, would become the first ever sponsor of the FC Barcelona shirt, a deal which lasted two years, upon which time Qatar Airways—Qatar's flagship airline carrier—took over; or when, in 2012, Qatar Sports Investments—a subsidiary of the state's sovereign wealth fund, the Qatar Investment Authority—became the sole shareholder of French Ligue 1 club Paris Saint-Germain (after starting to invest into the club in 2011), making it one of only two state-owned professional football clubs in major European football (the other being English Premier League club, Manchester City, owned by members of the Abu Dhabi royal family); and when, in 2015, the Qatar-based media network, beIN Sports, secured the Middle East and North African broadcasting rights to the 2018 and 2022 Winter Olympic Games and the 2020 and 2024 Summer Olympic Games (*IOC*, 27 July 2015). Thus, while our focus here is predominantly on the 2022 World Cup, so too do we look to shed light on the political motives behind, and responses to, Qatar's broader sports strategy. Before doing so, however, we first offer brief comment on the theoretical framework we seek to adopt in our forthcoming analysis of Qatar and the 2022 World Cup.

THEORETICAL FRAMEWORK: SMALL STATES AND INTERNATIONAL RELATIONS

Why might the study of small states be important? One reason would surely be that, if we were to ignore small states altogether, we would be failing to analyse a significant proportion of the international system: indeed, out of the 193 member states who make up the United Nations, 75 (more than one-third) have populations under five million, and, by most accounts, can be considered 'small'. Furthermore, not only do these states form a substantial chunk of the world map as we know it, they also play a vital role within contemporary global society: small states such as Hong Kong and Singapore, for example, boast some of the most lucrative and sought-after financial services worldwide (see: *Global Financial Centres Index*, 2020); then there is the European small state of Norway, which is repeatedly held up as the international benchmark for achievements in human development, standards of living and social equality (see: *UNDP Human Development Index*, 2019); and finally there is the small Trucial State of Dubai, which, in just over a decade, has built 'the region's first successful post-oil economy' (Krane, 2019, p. 19), and emerged as one of the most-visited business and leisure destinations on the planet (see: *MasterCard Global Destinations Cities Index*, 2019). In short, despite their size, small states matter.

Defining what exactly a small state is, nonetheless, is notoriously difficult, and, as is the case with most social science concepts, any definition can only ever be arbitrary. To some, 'small' states can be defined by the relative *size of their population*: the World Bank and the Commonwealth, for example, signify small states as 'sovereign countries with a population of 1.5 million people or fewer', while others more commonly define small states as those with populations exceeding no more than five million (see: World Trade Organization, 2004). Going along with the latter, we could suggest therefore that a state such as Qatar (with a population of just under three million) qualifies as 'small', while Sudan (with a population of just under 44 million) is what we might call a 'medium'-sized state, and China (with a population of 1.4 billion) is most certainly 'large'.

Quantitative measurements of a state's population nonetheless tell us little about state behaviour and, more importantly, the resources at their disposal. This reminds us that 'smallness' is a comparative concept, and is highly dependent on what exactly is being compared (Ingebritsen et al., 2012). Certainly, while Qatar is a smaller state than Sudan from a demographic and geographic standpoint, it is a much larger state in economic terms: Qatar's nominal GDP per capita is currently the 10th highest in the world, standing at $59,143, while it is ranked the 4th highest in the world for its GDP per capita at purchasing power parity, which presently stands at $97,262; in comparison, Sudan currently has the 180th highest nominal GDP per capita, standing at $787, and the 146th highest GDP per capita at purchasing power parity figure, at $4082 (International Monetary Fund, 2021). Additionally, while Sudan lags behind the majority of the world's states in areas of social and human development, Qatar has attracted some of the globe's leading universities to set up branch campuses in its capital city, Doha, and, in doing so, the state has emerged as a regional hub for health, science and technology research and training (see: Khodr, 2011). Thus, small states cannot be summed up by their relative geographic or demographic size alone, as their *resources and capacity* to be innovative and to influence the international system also needs to be taken into account.

Our forthcoming analysis of Qatar and the 2022 World Cup can best be situated in-and-amongst the literature on small states in international relations (henceforth 'IR'). As a field of study, IR seeks to understand the political, economic and cultural (in)actions, strategies and (positive and negative) relations of *states* on the global level. IR thus takes its central unit of analysis to be the 'state', or rather the international state system. A state refers to the 'political apparatus (government institutions, plus civil service officials) ruling over a given territory' (Giddens & Sutton, 2013, p. 1071). The two defining features of a state are that 'it possesses a monopoly over the legitimate use of force' within its borders, and 'its sovereignty is recognized by other states in the international system' (Baylis & Smith, 2005, p. 780). The state occupies such importance to IR scholars due to there being no higher governing power (or 'world government') in existence that exerts authority over sovereign states,[2] thus leaving said states as the dominant actors and key players in international politics (Handler, 2013). In IR, this lack of formal, centralized authority is known as 'anarchy'. Important to note is that, alongside analyses of the state, scholars of IR are also concerned with areas that extend beyond—but nonetheless impact—purely state-to-state relations, such as the role played by non-state actors in international affairs, as well as contemporary threats posed by 'global issues', related to the environment, terrorism or cybercrime.

If indeed the state is IR's main unit of analysis, then the discipline's central concept is that of 'power'. In broad terms, power refers to the ability to 'make or receive change, or to resist it' (Lukes, 2005, p. 478); that is, on the one hand, power is the ability to bring about change in a bid to get what one wants, while on the other it is the capacity to take advantage of or resist the power attempts of others in given—and at times rapidly changing—scenarios. Power analyses thus focus on how actors go about getting what they want. In IR, such a focus centres on the strategies and actions employed by state (and non-state) actors in attempts to get what they want within the international system. Consequently, if IR were a game, with states as the main players, a focus on power would be a focus on how the game is played, who wins and who loses, and why some moves are more effective than others. Power is thus so significant in understanding the dynamics of international politics that, for many, the study of IR can quite simply be defined 'as the analysis of the nature, exercise and distribution of power' (see: Hay, 2002, p. 168).

Despite this significance, power nonetheless remains a highly contested concept, one that has witnessed a sincere lack of consensus within IR. Indeed, as Joseph Nye (1990, p. 177) once remarked: power is like love—it continues to be much 'easier to experience than to define or measure'. This lack of consensus stems from IR's competing theoretical perspectives, and their subsequent treatment of what constitutes 'power' and who has the capacity to wield it. Historically, 'neorealist' and 'neoliberalist' understandings have dominated IR scholarship. In the case of the former, power equates to material possession—that is, economic and, in particular, military strength. Crucially, in an archaic international system, neorealists believe states are rationale, self-interested actors who, above all else, are concerned with external threats and matters of national security. In continuously seeking to ensure their survival, it is believed here that states are most occupied with maximizing their share of material resources, based on the assumption that the balance of power always lies with those who have the largest populations, armed forces and share of global wealth (Mearsheimer, 2007). As small states tend to lack the material resources of their larger neighbours, neorealists have largely deemed them unworthy of investigation. When they have approached the analysis of small states, they have done so from the perspective of *vulnerability*—that is, how and in what ways these states can make up for their lack of material resources in the face of adversity. From a neorealist perspective, small states are therefore considered to be 'weak powers' who exert little influence in their own right, and are left with little choice but to safeguard their survival through cuddling up to 'great (material) powers', a strategy known as 'bandwagoning' (see: Cooper & Shaw, 2009).

In the mid-1970s, a new school of thought emerged which begun to challenge neorealism's dominance in IR: 'neoliberalism'. In particular, neoliberalism questioned neorealism's focus on state security and survival. Like the neorealists, neoliberalists believe in the existence of an anarchic system of self-interested states; however, whereas neorealists perceive anarchy as an all-encompassing, uncontrollable environment which naturally leads states into a position of paranoia, neoliberals argue that over time this system has, in many ways, pacified, allowing states a greater degree of control over external threats (see: Sterling-Folker, 2001). Significantly, neoliberalists argue that the international system has largely become characterized by interdependence and cooperation (as opposed to fragmentation, as is the case of the neorealist account) (Ingebritsen et al., 2012). In particular, neoliberalists point to the emergence of international organizations—such as the United Nations (UN), World Trade Organization (WTO) and the World Bank—who have created opportunities for states to get what they want through cooperation and mutually dependent strategies. Here, the picture for small states somewhat changes from one of vulnerability to one of *resilience*: scholars have pinpointed, for instance, how many international organizations operate on a 'one state, one vote' system, which not only permits small states equal voting rights with their larger peers but also allows them to work together in order to increase their influence on international decision-making (Neumann & Gstöhl, 2004). Nonetheless, for the neoliberals, material clout is still considered to be the greatest source of power, and thus small states are not considered to be able to wield much influence beyond pooling together and voicing their collective concerns at international gatherings, a strategy known as 'balancing' (Braveboy-Wagner, 2010). Thus, for the neoliberalists, acting alone, small states are still considered to be relatively 'weak powers'.

By the 1990s, constructivism emerged which challenged the neorealist and neoliberalist understanding of IR. To the constructivists, the international system is far from simply an objective reality, but rather global politics is, in many ways, a 'world in our making' (Onuf, 1989). In opposition to seeing the interstate system as a static, anarchic one, with material power acting as the greatest influence of self-interested states, constructivists argue that interstate relations are continuously formed by various subjective factors (ideas, rules, norms), which themselves are the products of historical and cultural contexts (Dunne et al., 2013). Constructivists would highlight how, throughout history, national leaders have not solely been concerned with material interests alone, but have equally sought to promote various ideologies, identities and values—take, for example, the Cold War, which, much to the surprise of neorealist and neoliberalist thinkers, ended not through armed conflict, but rather thanks to the revolutionary impact of an idea, specifically Soviet President Mikhail Gorbachev's new way of thinking (see: Snyder, 2005). Key for constructivists is the notion of 'intersubjectivity'—that is, the *shared* norms, values and beliefs that exist amongst states. This is because, for constructivists, the meanings that actors lend to their actions derive not from individual, private beliefs, but rather 'meaningful' action and behaviour is only possible in a sociocultural context based on some form of shared understanding—of what are considered to be 'right' or wrong' actions, or 'attractive' or 'unattractive' behaviours. In this sense, without such shared norms, the very constitution of what 'power' is becomes meaningless (see: Barnett, 2005). Here, the potential for small states to make an impact on the international state system increases greatly. Indeed, for small states whose power is less likely to be found through military means, constructivism opens up the possibility for influence to be wielded via what we may term 'strategic social construction'—that is, the deliberate attempt to (re)shape and influence shared ideas, beliefs and norms (see: Finnemore & Sikkink, 1998).

For the purposes of theoretical transparency, it should be noted that the authors adhere to what can be said to be a social constructivist take on international relations, and, furthermore, seek to apply such a perspective to our forthcoming analysis of Qatar and the 2022 World Cup. In particular, we share the main constructivist critique of neorealism and neoliberalism, that, firstly, 'anarchy' is not a 'one size fits all' model and that states' understanding of an anarchic world is not uniform. Indeed, by locating the subjectivity of actors within the international system, we can suggest that, rather than the existence of one, homogenous form of anarchy, multiple forms of anarchy and world views are in existence, some at different levels of maturity, but which nonetheless all dictate actors' preferences and customs and, ultimately, underpin their behaviour, decision-making and (in)actions. Constructivism thus critiques the neorealist and neoliberalist assumption that all states have the same a priori interests (for more on this, see: Hopf, 2013).

Second, we adhere to the constructivist criticism that neorealist and neoliberalist thinking has, in many ways, failed to appreciate the major changes that have occurred within international society since the end of the Cold War. One such change has been the spread of state capitalist logic beyond the Western, developed world, spurred on by the subsequent global stability brought about by the hegemonic rise of the United States. An evidential outcome of this is that the use of military force has largely given way to the desire to maintain economic prosperity. Ensuring such prosperity requires the free movement of goods, services and capital, which, in turn, necessitate the maintenance of lawful, just and peaceful societies, and thus, in the contemporary epoch, the use of force comes to severely jeopardize one's economic objectives and ability to maintain international competitiveness (see: Cerny, 1997). Linked to this has been advances in information and communications technologies, as well as the growth of international non-governmental organizations, transnational civil society groups and global media networks. Together, these non-state actors have taken advantage of the opportunities provided by the internet and social media in order to more effectively raise their own concerns, many of which go beyond traditional (realist) security matters, related to such areas as human rights, environmentalism, social equality and the like. This, in turn, has not only made publics more aware of issues within and beyond their borders, but has also led them to become more critical of leaders' decisions, exploits and policies, particularly when they are perceived to be immoral, unethical or inhumane. The result is that, in the contemporary epoch, not only has the use of force become less tolerated, but there is now a greater need for political leaders to align their policies to the ideas, values and visions of their—and others'—publics (see: Nye, 2004).

Important to note, nonetheless, is that we are not claiming materialist interests do not matter, which is a common, yet misplaced, critique of constructivist thinking. Rather, our key point here is that, whilst neorealism and neoliberalism consider material power as the greatest form of influence, we suggest that the international state system is driven by *both* material factors (migration, trade, production, security etc.) and subjective patterning (ideologies, values, beliefs etc.); that is, that material and subjective factors constitute a mutual relationship, and it is this mutual relationship which shapes international relations, with the latter playing a significant role in the underpinning and direction of the former (see also: Scholte, 2005; Ritzer, 2010). Note, for instance, how the global stock exchange, a key facet of the international financial economy, is, in-part, run on speculation, belief and hope. Note, too, how threats to state's national security do not solely depend on military capability alone, but can also rest on specific historical and/or sociocultural tensions—on this latter point, take, for example, the attacks of 9/11, which were motivated not by the desire for greater material possession, but were rather the result of a clash of values between the U.S./'western' world, on the one hand, and Islamic fundamentalism, on the other.

Moreover, we are not claiming that there are never any structural limitations to states' actions, nor that (small) states are simply 'free' to do as they like. Indeed, while Qatar's natural resources provide it with more capital and thus more possibilities than most (small, medium or even some large) states, its geographic size nonetheless means it is unable to escape many of the constraints facing all small states, such as a relative lack of available human resources, or the threat of invasion by larger neighbours. Additionally, we recognize that choices are always constrained by intersubjectivity and a shared set of meanings, rules, codes, norms and social practices that govern behaviour and action (see also: Guzzini, 2000). Or, put differently, that structural forces and the agency of actors are 'mutually causative'; that is to say, that there is a complex interplay at work between the constraints of structures on the one hand and the autonomy of actors on the other. This creates a 'double involvement' or interdependence in which actors (states, non-state actors, transnational corporations etc.) collectively create the rules and norms that constitute the international normative system, and are, at the same time, created, guided and reproduced by these same set of rules and norms (see: Bilton et al., 2002).

Consequently, in adopting a social constructivist IR stance, and through our case study of Qatar and the 2022 World Cup, in what follows we seek to join those who have sought to identify how small states seek to strategically and creatively innovate in a bid to make up for their structural vulnerabilities in material *and* symbolic terms (see: Cooper & Shaw, 2009; Lee & Smith, 2010). In doing so, we also look to pinpoint how, in turn, such endeavours also generate certain consequences and responses from others, responses which at times potentially come to add new constraints and limitations for small states to confront—in the case of Qatar, note, for instance, the negative media scrutiny the state has had to endure since its awarding of the World Cup in December 2010; or the regional backlash to Qatar's independent foreign policy attempts, culminating in June 2017 in an air and sea blockade and the cutting of diplomatic ties by four of its Middle Eastern neighbours (Saudi Arabia, the United Arab Emirates, Bahrain and Egypt).

STRUCTURE AND MAIN ARGUMENTS

The remainder of the book proceeds as follows. In Chap. 2, we provide a brief history of Qatar, and, in doing so, we chart the state's development from a small pearl fishing settlement in the nineteenth century, to its modern-day foundations as a major natural gas exporting country and international hub for politics, science and culture. Within this chapter, we also highlight many of Qatar's concerns: namely, anxieties over its security and survival as a small state, as well as its desire to retain an independent foreign policy; the need to diversify its national economy and move away from its heavy reliance on hydrocarbon revenues; the health and well-being of its citizens; and confronting the negative scrutiny that has occurred after the awarding of the forthcoming 2022 World Cup finals. Then, in Chap. 3, we identify the ways in which global sport and the 2022 World Cup seek to be used to achieve Qatar's broader, non-sporting objectives; in doing so, we seek to be the first to analyse Qatar's sporting pursuits from a small state perspective, arguing how the staging of major sports events not only help the state to overcome many of its (small state) vulnerabilities, but also how they provide Qatar with a competitive niche within the international state system. Next, Chap. 4 focuses on the negative scrutiny that has surrounded the 2022 World Cup, and, in doing so, identifies the range of non-state actors who have sought to globally highlight Qatar's fallacies. We argue in this chapter that international critique from non-state actors—particularly specific non-governmental organizations and the global media—has revolved around three key areas: *Qatar's human rights record; accusations of bribery and corruption; and Qatar as a sports event destination.* We discuss each in turn, and pinpoint how such scrutiny has come to significantly damage the state's soft power attempts. Chapter 5 is our final, and concluding, chapter, and looks to identify the key opportunities and challenges facing Qatar leading up to, and beyond, 2022. Within this chapter, we pinpoint and discuss three overarching areas that we argue will be of crucial significance to Qatar in the coming years: *delivering a successful World Cup; maintaining an independent foreign policy; and continuing with domestic reforms.* In this closing chapter, we also identify areas for potential future research on Qatar and the 2022 World Cup.

NOTES

1. This was a point echoed by Hassan Al-Thawadi, the secretary general of the Supreme Committee for Delivery & Legacy (SC), shortly after Qatar was awarded the tournament: 'We acknowledge there is a lot of work to do and we stand by our promise and we will honour the sacred trust given to us today' (*The Guardian*, 3 December 2010).
2. Although we might point here to organizations such as the United Nations or the World Trade Organization as examples of such 'world governments', we must remember that these organizations are, to a great or lesser extent, 'creatures of their members'—that is, they can do no more than their sovereign member states allow them to do (see Heywood, 2014, p. 8); furthermore, in the case of the United Nations, one needs to remember that (veto) power and key decision-making lie with the Security Council, which is made up of only five permanent member states (China, France, Russia, the United Kingdom and the United States).

REFERENCES

Barnett, M. (2005). Social constructivism. In J. Baylis (Ed.), *The globalization of world politics: An introduction to international relations.* Oxford University Press.

Baylis, J., & Smith, S. (2005). *The globalization of world politics: An introduction to international relations.* Oxford University Press.

BBC. (2014, June 14). Qatar 2022 World Cup a 'high security risk', report claimed [online]. Retrieved February 18, 2021, from https://www.bbc.co.uk/sport/football/27852582

BBC. (2018, November 21). Qatar World Cup 2022: Four years out, what do we know sao far? [online]. Retrieved February 11, 2021, from https://www.bbc.co.uk/sport/football/46294929

Bilton, T., Bonnet, K., Jones, P., Lawson, T., Skinner, D., Stanworth, M., & Webster, A. (2002). *Introductory sociology.* Palgrave.

Brannagan, P. M., & Giulianotti, R. (2015). Soft power and soft disempowerment: Qatar, global sport and football's 2022 World Cup finals. *Leisure Studies, 34*(6), 703–719.

Brannagan, P. M., & Giulianotti, R. (2018). The soft power–soft disempowerment nexus: The case of Qatar. *International Affairs, 94*(5), 1139–1157.

Braveboy-Wagner, J. (2010). Opportunities and limitations of the exercise of foreign policy power by a very small state: The case of Trinidad and Tobago. *Cambridge Review of International Affairs, 23*(3), 407–427.

Cerny, P. G. (1997). Paradoxes of the competition state: The dynamics of political globalization. *Government and Opposition, 32*(2), 251–274.

CNN. (2015, May 27). FIFA in crisis: The men who have been charged [online]. Retrieved July 25, 2021, from http://edition.cnn.com/2015/05/27/football/fifa-arrests-webb-warner-marin/

Cooper, A. F., & Shaw, T. (2009). *The diplomacies of small states.* Palgrave Macmillan.

Dunne, T., Kurki, M., & Smith, S. (2013). *International relations theories: Discipline and diversity* (3rd ed.). Oxford University Press.

Finnemore, M., & Sikkink, K. (1998). International norm dynamics and political change. *International Organization, 52*(04), 887–917.

Giddens, A., & Sutton, P. W. (2013). *Sociology* (7th ed.). Polity.

Global Financial Centres Index. (2020). The Global Financial Centres Index [online]. Retrieved November 10, 2021, from https://www.longfinance.net/programmes/financial-centre-futures/global-financial-centres-index/

Guzzini, S. (2000). A reconstruction of constructivism in international relations. *European Journal of International Relations, 6*(2), 147–182.

Handler, S. P. (2013). *International Politics: Classic and Contemporary Readings.* CQ Press.

Hay, C. (2002). *Political analysis: A critical introduction.* Palgrave Macmillan.

Heywood, A. (2014). *Global Politics.* Basingstoke: Palgrave Macmillan.

Hopf, T. (2013). The promise of constructivism in international relations theory. In S. P. Handler (Ed.), *International Politics: Classic and contemporary readings.* Sage.

Human Rights Watch, World Report. (2020). [online]. Retrieved February 14, 2021, from https://www.hrw.org/world-report/2020#

Ingebritsen, C., Neumann, I., & Gsthl, S. (Eds.). (2012). *Small states in international relations.* Washington: University of Washington Press.

International Monetary Fund. (2021). GDP per capita [online]. Retrieved July 07, 2021, from https://www.imf.org/external/datamapper/NGDPDPC@WEO/OEMDC/ADVEC/WEOWORLD

IOC. (2015, July 27). IOC awards 2018–2024 broadcast rights in Middle East and North Africa [online]. Retrieved July 26, 2021, from https://www.olympic.org/news/ioc-awards-2018-2024-broadcast-rights-in-middle-east-and-north-africa

Khodr, H. (2011). The dynamics of international education in Qatar: Exploring the policy drivers behind the development of Education City. *Journal of Emerging Trends in Educational Research and Policy Studies, 2*(6), 514–525.

Krane, J. (2019). *Energy kingdoms.* Columbia University Press.

Lee, D., & Smith, N. J. (2010). Small state discourses in the international political economy. *Third World Quarterly, 31*(7), 1091–1105.

Lukes, S. (2005). Power and the battle for hearts and minds, *Millennium-Journal of. International Studies, 33*(3), 477–493.

MasterCard Global Destinations Cities Index. (2019). [online]. Retrieved February 15, 2021, from https://newsroom.mastercard.com/wp-content/uploads/2019/09/GDCI-Global-Report-FINAL-1.pdf

Mearsheimer, J. J. (2007). Structural realism. *International Relations Theories: Discipline and Diversity, 83,* 77–94.

Millward, P. (2017). World Cup 2022 and Qatar's construction projects: Relational power in networks and relational responsibilities to migrant workers. *Current Sociology, 65*(5), 756–776.

Neumann, I. B., & Gstöhl, S. (2004). *Lilliputians in Gulliver's World?: Small states in international relations.* Centre for Small State Studies, Institute for International Affairs, University of Iceland.

Nye, J. S. (1990). Soft power. *Foreign Policy, 80,* 153–171.

Nye, J. S. (2004). *Soft Power: The means to success in world politics.* Public Affairs.

Onuf, N. G. (1989). *World of Our Making: Rules and Rule in Social Theory and International Relations.* Columbia: University of South Carolina Press.

Reiche, D. (2015). Investing in sporting success as a domestic and foreign policy tool: The case of Qatar. *International Journal of Sport Policy and Politics, 7*(4), 489–504.

Ritzer, G. (2010). *Globalization: A basic text.* Wiley-Blackwell.

Scholte, J. A. (2005). *Globalization: A critical introduction.* Palgrave Macmillan.

Snyder, R. S. (2005). Bridging the realist/constructivist divide: The case of the counterrevolution in Soviet foreign policy at the end of the Cold War. *Foreign Policy Analysis, 1*(1), 55–71.

Sterling-Folker, J. (2001). Evolutionary tendencies in realist and liberal IR theory. In *Evolutionary Interpretations of World Politics* (pp. 62–109). Routledge.

The Guardian. (2010, December 03). Football crosses new frontier as Qatar wins World Cup vote for 2022 [online]. Retrieved January 11, 2021, from https://www.theguardian.com/football/2010/dec/03/qatar-world-cup-2022

The Guardian. (2014, November 03). Fifa confirms 2022 World Cup in Qatar is likely to be held in winter [online]. Retrieved June 12, 2021, from https://www.theguardian.com/football/2014/nov/03/fifa-qatar-2022-world-cup-winter

The New York Times. (2015, March 19). FIFA confirms winter World Cup for 2022 [online]. Retrieved September 05, 2021, from https://www.nytimes.

com/2015/03/20/sports/soccer/fifa-confirms-winter-world-cup-for-2022.html

The New York Times. (2020, April 06). U.S. says FIFA officials were bribed to award World Cups [online]. Retrieved April 11, 2021, from https://www.nytimes.com/2020/04/06/sports/soccer/qatar-and-russia-bribery-world-cup-fifa.html

The Sunday Times. (2019, March 10). Take it or leave it: Qatar's lucrative World Cup offer to FIFA [online]. Retrieved February 04, 2021, from https://www.thetimes.co.uk/article/take-it-or-leave-it-qatars-lucrative-world-cup-offer-to-fifa-qdj5fkxxm

The Telegraph. (2014, December 17). Fifa report into World Cup bid process 'misrepresented' says investigator Michael Garcia [online]. Retrieved May 13, 2021, from http://www.telegraph.co.uk/sport/football/world-cup/11228523/Fifa-has-misrepresented-my-report-says-investigator.html

The Telegraph. (2015a, March 19). World Cup 2022 final in Qatar will be on December 18 [online]. Retrieved May 26, 2021, from https://www.telegraph.co.uk/sport/football/world-cup/11483629/World-Cup-2022-final-in-Qatar-will-be-on-December-18.html

The Telegraph. (2015b, February 24). Qatar 2022 World Cup—the logistical nightmare before Christmas that will make Die Hard 2 look tame [online]. Retrieved March 27, 2021, from https://www.telegraph.co.uk/sport/football/world-cup/11432515/Qatar-2022-World-Cup-the-logistical-nightmare-before-Christmas-that-will-make-Die-Hard-2-look-tame.html

UNDP Human Deveopment Index. (2019). Annual Report [online]. Available at: https://hdr.undp.org/sites/default/files/hdr2019.pdf (Accessed 12.03.20)

World Trade Organization. (2004). Income volatility in small and developing economies: Export concentration matters [online]. Retrieved February 03, 2021, from https://www.wto.org/english/res_e/booksp_e/discussion_papers3_e.pdf

CHAPTER 2

The State of Qatar: A Background

Abstract This chapter offers up a background to Qatar. It does so by first focusing on the early formation of the 'state' of Qatar in nineteenth century, as well as highlighting the key moments in the state's political and economic developments throughout the twentieth century. Finally, the chapter discuss Qatar's more recent foreign policy endeavours, and pinpoints the (small state) concerns the state currently faces in the contemporary epoch. The chapter concludes by drawing together a number of evidential small states trends that have come to define Qatar's approach to regional and international affairs.

Keywords Qatar • Arabian Gulf history • Middle East politics • Small state foreign policy

The 'State of Qatar' is a sovereign state, located on the peninsula of the Arabian Gulf (also known as the 'Persian Gulf', or simply 'the Gulf'). Covering an area of 4473 square miles, the state is the seventh smallest country in Asia by landmass, and the third smallest in the Middle East (World Bank, 2019). Qatar is connected by land only to Saudi Arabia, its larger neighbour to the south, with the rest of the state's territory surrounded by the Persian Gulf Sea. To the northwest lies Qatar's smaller

© The Author(s), under exclusive license to Springer Nature   19
Switzerland AG 2022
P. M. Brannagan, D. Reiche, *Qatar and the 2022 FIFA World Cup*,
https://doi.org/10.1007/978-3-030-96822-9_2

neighbour, Bahrain, and to the east are the seven emirate states who form the United Arab Emirates. To the north lies the state of Iran, with whom Qatar shares a maritime border. Qatar's territory also comprises a number of smaller islands, most notable of which is Halul (to the east of the mainland), which acts as a strategic storage site for the state's natural oil extraction. Like its Gulf neighbours, Qatar's terrain can be described as a mostly sandy, barren desert, one that endures extreme temperatures—in the summer months of June, July and August, temperatures in Qatar can reach more than 40 °C, while in the cooler months of December and January, temperatures rarely drop below 15 °C.

As of 2021, Qatar's total population stands at 2.642 million, consisting of roughly 1.895 million males, and 746,687 females (Qatar Ministry of Planning and Statistics, 2021). The capital city, Doha, is located on Qatar's eastern shoreline, and is by far the state's most populated area, with 77% of the state's entire population living either in the city itself, or in the surrounding suburbs of Al Rayyan and Al Wakra (Qatar Ministry of Planning and Statistics, 2020). Of note is that 89% of Qatar's total inhabitants are expatriate workers, the majority of whom hail from some of the poorest countries in South Asia, including Bangladesh, India, Nepal, Sri Lanka and the Philippines (see: Snoj, 2019). The result is that Qatari's themselves account for a mere 333,000 of the state's overall population, acting as the fourth largest national group in the country after people from India (700,000), Bangladesh and Nepal (400,000 each) (see: Snoj, 2019). The composition of this numerically smaller group is 51% Qatari females, compared with 49% Qatari males (Qatar Ministry of Planning and Statistics, 2018). Although the official language of Qatar is Arabic, English has become the de facto second language, due to the majority of the state's indigenous citizenry receiving some form of English-taught education, either in Qatar itself or abroad. Islam is the dominant religion amongst Qataris, with 90% following the Sunni doctrine of Islam, while 10% adhere to Shia Islam.

Politically, Qatar is governed as an 'absolute monarchy'—that is, a form of governance within which the monarch holds supreme monocratic authority. The Emir of Qatar is Sheikh Tamim bin Hamad Al Thani, who has ruled over the state since his father, Sheikh Hamad bin Khalifa Al Thani, voluntarily abdicated power in 2013—a move seldom witnessed anywhere in the Middle East. Regionally, Qatar is a member of the Gulf Cooperation Council (GCC), an interstate grouping of neighbouring countries—Bahrain, Kuwait, Oman, Qatar, Saudi Arabia and the United

Arab Emirates—with the goal of ensuring a politically stable environment for fast-paced national and regional development. Furthermore, since 2003, Qatar's Al Udeid Air Base has acted as the United States' Middle East Central Command headquarters. As we discuss further in this chapter, the housing of a U.S. Air base offers Qatar much needed security and, in many ways, makes up for the state's relative lack of its own military—latest figures show that Qatar has an active military personnel of just 16,500; 12,000 of whom form the state's national army, 2500 its naval forces and 2000 its air force (see: International Institute for Strategic Studies' Military Balance Report, 2020).

Despite its relative lack of military resources, economically, Qatar records some of the highest gross domestic product (GDP) per capita incomes worldwide. Indeed, as we saw in Chap. 1, Qatar's nominal GDP per capita is currently the tenth highest in the world, standing at $59,143, while it is ranked the fourth highest in the world for its GDP per capita at purchasing power parity, which presently stands at $97,262 (see: International Monetary Fund, 2021). Such wealth is derived chiefly from the state's sale of hydrocarbon resources. Qatar has proven oil reserves of 25.2 billion barrels, and produces on average 1.5 million barrels per day (b/d), making it the 17th largest exporter of crude oil worldwide (see: U.S. Energy Information Database, 2019). Most notable in this regard however is Qatar's exploits in the sale of natural gas. Qatar is the world's largest exporter of liquefied natural gas (LNG), exporting on average 77 million metric tons per year (Dourian, 2020). In reserve, the state holds 872.1 trillion cubic feet of natural gas, the third largest reserve held by any one state, and equivalent to 12.5% of total reserves held worldwide (ibid.)

Such wealth has come to radically transform Qatar's urban landscape, as well as provide its citizens with the kind of life rarely found elsewhere, in part for their political allegiance and support. Qatar's capital, Doha, for instance, has been developed from a small fishing town into a large, glitzy metropolis in a matter of decades. Such changes have been driven by what Rizzo (2014, p. 51) calls Qatar's 'megaproject phase', referring to the state's 'tendency to build large, themed urban projects in an effort to emulate similar, popular developments taking shape in the rest of the Gulf region', most particularly in neighbouring Abu Dhabi and Dubai. Take, for example, the 2022 World Cup, a project that Qatar is dedicating $500 million a week towards the construction of related infrastructure, including the building of Lusail, an entire new city 10 miles north of

Doha, which, upon completion, will host the final of the tournament (*The Guardian*, 7 February 2017). Furthermore, for Qataris themselves, a well-paid job in the public sector is guaranteed to all high school and university graduates, no national citizen is required to pay tax, healthcare or utilities bills, education costs are fully subsidized, and Qataris are eligible to receive plots of land and an interest-free loan of up to QR850,000 (equivalent to $233,452) towards its development (Rathmell & Schulze, 2006).

Its hydrocarbon wealth has also allowed Qatar to ambitiously invest in numerous lavish ventures abroad. The Qatar Investment Authority (QIA), Qatar's state-owned, sovereign wealth fund, which holds assets in the region of $295 billion (*Reuters*, 14 October 2020a), has been a key player in this regard, and, in recent years, has acquired shares in Barclays Bank PLC, Miramax Films, Royal Dutch Shell, J Sainsbury PLC and Volkswagen; in London alone, Qatar Holdings, the real-estate arm of the QIA, owns shares in Heathrow Airport, Harrods, Canary Wharf, the newly built Shard building, Chelsea Barracks and the London 2012 Olympic Village (see: Brannagan, 2017; Brannagan & Rookwood, 2016). Adding to this is, of course, the 2011 purchase of Paris Saint-Germain by the QIA's sports subsidiary, the Qatar Sports Investment Group, for a reported fee of €100 million (£89 million).

As we discuss in detail in Chap. 3, global endeavours such as the above break with many understandings of what small states 'should' be able to achieve in international affairs, and, in many ways, so too do they help Qatar punch far above its weight in both real and symbolic terms. Before delving deeper into Qatar's international sporting pursuits, in this chapter we first offer a crucial background to the state. We do so by starting with the early formation of the 'state' of Qatar, as well as highlight the key moments in the state's political and economic developments throughout the twentieth century. Finally, we discuss Qatar's more recent foreign policy endeavours and pinpoint the (small state) concerns the state currently faces in the contemporary epoch. We conclude by drawing together a number of evidential small states trends that have come to define Qatar's approach to regional and international affairs.

QATAR: STATE FORMATION

For many, the formation of the 'state' of Qatar started with Sheikh Muhammed bin Thani in the mid-nineteenth century. Up until this period, Qatar was not the unified nation that it is today, but was rather occupied by groups of dispersed tribes. There were, for example, the various nomadic Bedouin tribes, who roamed Qatar's desert lands, settling in one area for only a short time. Then there was the 'hadar'—that is, the coastal 'settled' tribes, who occupied the various small towns across the Qatari peninsula, and whose principal activities included pearl diving, fishing and the trading of local goods (Zahlan, 1979; Al-Hammadi, 2018). During the mid-eighteenth century, one of the largest populated towns was Al Zubara, located on Qatar's north-western shoreline. Benefiting from its central location within the Arabian Gulf, as well as its immediate access to one of the most abundant pearling seas in the world, in the later-part of the eighteenth century, Al Zubara had developed into Qatar's most vibrant commercial town, and one of the principal trading hubs across the Arab world.

Al Zubara's growing commercial success, nonetheless, generated external interest amongst its rivals, and from 1777 onwards, the town came under regular attacks by the Persian Governor of neighbouring Bahrain (Wright, 2011). For most of the eighteenth century, Al Zubara had largely been ruled by the Kuwaiti-derived Al-Khalifa tribe, who, in 1783, along with local Qataris, launched a successful counterattack on Persian forces in Bahrain. Seeing an opportunity, the Al-Khalifa subsequently took control of the islands of Bahrain, but, in doing so, ceased much of their rule over Al Zubara (ibid.; see also: Zahlan, 1979). In 1800, Bahrain was then invaded by Oman, after a tax dispute developed between the Al-Khalifa and the Imamate of Muscat. At the time, Muscat and the Saudi Arabian Al-Saud tribe were involved in a long-standing rivalry, which prompted Qatari tribes loyal to the Al-Saud to launch a counterattack, one that largely defeated Muscat forces in Bahrain, and, in doing so, handed rule over both Bahrain and Al Zubara to the Al-Saud. In a twist of events, in 1811 a coalition of Ottoman and Egyptian forces then attacked the Najd region of Saudi Arabia, which resulted in the majority of Al-Saud forces in Bahrain and Zubara being ordered to return home. Once again seeing an opportunity, the Al-Khalifa took advantage of this now political void by signing an agreement with the Imamate of Muscat, one that effectively made them an Oman tributary if they were restored to power in Bahrain

(Wright, 2011). In seeking to quash any further Al-Saud or Qatari counters in Bahrain, Muscat forces carried out targeted attacks on Qatar's western shoreline, which, in 1811, resulted in the burning and flattening of Al Zubara (see: Rahman, 2005).

The fall of Al Zubara opened up the opportunity for other towns across the Qatari peninsula to benefit from new commercial activities. One such town was Doha, which had grown from a tiny fishing village in the eighteenth century into a large town by the mid-nineteenth century (Zahlan, 1979). In 1849, Sheikh Muhammed bin Thani moved to Doha. Although moving to Doha initially for commercial reasons, he was soon able to establish himself as 'Chief of Doha'. In 1851, Emir Faisal bin Turki Al-Saud from the Nejd region of Saudi Arabia sought Qatar's assistance in regaining control over Bahrain. In doing so, Emir Faisal first reached out to Sheikh Muhammed, the latter of whom was only too happy to unite with Al-Saud forces, due to ongoing fears of a further invasion of Qatar by the Bahraini Al-Khalifa tribe (see: Wright, 2011). Importantly, this mutual agreement between Qatar and the Al-Saud helped symbolically position Sheikh Muhammed as not only Chief of Doha, but now also 'Ruler of Qatar' (ibid.).

Sheikh Muhammed's position as the 'Ruler of Qatar' was further solidified when British Forces entered the Arabian Gulf in the late-1860s. In 1868, due to continued tensions between Qatar and Bahrain, a dispute broke out between the countries which resulted in Sheikh Muhammed's son, Sheikh Jassim bin Muhammed Al-Thani, being captured and arrested by Bahraini forces (Wright, 2011). In 1867, Bahraini militaries, along with the help of Abu Dhabi, led an assault on Doha, with Qatari forces responding the following year with a counter-invasion of Bahrain, during which Qatar was able to secure the release of Sheikh Jassim. The back-and-forth events of the late-1880s led British forces to get involved in the despite, which ended when Britain mediated a peace treaty between Bahrain and Qatar in September 1868 (Zahlan, 2016). Crucially, this also signalled Britain's formal recognition of Sheikh Muhammed as Qatar's ruler, which, in turn, allowed him the greater ease through which to consolidate his power. Sheikh Muhammed is thus considered to be the first ruler of Qatar, and played a vital role in setting the groundwork for the future unification of Qatari tribes, and the very statehood of Qatar itself.

In 1878, Sheikh Muhammed died, at which point Sheikh Jassim, succeeded him. Although Sheikh Muhammed is credited with laying the foundations for Qatar's unification, it is Sheikh Jassim who is today celebrated as the 'founder of Qatar'. Such a title is symbolic of Jassim's vital role during the Ottoman expansion efforts into Qatar during the late nineteenth century. At the time, the two dominant powers across the Gulf were the British and Ottomans, whose rivalry grew as they simultaneously expanded their control. This was something that Jassim and Qatar took advantage of. While the British, with its dominant navy, controlled the sea, the Ottoman expansion was an increasing land-threat for Qatar and its neighbours. Whilst maintaining good terms with the British, in 1872 Qatar simultaneously became an officially recognized 'Kaza' (small district) of the Ottoman Empire, with Jassim occupying the role of 'Qaim Maqam', or 'regional governor' (Fromherz, 2012). This suited Qatar in two specific ways. First, by keeping close relations with the two dominant powers of the day, Qatar helped to ensure its survival—indeed, as Wright (2011, p. 116) asserts on Qatar's dealings with the Ottomans, 'the trend of Qatar pragmatically using a foreign power as a guarantor of its security had [by this time] thus become firmly established'. Second, Qatar was also able to strategically play international powers off against one another, which not only guarded against security 'mono-dependence', but also provided the state with a degree of control over its fate, a tactic Qatar would come to employ again and again (see: Wright, 2012, p. 298).

In the case of the Ottomans, such a tactic did, nonetheless, last only so long for Qatar. Over time, relations between the Ottomans and Qatar broke down, after it became apparent that the former were more interested in repelling British expansion attempts than actually benefitting the Al Thani; added to this was Jassim's unwillingness to ever allow the Ottomans to truly establish any effective presence in Qatar (see: Fromherz, 2012). On the back of this growing tension, in 1892 the Ottomans sent 200 armed soldiers to Doha to establish a greater Ottoman presence in Qatar. Such an act prompted Qatari tribes to unite against this external invader. Held up at the fortress of Wajbah on the outskirts of Doha, Jassim and a small contingent of Qatari tribes successfully repelled Ottoman forces. Symbolically, this showed the Ottomans that the Qataris 'were not simply a dispersed group of tribes that happened to inhabit a strategic peninsula', but rather they were a collective force to be respected (ibid., p. 61; see also: Kurşun, 2002). From then on, although Ottoman presence in Qatar continued, the Qataris were treated as allies rather than foes. Crucially, in successfully uniting Qatari tribes against the Ottomans, Jassim and the Al Thani's rule was further solidified, and the unified 'state' Qatar was born. Since 2007, the Qatar National Day (also known as 'Founder's

Day'), which is a national holiday that takes place on 18 December each year, celebrates the state's unification in the late nineteenth century, and commemorates Sheikh Jassim's role as the 'founder of Qatar'.

QATAR AS A BRITISH PROTECTORATE

In 1913, Sheikh Abdullah bin Jassim Al-Thani came to power, after Sheikh Jassim retired. In the same year, the Anglo-Ottoman convention took place, which effectively renounced much of Ottoman control across the Gulf, including influence over Qatar (Rahman, 2005). Importantly, the convention cleared the way for Sheikh Abdullah to sign a protection treaty with the British in 1916. Unlike the 1868 agreement between Qatar and the British, the 1916 treaty was a more formal, legal arrangement, and provided Qatar with official 'protectorate' status (Exell & Rico, 2013). The guarantee of British protection was crucial, as it was around this time that tensions escalated between Qatar and Saudi Arabia. The death of Sheikh Jassim had provided a brief period of political instability in Qatar, something that Sheikh Abdullah feared might be used by the Saudi's in any expansion attempts. Thus, in looking to ensure Qatar's safety and his own position, Sheikh Abdullah's signing of the 1916 treaty with the British was not only personally symbolic, but it also guaranteed that Britain would protect both Abdullah and Qatar from any external aggressor (Fromherz, 2012). Like before, Qatar had thus once again sought to ensure its survival by forging strategic external relationships, with both the state and Abdullah now formally supported and protected by *the* super-power of the day (Kamrava, 2013).

Although the 1916 agreement gave up Qatar's rights to act as an independent actor in foreign affairs, the state did retain autonomy over its domestic decision-making. This was crucial to Qatar's overall development. Indeed, Wright (2011) notes how the 1916 treaty with Britain allowed Qatar a long-period of peace and stability; this, in turn, ensured the state the time and space to mature, both politically and economically, as well as further cemented the Al-Thani's position as the 'rightful' rulers of Qatar—indeed, by the time Qatar gained its independence from the British in 1971, the Al-Thani's had ruled over the state for over 100 years, with Sheikh Ali bin Abdullah Al-Thani taking over after Sheikh Abdullah's abdication in 1949, and then Sheikh Ahmad bin Ali Al-Thani assuming power from 1960–1972 (see Fig. 2.1).

Fig. 2.1 Timeline of the Al-Thani rule over Qatar

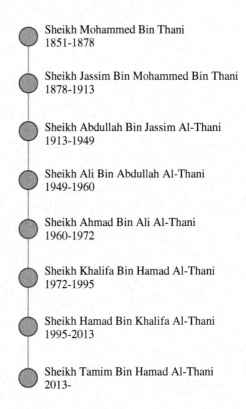

Sheikh Mohammed Bin Thani
1851-1878

Sheikh Jassim Bin Mohammed Bin Thani
1878-1913

Sheikh Abdullah Bin Jassim Al-Thani
1913-1949

Sheikh Ali Bin Abdullah Al-Thani
1949-1960

Sheikh Ahmad Bin Ali Al-Thani
1960-1972

Sheikh Khalifa Bin Hamad Al-Thani
1972-1995

Sheikh Hamad Bin Khalifa Al-Thani
1995-2013

Sheikh Tamim Bin Hamad Al-Thani
2013-

Nonetheless, during Sheikh Abdullah's rule, Qatar came to witness severe economic hardship, something almost unimaginable today. Indeed, with the collapse of the pearl trade in the 1930s, and the negative impact on oil exportation caused by the outbreak of the Second World War, Qatar's national economy witnessed a significant downturn, so much that there were reports of Qataris dying of starvation—hence, this period of Qatar's history is known as the 'years of hunger' (see: Fromherz, 2012; Boussaa, 2021). During this time, Qatar continued to feel the need to symbolically showcase its independence, as throughout the early 1930s, Saudi Arabia regularly made claim to Qatari oil fields. In was in the context of these two pressures that, in 1935, Abdullah signed an oil concession agreement with the Anglo-Persian Oil Company (APOC), which, at the time, was the primary oil supplier of the British Navy (Fromherz, 2012).

It wasn't however until 1949 that Qatar's oil exportation operation took off, and the first large tanker left Qatari shores (see: El Mallakh, 2014). By the time Sheikh Ahmed bin Ali Al-Thani took power in 1960, Qatar was emerging as an incredibly wealthy state. During his reign, Sheikh Ahmed spent little time in Qatar however, instead opting to spent most of his time in some of Europe's wealthiest destinations (Fromherz, 2012). Despite this economic boom, politically, Qatar's future and independence was once again in threat after Britain's announcement in 1968 that it intended to withdraw from the Gulf in 1971. Mindful of the security void it would leave behind, before its formal withdrawal, Britain attempted to assemble a union of Gulf States, one that would include Qatar, Bahrain and the seven Emiratis sheikhdoms formally known as the Trucial States. However, in late 1971, Qatar—along with Bahrain—withdrew from talks, and, in doing so, became a fully independent state, leaving the seven Emiratis sheikhdoms to form the United Arab Emirates (UAE) (see: Zahlan, 2016).

QATAR'S MODERNIZATION AGENDA

In 1972, Sheikh Khalifa bin Hamad Al-Thani came to power after ousting Sheikh Ahmed on the back of a peaceful coup. As mentioned, throughout his reign Ahmed spent most of his time in Europe, and had thus largely remained absent from fulfilling his constitutional duties. There was therefore little complaint by Qataris when Khalifa took the throne for himself, a move that took place whilst Ahmed was on a hunting trip in Iran (Fromherz, 2012). Upon taking up his position, Khalifa promised sweeping reform across Qatar, and intended to focus on modernizing the state. Because of this, it may be said that Khalifa can be referred to as the 'father' of the modern state of Qatar. Indeed, he helped to expand the authority of the state, increased the size of the armed forces and introduced public housing benefits and state pensions (Kamrava, 2013). In 1972, the Basic Law of Qatar was revised from its earlier 1970 introduction. This revision was overseen by Khalifa, and helped set in place a more traditional, codified form of governance—as opposed to the more personalized one that had been in place up to this point (Wright, 2011). Crucially, the Basic Law revision laid the foundations for the creation of government-run entities across Qatar, including the Ministry of Education and Culture, the Ministry of Finance, the Ministry of Public Works, the Ministry of Public Health, the Ministry of Labour and Social Affairs and the Ministry of

Table 2.1 Qatar's year of membership to international (non) governmental organizations

International organization	Year of membership
Organization of the Petroleum Exporting Countries	1961
Fédération Internationale de Football Association	1970
United Nations	1971
International Monetary Fund	1972
World Bank	1972
International Telecommunication Union	1973
Interpol	1974
International Atomic Energy Agency	1976
International Red Cross	1978
International Olympic Committee	1980
Organization for the Prohibition of Chemical Weapons	1993
World Trade Organization	1996
World Health Organization	1996
Group of 77	2004
International Organization for Migration	2007
International Renewable Energy Agency	2010

Foreign Affairs (see: Wright, 2011). In 1973, Khalifa then oversaw the establishment and opening of Qatar University, the state's first public university (Fromherz, 2012).

During Khalifa's reign, Qatar also become a member of a number of various international governmental and non-governmental organizations (see Table 2.1). Indeed, throughout Khalifa's rule, Qatar formally joined no less than nine international (non-)governmental organizations, including the United Nations, the World Bank and the International Olympic Committee (IOC). For small states, membership to these organizations can act as one way to resonate their right to sovereign independence by enlarging their voice and visibility through their participation in transnational pursuits. Their existence in what Cooper and Shaw (2009, p. 10) call 'club-membership' offers small states significant image enhancement opportunities via participation in key global decisions and causes, as well as through hosting various 'member-only events', such as, for instance, a

World Cup. Most importantly, affiliation with such organizations can also offer small states judicial and political protection, and support and advice if and when larger states seek to interfere in their affairs (see: Karns & Mingst, 2004). Thus, for Qatar, we can argue that membership to such organizations sought to act as one way to not only showcase the state's independence but also offer some national security—on this latter point, note, for instance, the amount of organizations Qatar joined in the years immediately following the British withdrawal from the Gulf in 1971.

One interregional organization Qatar situated itself under Khalifia was the formation of the Gulf Cooperation Council (GCC). In 1981, Qatar, along with Saudi Arabia, Kuwait, Bahrain, the UAE and Oman, established the GCC as part of a combined attempt to create a fast-paced, fruitful and stable environment for global capital accumulation (De Boer & Turner, 2007). At the time, many of the smaller GCC states suffered from lingering suspicions that such a forum would come to informally legitimize Saudi Arabia's hegemony over the Gulf, particularly given how the GGC headquarters would be based in Riyadh, the capital of Saudi Arabia (see also: Kamrava, 2013). Nonetheless, for these smaller states in particular, and for leaders such as Khalifa, a combined security coalition was necessary given persistent fears over invasion from neighbouring Iraq and Iran, fears that were fully realized in August 1990 with Iraq's invasion and annexation of Kuwait, which prompted the start of the first Gulf War. At the time, it was due to Kuwait's membership to the GCC, and particularly the United Nations, that allowed the state to greatly succeed in mobilizing swift regional and international action against Iraq in January 1991, and towards bringing a rapid end to the first Gulf War in February 1991 (six weeks later) (see: Karns & Mingst, 2004).

Nonetheless, despite all of Khalifa's attempts at state modernization, by the early 1990s Qatar started to experience significant economic downturn. At this time, Qatar's wealth was heavily dependent on the exportation of oil, and thus falling global oil prices in the late 1980s had severely impacted state revenues, leading to government deficits and a significant reduction in per capita income (Wright, 2012). It was in this context that Khalifa's son, Sheikh Hamad bin Khalifa Al-Thani, gained traction for the successful staging of a peaceful coup against his father in 1995. With support from the Qatari military, as well as a number of prominent Al-Thani's, Hamad staged the coup whilst Khalifa was on vacation in Switzerland. It is reported that, in response to Hamad's coup, Khalifa left with much of the state's cash reserves (estimated to be between $2.5–$7.5 billion), leading to further tightening of government spending through to the mid-1990s (Fromherz, 2012).

Notwithstanding the success of the 1995 coup, Hamad was still nonetheless fearful of threats to Qatar's independence and his own position. This was particularly so after 1996, the year in which Khalifa staged an unsuccessful counter-coup, one supposedly backed by Saudi Arabia (Kamrava, 2013; Roberts, 2017). Matters were made worse by Saudi Arabia's continuous claim that Saudi 'land' should extend into Qatar, a notion that even some Qatari's might have entertained—indeed, not only do many Qataris still practise a light form of Saudi Wahhabism, but some of the Al-Thani royal family have previously openly traced their ancestry back to Saudi Arabia. It is because of this that Fromherz (2012, p. 925) suggests that the Qatari hierarchy have, for some decades now, been in somewhat of a 'cold war' with Saudi Arabia, a war that has, to varying degrees, become both 'warm' and 'hot'—in 1992, a clash broke out on the Qatar-Saudi Arabia border, leading to the death of three; and, as discussed further below, there was the more recent Saudi Arabia-led blockade of Qatar, which was bought into effect in June 2017.

It was in the context of these internal and external pressures that Hamad's reign heralded in significant changes. On the political front, Hamad set about removing old guard Al-Thanis from power, replacing them with younger, more progressive and loyal members of his family and, in doing so, bringing heightened degrees of discipline, unity and stability to the Al-Thani family (Kamrava, 2013). In 1996, Hamad then commissioned the construction of the Al Udeid Air Base, at a reported cost of $1 billion (*The New York Times*, 28 April 2003). In arguably one of the state's most savvy political moves, in 2003 Hamad then convinced the U.S. Armed Forces to move their Middle East Central Command headquarters from Saudi Arabia's Prince Sultan Air Base to Al Udeid. Qatar and the United States had signed a mutual Defence Cooperation Agreement back in the early 1990s, something Hamad sought to greatly expand, to the point that American soldiers would now be stationed on Qatari soil. Today, the base is the jewel in crown of Qatar's diplomatic relationship with the United States, acting as the latter's command centre for over 18 nations across the Middle East and central Asia, and housing up to 11,000 U.S. military personnel and 120 aircraft at any one time (Lendon, 2017). Thus, just like it had done previously with the British and the Ottomans, Qatar had once again safeguarded its—and Hamad's—security by strategically cuddling up to *the* superpower of the day.

Having shored up Qatar's security, Hamad then set about rolling out his ambitious plans for the state. In seeking to positively make use of its natural resource wealth, Hamad's vision for Qatar centred on the belief that the state should seek to carve out for itself a proactive and independent foreign policy, one where it would play a key role on regional and international stages. One way this looked to be achieved was through Al Jazeera, the state's foremost media network, which the Qatari government has financially backed since its establishment in 1996 (Cooper & Momani, 2011). As the Middle East's first 24-hour news channel, Al Jazeera gained regional recognition when it became the only Arab alternative to America's CNN (Khatib, 2013). Its international reputation then soared when it became the first media network to air video messages of Osama bin Laden after the 2011 attacks of 9/11. The key to Al Jazeera's success has been its ability to break media norms in the Arab world by unorthodoxly criticizing various repressive and undemocratic governments (Lynch, 2006). Although this has led to the closure of its offices in a number of states across the Middle East, it has ultimately won significant admiration from both Arab and international audiences for its ability to create a platform for the voice of the suppressed to be heard. Indeed, in 2011 Hillary Clinton proclaimed that the network had truly become a global media 'leader', thanks to its continuous dedication towards 'changing people's minds and attitudes' (*ABC News*, 21 March 2011). Through becoming synonymous with the 'Al Jazeera brand', the network has thus become a vital cog in the state's independent foreign policy push, providing Qatar with a crucial outlet through which to take a leading role in shaping regional and international opinion.

Then came developments in education. Education City was established in 1997, with the goal to provide 'a unique model of academic and research excellence...that benefit Qatar and the rest of the World' (Qatar Foundation, n.d.). Encompassing a 14 sq km campus, by 2010, Education City played home to overseas branches of some of the world's leading universities, including Carnegie Mellon, Georgetown, Northwestern, Texas A&M, University College London, Virginia Commonwealth and Weill Cornell Medicine. Crucial in this regard has been Hamad's second wife, Sheikha Moza bint Nasser, who is chairperson of the Qatar Foundation—the state's umbrella organization for education, science and community development. Since its formation, Education City has since become the largest enclave of American universities outside the United States (*Financial Times*, 20 October 2013). The housing of illustrious universities helps position Qatar as a vital regional hub for education. In doing so, such institutions not only raise the educational proficiency of Qataris themselves but also provide Qatar with an opportunity to shape the minds of the many Arab students who are hesitant to study in the West, and thus see Education City as a suitable alternative. Through this, Qatar can also seek to forge independent and lasting relationships with both the regional leaders of tomorrow and the Western home countries of foreign universities, particularly the United States, making Education City, with its international workforce and student body, an additional security feature for Qatar, beyond the U.S. military base (see: Khodr, 2011; Antwi-Boateng, 2013).

The 2000s then heralded in the rolling-out and completion of a number of high-profile infrastructure projects that have since come to significantly change the built environment of Qatar. In 2004, plans were revealed for the construction of 'The Pearl'—a human-made island, reclaimed from the sea, which today houses state-of-the-art apartments with marina views, high-end restaurants and shops, and leisure facilities. A year later, a far more ambitious project was announced in the form of Lusail—the building of an entire new city just north of Doha that would be completed before the 2022 World Cup, and would comprise a mix of residential and commercial neighbourhoods, hotels, a golf course, high-end restaurants and shops, and a theme park. Upon completion, Lusail will be able to house up to 450,000 residents (see: *The Independent*, 25 March 2021). Then, in 2008, came the opening of the Museum of Islamic Art, which today houses one of the world's most comprehensive collections of Islamic paintings and artefacts. All this took place alongside the ongoing expansion of Qatar's central business district (known as 'West Bay')—over a 15-year period, starting in the late 1990s, 88 high-rise skyscrapers were erected in the West Bay area alone (see: Mirincheva et al., 2013). Combined, these infrastructure developments have helped situate Qatar as a notable international destination for business, living and cultural tourism. The building of such projects has of course also required an influx of overseas blue-collar workers, particularly from South Asia, and thus, while between 2004 and 2010 Abu Dhabi's population grew by 11% and Dubai's by 21%, Doha's grew by 93%, and Qatar's overall population grew by a significant 128% (Rizzo, 2014).

Under Hamad, Qatar furthermore established itself as a significant actor in regional military affairs. In 2011, Qatar was pivotal in rallying Arab backing for the NATO-led campaign to oust Libyan leader, Colonel

Muammar Gaddafi (*Foreign Policy*, 30 September 2014); and in 2014, Qatar partook in various U.S.-led airstrikes in Syria against the terrorist group, Islamic State (*Doha News*, 13 March 2015). Nonetheless, Qatar has also retained close ties to countries and organizations such as Iran, the Taliban, Al Qaeda and Hamas, all of whom exert strained relations with the West (*The Telegraph*, 20 September 2014). Of note here too was Qatar's support of the Muslim Brotherhood in Egypt during the 2011 Arab Spring, a move that was in direct conflict with Saudi Arabia's support of then Egyptian president, Hosni Mubarak, who in turn sought to supress the Brotherhood's sway across the country (see: Nuruzzaman, 2015). Thus, in the same way Qatar sought to balance its interests with rivals in the form of the British and the Ottomans in the late nineteenth century, in recent decades a similar approach has taken shape, with the state maintaining good relationships with both friends and the enemies of friends. In the small state literature, this is known as 'hedging'—that is, a 'strategy [that] offers actors unprecedented flexibility to deal with strategic uncertainties in relation to their partners' future behaviour, while also enabling them to benefit from the existing relationship' (Suorsa, 2017, p. 8).

Of particular importance for Qatar are good relations with its Shiite neighbour Iran, a much larger country with more than 80 million people and a landmass about 150 times larger than that of Qatar. Iran's population is larger than all GCC countries combined. Bahgat writes in his analysis of Iran's relations with the Gulf States: "Qatar has been traditionally more accommodative to Iran than the other GCC states" (Bahgat, 2015, p. 20). He gives two reasons for the close economic and strategic cooperation between the two countries. Firstly, Qatar wants to balance the influence of Saudi Arabia, the by far largest GCC state. Secondly, Qatar and Iran share the largest natural gas field in the world, and natural gas is the primary source of income for Qatar. 'Maintaining good relations with Iran has helped Qatar to develop its share of the field with no political or security hurdles' (Bahgat, 2015, p. 20).

Hedging strategies not only provide small states with added choice, and thus security, if and when certain actor's behaviours change, but also puts them in a central position for regional/international mediation. Indeed, for Qatar, its multifarious ties have enabled the state to position itself visibly as a 'non-stop mediator' and conflict negotiator. In 2008, for example, Qatar persuaded the rival Lebanese Sunni-led government and Shiite Hezbollah group to sign the Doha Agreement, marking the end of an eighteen-month-long political deadlock—this led to flags of Qatar being raised in Lebanon's capital, Beirut, as well as placards that read 'Thank you Qatar' (see: Roberts, 2017, p. 239); in 2011, Qatar then initiated the 2011 Doha Agreement (also known as the Darfur Peace Agreement), signed between the Sudanese government and rebel group, the Liberation and Justice Movement, to establish a compensation fund for the victims of the Darfur conflict (*The New York Times*, 23 November 2014). In 2014, U.S. officials—including then secretary of state, John Kerry—implored Qatar 'to use their influence' in securing the release of kidnapped Israeli soldiers (*Reuters*, 1 August 2014b); in May 2014, Qatar was then central in securing the release of U.S. Army sergeant, Bowe Bergdahl, who was being held in Afghanistan by Taliban forces (*The Guardian*, 24 August 2014); and in August 2014, Qatar negotiated the release and return of U.S. writer and journalist, Peter Curtis, who was held hostage for two years in Syria by Al-Nusra Front (*Reuters*, 28 August 2014a). It is because of feats such as this—and those mentioned above—that Qatar's Hamad-led foreign policy has been described as 'a fascinating example of a small state achieving an international presence far beyond its size' (Wright, 2011, p. 127).

During Hamad's reign, Qatar also started to carve out for itself the reputation as a significant financier of various humanitarian causes, some-thing which has continued to this day: after Hurricane Katrina in 2005, for example, Qatar donated $100 million to help rebuild housing, hospi-tals and schools in New Orleans and surrounding areas (*The New York Times*, 30 April 2008); in 2012, Qatar held the UN Conference on Trade and Development, during which time 155 World Trade Organization members agreed to sign the 'Doha Development Agenda', which empha-sized a stronger commitment towards helping developing countries join the global economy (*The Economist*, 9 December 2013; see also: Lee, 2012); in 2015, the Qatar Red Crescent sent staff to Nepal to treat more than 300 patients after the devastating Kathmandu earthquake, which killed more than 7000 people (*Doha News*, 7 May 2015); in the same year, Qatar donated around $1.6 billion worth of food, clothing and medical supplies to help those caught up in the Syrian civil war (*The Telegraph*, 10 February 2015); and more recently, in 2021, Qatar pledged to pay $500 million for the reconstruction of the Gaza Strip, after the area wit-nessed some of the most damaging fighting in years between Israel and the Palestinian group Hamas (*Al Jazeera*, 26 May 2021). Such efforts have arguably helped Qatar establish its standing as a 'good global citizen'. Through this, Qatar not only garners benevolence and friendship amongst

those it helps—which it can seek to exploit during times of potential instability—but such generosity also helps showcase the state's desire to be a
key international actor in its own right, one committed to positive causes
that take place well beyond its borders.

It was also under Hamad's rule that Qatar was awarded by FIFA in
December 2010 the rights to host the 2022 World Cup. However, it was
in fact Hamad's son, Sheikh Tamim bin Hamad Al Thani, who was the
central instigator behind the state's bid for the World Cup, as well as
Qatar's other regional and international sporting events. Tamim was
handed power in 2013 after Hamad voluntarily abdicated the throne, a
move seldom witnessed in the Middle East. Hamad had preferred Tamim
to his older sons, and at just thirty-three years of age, Tamim became the
youngest ever ruler of Qatar. Having previously been labelled as 'the best
sport personality in the Arab world', Tamim has been at the forefront of
Qatar's use of sport for foreign policy and domestic reform (topics we
discuss in detail in subsequent chapters). He has previously occupied the
positions of chair for the 2006 Asian Games and for Qatar's (failed) bid for
the 2020 Summer Olympic Games (*BBC*, 25 June 2013).

QATAR TODAY: INTERNATIONAL, REGIONAL AND DOMESTIC CONCERNS

Like his father before him, upon assuming power of the state, Tamim was
quick to substitute several key members of the previous political elite,
replacing them with younger members of his family (see: Ulrichsen,
2017). Although he has largely sought to maintain his father's approach
to foreign affairs since taking the throne, under Tamim there has been a
greater focus on addressing the state's international, regional and domestic concerns, many of which are common in particular to naturally
resource-rich, small states. The first is Qatar's (over)reliance on the sale of
oil and natural gas. As mentioned in the introduction to this chapter,
Qatar is currently the world's 17th largest exporter of crude oil, and the
largest exporter of liquefied natural gas (LNG). On the latter, Qatar ships
on average 77 million metric tons per year of liquefied natural gas, contributing to 12% of China's total LNG yearly intake, 40% of India's entire
annual supply and 50% of the United Kingdom's (see: UK Government,
2019; *Reuters*, 27 January 2020b; S&P Global, 2021).

One the one hand, Qatar's exportation of its natural resources does provide the state with added security—indeed, as states such as China, India and the United Kingdom come to strongly rely on Qatar's LNG supplies, they too have a strong vested interest in the state's security and survival. On the other hand, however, such a reliance on hydrocarbon sales has resulted in Qatar's oil and gas sector contributing to 70% of the state's total annual revenues, 85% of its export earnings and 60% of its gross domestic product (see: Mahmood & Earley, 2019). This heavy reliance on the sale of natural resources means that Qatar is prone to the instability of global markets, something that Tamim was reminded of a year into his tenure, when a slump in oil prices occurred in 2014, forcing the tightening of domestic fiscal spend. Since then, state spending has continued to dwindle under Tamim, to the point that the decision was made in 2016 to close Al Jazeera America, leading to the loss of over 700 jobs, as a result of significant losses Qatar had witnessed due to 'falling oil prices' (CNN, 27 March 2016). In commenting on this, Ulrichsen (2017, p. 100) notes that, in the late 2010s, it was evident that under Tamim 'nothing was safe from the sacrificial axe save perhaps for expenditure directly related to the World Cup itself'.

It is because of this precarious overreliance on its sale of natural recourses that the state has actively sought to take measures to diversify its economy. The Qatar National Vison 2030, released in July 2008, is the state's blueprint document for future development. It seeks to chart out the ways in which the state will endeavour to become 'an advanced country by 2030, capable of sustaining its own development and providing for a high standard of living for all of its people' (Qatar National Vision: 2). A major pillar of the National Vision centres on 'economic development', and in particular the 'development of a competitive and diversified economy capable of meeting the needs of, and securing a high standard of living for, all its people for the present and for the future' (ibid., p. 11). This seeks to be achieved via successfully confronting the challenge of positioning Qatar as a 'regional hub for knowledge and for high value industrial and service activities', and by creating 'open and flexible markets' in order to bring about a more 'diversified economy that gradually reduces its dependence on hydrocarbon industries, enhances the role of the private sector and maintains its competitiveness' (ibid, pp. 24–29).

A second concern centres on Qatar's relationship with its GCC neighbours, and existing tensions around the state's desire to be seen as an independent actor in its own right. As we have seen in this chapter, Qatar has a long and strained relationship with some of its neighbours, particularly the much larger state of Saudi Arabia. During his first year in power, alongside having to confront Qatar's economic vulnerabilities, Tamim was also reminded of the strained relations that existed with some of his fellow Gulf leaders. In March 2014, the coalition of Saudi Arabia, Bahrain the UAE and Egypt withdrew their ambassadors from Doha in protest of Qatar's support of the Muslim Brotherhood in the aftermath of the Arab Spring, which erupted in 2011. After the 2013 overthrow of Mohamed Morsi in Egypt—which led to the arrest of thousands of Brotherhood members—Qatar openly granted refuge to senior Brotherhood leaders, acting as the group's foremost safe haven, as well as providing its leadership with regular airtime on Al Jazeera to preach their message (*Reuters*, 5 March 2014c). Such an action was purported to threaten the stability of the region, with Saudi Arabia, Bahrain and the UAE claiming the Brotherhoods' desire to create a transnational movement equated to a serious threat to the GCC's security and sovereign order. In other words, this was a direct reaction to Qatar's desire to act independent of the GCC and, in doing so, to implement strategies that 'vary drastically from those adopted by its neighbours' (Abdullah & Al-Nasiri, 2014, p. 5). In September 2014, after intense pressure from the GCC, Qatar finally asked senior Muslim Brotherhood leaders to leave the country (*Gulf News*, 25 April 2014).

Regional anxieties over Qatar's continued support for groups such as the Brotherhood culminated in June 2017 when the above-mentioned coalition of four states—initially supported by countries such as Mauritania and the Maldives, amongst others—blockaded Qatar, cutting all diplomatic and trade links, as well as suspending all shipping and air routes to their Gulf neighbour. The coalition governments claimed that such actions were in response to Qatar's continual support of the Brotherhood and other 'extreme Islamist' groups such as the Hamas movement, as well as the state's growing ties with regional rival, Iran. To end the blockade, the coalition states made thirteen demands, including that Qatar sever all ties to terrorist organizations, end all support and funding of 'fundamentalist' groups, close Al Jazeera and its affiliate stations, and refrain from interfering in other countries' internal affairs. Qatar denied all of these accusations, claiming they were politically motivated by others' attempts to secure hegemony across the region (see: Bayoumy, 2017). Crucially, some reports indicated that the Gulf crisis had been engineered by neighbouring nations who felt weakened by Qatar, and were provoked more by its successful 2022 World Cup bid than by its acting as a safe haven for terrorist groups. On this reading, the Gulf crisis would end if Qatar gave up its prize asset—the World Cup finals—so that regional and international balances could be restored (see: Brannagan & Giulianotti, 2018). As we discuss in detail in Chap. 5, the blockade was not resolved until January 2021, after Kuwait and the United States helped broker a deal between Qatar and its regional neighbours.

A third concern centres on Qataris themselves, and in particular issues of health and well-being. Most notable in this regard is the high prevalence of lifestyle diseases present amongst Qataris, most significant of which are diabetes and obesity. The World Health Organization (2017) estimates that 18.9% of Qataris have diabetes, 71.7% are 'overweight' and 35% are 'obese'. As previous research has shown (Brannagan & Giulianotti, 2014), this public health issue is due to three interlinked causes: high levels of wealth and affluence amongst Qataris; the rapid increase across Doha of western-style, high-calorie fast-food outlets; and a general lack of physical activity across the population—indeed, on this last point, it is estimated that 41.6% of all Qatari adults are 'physically inactive' (33.4% of males and 49.7% of females), while, more concerning, 90.1% of adolescents are also physically inactive (88.3% in boys and 91.6% in girls) (see: Global Health Observatory, 2017).

A fourth and final concern to note here is of course the negative international scrutiny that has been manifested in response to Qatar's forthcoming 2022 World Cup, and how the state continues to respond to these accusations. As set out in Chap. 1, and as discussed further in Chap. 4, the 2022 World Cup has ensued three key forms of criticism: that Qatar is an unsafe destination for the staging of such a tournament, largely due to its searing summer temperatures; that the state unfairly acquired the World Cup, through forms of bribery and corruption; and that Qatar exhibits 'inhumane' working conditions, leading to degrees of 'modern-day-slavery' for its plethora of South Asian expatriates, particularly those blue-collar workers who work on the state's multitude of (World Cup) construction projects. Notable will be how these accusations play out as we move closer to the start of the 2022 World Cup, as well as how the state meaningfully responds to calls to bring its domestic policies and practices in line with western/global notions of democracy and human rights (issues we discuss in detail in Chap. 5).

Conclusion

This chapter set out to offer a historical and political background of Qatar, starting in the mid-nineteenth century and leading through to the contemporary epoch. Having done so, it is evident that a number of key trends have emerged, many of which are common to small states. When looking back at Qatar's most notable moments throughout its history, it is clear that—in typical small state fashion—the state's survival and security have continued to be of paramount concern. Indeed, as we have seen, a prominent trend centres on how the state has repeatedly sought to benefit from cuddling up to—or 'bandwagoning'—the major powers of the day, starting with the British, then the Ottomans, the British again and, in more recent years, the United States. In large part, the desire to bandwagon has been driven by anxieties over the need for Qatar to shield itself from any possible expansion attempts by regional neighbours.

Although such a bandwagoning approach appears to strongly resemble a more neorealist IR account—that states are most concerned with their survival, and that small states in particular suffer from deep security vulnerabilities—it is important to note that the ways in which Qatar has forged its relationships with external powers has been done with a great deal of strategy and deft diplomacy. Indeed, as we have seen with the Ottomans and the British in the nineteenth century, and more recently with the United States and nations such as Iran, a further trend is that Qatar has sought to go beyond simply relying on one major power and has rather looked to strategically position itself between friends and foes—a tactic known as 'hedging'. Not only does this ensure that the state avoids security 'mono-dependence', but it has left Qatar in a well-placed position where it can act as an effective go-between mediator, thus meaning, if needed, it can play international powers against one another. In short, Qatar has shown a great deal of strategy and innovation in getting itself into a position where it can have a degree of control over its own fate. This not only displays notions of *resiliency* (to use neoliberal terminology) on behalf of Qatar but also shows how the state can has come to wield degrees of international influence, despite its size—indeed, as we have seen, where once Qatar relied on the British, today it is, in many ways, the British who rely on Qatar and its significant annual supply of liquefied natural gas.

A further trend that has emerged from this chapter is that Qataris are not solely concerned with security for security's sake, but rather have looked to safeguard their national survival in order to allow themselves the time and space to forge an independent foreign policy, one that is formed by a great deal of 'strategic social construction'. Indeed, as we have seen, Qatar has come to occupy a regional and international role in the areas of media, education, mediation, conflict negotiation, humanitarianism, culture and leisure (including, of course, its role in the world of global sport). Through this, the state has put itself in the position where it can be a vital influencer of current affairs and, in doing so, can (re)shape opinions, practices and norms. Qatar's ability to wield power on the international stage through strategic social construction forms has led many to conclude that the state has, in recent decades, come to 'punch above its weight' in foreign policy terms (Woertz, 2012, p. 1); in doing so, we may also suggest that Qatar has come to break with many (neorealist) understandings of what small states 'can' do.

A final trend that has emerged from this chapter centres on the various contemporary concerns the state faces, some of which have been caused by Qatar's drive for an independent foreign policy. In Chap. 4, we explore this aspect in detail by looking closer at the negative international scrutiny the state has endured since its awarding of the 2022 World Cup in 2010. In Chap. 5, we then focus on some of the more domestic and regional concerns the state needs to confront leading up to, and after, the 2022 World Cup—including its relations with its Middle East neighbours, the health and well-being of its citizens, and changes to the kafala sponsorship system. In the next chapter, however, we first look to uncover and discuss how Qatar's endeavours in global sport and major sports events look to help the state significantly add to its international profile and, in doing so, to achieve economic diversification at home through engaging with global audiences and international markets. In other words, how sport acts as a key vehicle for Qatar to engage with 'globalization-for-state-purposes'.

References

ABC News. (2011, March 21). Clinton: Al Jazeera is 'real news' [online]. Retrieved September 16, 2021, from https://abcnews.go.com/Politics/video/hillary-clinton-al-jazeera-real-news-13042310

Abdullah, J., & Al-Nasiri, N. (2014). *Qatari foreign policy: Carryover or redirection?*. AlJazeera Centre for Studies. Retrieved September 12, 2021, from https://studies.aljazeera.net/sites/default/files/migration/ResourceGallery/media/Documents/2014/7/10/201471011483120 5734 Qatari%20Foreign%20Policy%20Carryover%20or%20Redirection.pdf

Al Jazeera. (2021, May 26). Qatar pledges $500 m for Gaza reconstruction [online]. Retrieved July 12, 2021, from https://www.aljazeera.com/news/2021/5/26/qatar-pledges-500-million-to-gaza-reconstruction

Al-Hammadi, M. I. (2018). Presentation of Qatari identity at National Museum of Qatar: Between imagination and reality. *Journal of Conservation and Museum Studies, 16*(1), 3.

Antwi-Boateng, O. (2013). The rise of Qatar as a soft power and the challenges. *European Scientific Journal, 2*(1), 39–51.

Bahgat, G. (2015). Geopolitics of energy: Iran, Turkey, and Europe. *Mediterranean Quarterly, 26*(3), 49–66.

Bayoumy, Y. (2017, June 23). UAE says will not back down in dispute if Qatar declines to cooperate [online]. Retrieved March 13, 2021, from https://www.reuters.com/article/uk-gulf-qatar-emirates-idAFKBN19E29B

BBC. (2013, June 25). Qatari emir Sheikh Hamad hands power to son Tamim [online]. Retrieved June 17, 2021, from https://www.bbc.co.uk/news/world-middle-east-23026870

Boussaa, D. (2021). The past as a catalyst for cultural sustainability in historic cities; the case of Doha, Qatar. *International Journal of Heritage Studies, 27*(5), 470–486.

Brannagan, P. M. (2017). *The state of Qatar and global sport: A case study of globalization, the nation-state and soft power* (Doctoral dissertation, Loughborough University).

Brannagan, P. M., & Giulianotti, R. (2014). Qatar, global sport and the 2022 FIFA world cup. In *Leveraging legacies from sports mega-events: Concepts and cases* (pp. 154–165). Palgrave Pivot.

Brannagan, P. M., & Giulianotti, R. (2018). The soft power–soft disempowerment nexus: The case of Qatar. *International Affairs, 94*(5), 1139–1157.

Brannagan, P. M., & Rookwood, J. (2016). Sports mega-events, soft power and soft disempowerment: International supporters' perspectives on Qatar's acquisition of the 2022 FIFA World Cup finals. *International Journal of Sport Policy and Politics, 8*(2), 173–188.

CNN. (2016, March 27). Al Jazeera announces 500 job cuts [online]. Retrieved February 24, 2021, from https://money.cnn.com/2016/03/27/media/al-jazeera-qatar-layoffs/index.html

Cooper, A. F., & Momani, B. (2011). Qatar and expanded contours of small state diplomacy. *The International Spectator, 46*(3), 113–128.

Cooper, A. F., & Shaw, T. (2009). *The diplomacies of small states*. Palgrave Macmillan.

De Boer, K., & Turner, J. (2007). Beyond oil: Reappraising the Gulf states. *McKinsey Quarterly, 13*(1), 7–17.

Doha News. (2015, May 07). Qatar relief workers arrive Nepal, extend mission to three months [online]. Retrieved February 14, 2021, from https://dohanews.co/qatar-relief-workers-arrive-in-nepal-extend-mission-to-three-months/
Dourian, K. (2020, July 20). Looming peak oil demand triggers Gulf race for natural gas [online]. Retrieved July 16, 2021, from https://agsiw.org/wp-content/uploads/2020/07/KateGasPaperONLINE.pdf
El Mallakh, R. (2014). *The economic development of the United Arab Emirates (RLE Economy of Middle East)*. Routledge.
Exell, K., & Rico, T. (2013). 'There is no heritage in Qatar': Orientalism, colonialism and other problematic histories. *World Archaeology, 45*(4), 670–685.
Financial Times. (2013, October 20). Doha's Education City is a boost for locals [online]. Retrieved September 12, 2015, from https://www.ft.com/content/b2fff52c-1711-11e3-9ec2-00144feabdc0
Foreign Policy. (2014, September 30). The Case against Qatar [online]. Retrieved June 18, 2021, from http://foreignpolicy.com/2014/09/30/the-case-against-qatar/
Fromherz, A. J. (2012). *Qatar: A modern history*. Georgetown University Press.
Global Health Observatory. (2017). Qatar [online]. Retrieved September 12, 2021, from https://apps.who.int/iris/rest/bitstreams/1139345/retrieve
Gulf News. (2014, April 25). Brotherhood leaders leave Qatar for Libya: Report [online]. Retrieved April 12, 2021, from https://gulfnews.com/world/gulf/qatar/brotherhood-leaders-leave-qatar-for-libya-report-1.1324196
International Institute for Strategic Studies' Military Balance Report. (2020). [online]. Retrieved February 03, 2021, from https://www.iiss.org/publications/the-military-balance/military-balance-2020-book
International Monetary Fund. (2021). GDP per capita [online]. Retrieved July 07, 2021, from https://www.imf.org/external/datamapper/NGDPDPC@WEO/OEMDC/ADVEC/WEOWORLD
Kamrava, M. (2013). *Qatar: Small state, big politics*. Cornell University Press.
Karns, M. P., & Mingst, K. A. (2004). *International organizations: The politics and processes of global governance*. Lynne Reinner Publishers.
Khatib, L. (2013). Qatar's foreign policy: The limits of pragmatism. *International Affairs, 89*(2), 417–431.
Khodr, H. (2011). The dynamics of international education in Qatar: Exploring the policy drivers behind the development of Education City. *Journal of Emerging Trends in Educational Research and Policy Studies, 2*(6), 514–525.
Kurşun, Z. (2002). *The Ottomans in Qatar: A history of Anglo-Ottoman conflicts in the Persian Gulf*. Isis Press.
Lee, D. (2012). Global trade governance and the challenges of African activism in the Doha Development Agenda negotiations. *Global Society, 26*(1), 83–101.

Lendon, B. (2017, June 06). Qatar hosts largest US military base in Mideast [online]. Retrieved May 12, 2021, from https://edition.cnn.com/2017/06/05/middleeast/qatar-us-largest-base-in-mideast/index.html

Lynch, M. (2006). *Voices of the new Arab public: Iraq, Al-Jazeera, and Middle East politics today*. Columbia University Press.

Mahmood, S., & Earley, M. (2019). Oil and gas regulation in Qatar: Overview [online]. Retrieved July 15, 2021, from https://uk.practicallaw.thomsonreuters.com/5-525-5499?transitionType=Default&contextData=(sc.Default)&firstPage=true

Mirincheva, V., Wiedmann, F., & Salama, A. M. (2013). The spatial development potentials of business districts in Doha: The case of the West Bay. *Open House International* [online]. Retrieved July 17, 2021, from https://www.emerald.com/insight/content/doi/10.1108/OHI-04-2013-B0003/full/html

Nuruzzaman, M. (2015). Qatar and the Arab Spring: Down the foreign policy slope. *Contemporary Arab Affairs, 8*(2), 226–238.

Qatar Foundation. (n.d.). Education city [online]. Retrieved March 14, 2021, from https://www.qf.org.qa/education/education-city

Qatar Ministry of Development Planning and Statistics. (2018). Total population [online]. Retrieved June 14, 2021, from http://www.mdps.gov.qa/en/statistics1/StatisticsSite/LatestStatistics/Pages/PopulationStats.aspx

Qatar Ministry of Planning and Statistics. (2020). Qatar Cenusus 2020 [online]. Available at: https://www.psa.gov.qa/en/statistics1/StatisticsSite/Census/Census2020/Pages/default.aspx (Accessed 13.03.2022)

Qatar Ministry of Development Planning and Statistics. (2021). Total population [online]. Retrieved June 14, 2021, from http://www.mdps.gov.qa/en/statistics1/StatisticsSite/LatestStatistics/Pages/PopulationStats.aspx

Rahman, H. (2005). *The emergence of Qatar: The turbulent years, 1627–1916*. Routledge.

Rathmell, A., & Schulze, K. (2006). Political reform in the Gulf: The case of Qatar. *Middle Eastern Studies, 36*(4), 47–62.

Reuters. (2014a, August 28). American released by Syrian militants thanks Qatar, U.S. officials [online]. Retrieved August 01, 2021, from http://uk.reuters.com/article/us-syria-crisis-usa-curtis-idUKKBN0GQ1GP20140828

Reuters. (2014b, August 01). Kerry seeks Qatari, Turkish help to find Israeli soldier [online]. Retrieved October 12, 2021, from http://uk.reuters.com/article/us-mideast-gaza-kerry-soldier-idUKKBN0G14KV20140801

Reuters. (2014c, March 05). UPDATE 5-Three Gulf Arab states recall envoys in rift with Qatar [online]. Retrieved June 12, 2021, from http://uk.reuters.com/article/gulf-qatar-ambassadors-idUKL6N0M21P420140305

Reuters. (2020a, October 14). Qatar investment authority bets big on private and public equity—CEO [online]. Retrieved July 09, 2021, from https://www.reuters.com/article/swf-qatar-markets-int-idUSKBN26Z2SX

Reuters. (2020b, January 27). India wants to delink Qatar gas supply deals from crude; Qatar says no [online]. Retrieved April 02, 2021, from https://www.reuters.com/article/us-india-gas-idUSKBN1ZQ0VA

Rizzo, A. (2014). Rapid urban development and national master planning in Arab Gulf countries: Qatar as a case study. *Cities, 39*, 50–57.

Roberts, D. B. (2017). *Qatar: Securing the global ambitions of a city-state.* C Hurst & Co Publishers Ltd.

S&P Global. (2021). Qatar signs 15-year deal to sell China 3.5 mil mt/yr LNG [online]. Retrieved October 11, 2021, from https://www.spglobal.com/platts/en/market-insights/latest-news/lng/092921-qatar-signs-15-year-deal-to-sell-china-35-mil-mtyr-lng

Snoj, J. (2019). Population of Qatar by nationality [online]. Retrieved April 04, 2021, from http://priyadsouza.com/population-of-qatar-by-nationality-in-2017/

Suorsa, O. (2017). Maintaining a small state's strategic space: Omnidirectional hedging, International Studies Association Hong Kong [online]. Retrieved September 12, 2021, from http://web.isanet.org/Web/Conferences/HKU2017-s/Archive/f40db849-cb90-4826-9b7a-e449b602f398.pdf

The Economist. (2013, December 09). Doha delivers [online]. Retrieved August 13, 2021, from http://www.economist.com/blogs/freeexchange/2013/12/world-trade-organisation

The Guardian. (2014, August 24). US denies paying ransom as Qatar secures release of journalist in Syria [online]. Retrieved February 02, 2021, from https://www.theguardian.com/world/2014/aug/24/us-denies-ransom-qatar-peter-theo-curtis-syria

The Guardian. (2017, February 07). Qatar spending $500m a week on World Cup projects [online]. Retrieved March 06, 2021, from https://www.theguardian.com/football/2017/feb/08/qatar-spending-500m-a-week-on-world-cup-projects-2022

The Independent. (2021, March 25). Qatar builds entire new city in preperation for World Cup [online]. Retrieved October 13, 2021, from https://www.independent.co.uk/travel/news-and-advice/qatar-lusail-new-city-world-cup-2022-tourists-b1822413.html

The New York Times. (2003, April 28). US will move air operations to Qatar base [online]. Retrieved April 11, 2021, from https://www.nytimes.com/2003/04/28/world/aftereffects-bases-us-will-move-air-operations-to-qatar-base.html

The New York Times. (2008, April 30). Emir of Qatar tours New Orleans to see fruit of his £100 million donations [online]. Retrieved February 17, 2021, from http://www.nytimes.com/2008/04/30/us/nationalspecial/30emir.html

The New York Times. (2014, November 23). Sudan and Rebels in Darfur begin peace talks [online]. Retrieved February 02, 2021, from https://www.nytimes.

com/2014/11/24/world/africa/sudan-and-rebels-in-darfur-region-begin-peace-talks.html
The Telegraph. (2014, September 20). How Qatar is funding the rise of Islamist extremists [online]. Retrieved October 11, 2021, from http://www.telegraph. co.uk/news/worldnews/middleeast/qatar/11110931/How-Qatar-is-funding-the-rise-of-Islamist-extremists.html
The Telegraph. (2015, February 10). Assad is an enemy of Isil, but not the West's ally [online]. Retrieved August 05, 2021, from http://www.telegraph.co.uk/news/worldnews/middleeast/syria/11403949/Assad-is-an-enemy-of-Isil-but-not-the-Wests-ally.html
U.S. Energy Information Database. (2019). Qatar [online]. Retrieved May 13, 2021, from https://www.eia.gov/international/overview/country/QAT
UK Government. (2019). Trends in trade of Liquefied Natural Gas in the UK and Europe [onine]. Available at: https://assets.publishing.service.gov.uk/government/uploads/system/uploads/attachment_data/file/875383/Trends_in_trade_of_Liquefied_Natural_Gas_in_the_UK_and_Europe.pdf (Accessed 12.04.20)
Ulrichsen, K. C. (2017). What's going on with Qatar?. *The Qatar Crisis* [online]. Retrieved July 13, 2021, from https://www.researchgate.net/profile/Youssef-Cherif-2/publication/340741312_Everyone_is_Taking_Sides_in_the_Qatar_Crisis_Here_is_Why_these_Four_North_African_States_Aren't/links/5ea01b284585150839f41ba7/Everyone-is-Taking-Sides-in-the-Qatar-Crisis-Here-is-Why-these-Four-North-African-States-Arent.pdf#page=7
World Bank. (2019). Land Area—Qatar [online]. Retrieved April 07, 2021, from https://data.worldbank.org/indicator/AG.LND.TOTL.K2? name_desc=true&locations=QA
World Health Organization. (2017). Qatar [online]. Available at: https://apps. who.int/iris/rest/bitstreams/1139345/retrieve (Accessed 17.01.20)
Wright, S. (2011). Qatar. In C. M. Davidson (Ed.), *Power and politics in the Persian Gulf monarchies.* Columbia University Press.
Wright, S. (2012). Foreign policies with international reach: The case of Qatar. In D. Held & K. Ulrichsen (Eds.), *The transformation of the Gulf: Politics, economics and the global order.* Routledge.
Zahlan, A. (1979). The Arab brain drain. *Population bulletin of the United Nations Economic Commission for Western Asia, 16,* 19–38.
Zahlan, R. S. (2016). *The creation of Qatar.* Routledge.

CHAPTER 3

The Politics and Power of Small States: The 2022 World Cup and Qatar's Global Sports Strategy

Abstract This chapter divulges Qatar's global sports strategy from an international relations perspective. It does so by first exploring why states seek to paint a positive image of themselves on the international stage, and how this can equate to the acquisition of (small state) power. This is achieved by focusing on the work of Joseph Nye, and his conceptualization of 'soft power'. Following this, the chapter then turns to Qatar's World Cup strategy, and sheds light on how the tournament seeks to acquire the state power regionally and globally, as well as how its broader investment in sport also seeks to help it achieve the objectives set out in its Qatar National Vision 2030, the blueprint for future development.

Keywords Power • Soft power • Global sport • Nation branding • Mega-event legacy

In December 2013 (and again in December 2014), one of the authors was invited to attend the 'Doha Goals Forum', held at the Aspire Zone, Qatar's 'Sports City', located on the outskirts of the state's capital. The Forum was held, in part, to showcase Qatar's commitment and contribution to sport-for-international development initiatives. Indeed, it was self-labelled as the 'world's premier platform for world leaders to create initiatives for global progress through sport' (Doha Goals, n.d.). Attracting over 1500 guests—the majority of whom the state fully funded to attend—the Forum welcomed over 450 students from around the world, as well as a plethora of current and former athletes, sports policymakers and other world leaders. In 2013, for instance, the guest list included, among others, then FIFA president, Joseph 'Sepp' Blatter, former French president, Nicolas Sarkozy, the ex-track and field athlete and British politician, Lord Sebastian Coe, and former tennis champion Boris Becker (who had won the first ATP tennis tournament in Doha, the Qatar Open, in 1993). The high-profile nature of the three-day Forum also attracted the highest dignitaries from Qatar, including the Emir himself, Sheikh Tamim.

A further notable Qatari who was in attendance at the 2013 Forum was Hassan Al-Thawadi, the Secretary General of the Supreme Committee for Delivery and Legacy, the organization established in 2011 to oversee the planning, delivery and staging of the 2022 World Cup. In the afternoon of day two, Hassan Al-Thawadi was interviewed by one of the Forum's presenters. The topic of his interview centered on Qatar's increasing investment in global sport, and specifically its desire to stage the World Cup, one of the, if not *the*, largest event in existence. When asked what he thought would be the 'biggest' legacy of Qatar's 2022 World Cup, he replied by saying:

> I think the biggest legacies that we'd like for the World Cup to leave in the Middle East is .... for the outside people to really understand who we are, and what we are .... there have always been elements if you will of misperception about the Middle East. Now I think one of the elements a World Cup offers is shining the spotlight on a region. And if shining the spotlight correctly, it allows people from the outside world to look and understand who the people of the Middle East are. We're a population who has a great sense of humour, we're people who are friendly, we're known for our hospitality. So, it's an opportunity to bridge that gap that the outside world may have on the stereotypes of the Middle East. (Hassan Al-Thawadi, interview at Doha GOALS Forum, 11 December 2013)

Almost exactly five years later, both authors then attended a conference at the University of Oxford, UK, entitled '*Sports Diplomacy: a vision for the future*'. Once again, in attendance was Hassan Al-Thawadi, and, once more, he was asked to sum up Qatar's underlying desire to stage the World Cup, to which he replied:

Nothing brings people together, and breaks down social barriers, like sport. Peoples' passion for sport—in particular football—transcends linguistic and sociocultural differences. In 2022, fans from across the world will visit Qatar, with the vast majority visiting an Arab and Middle Eastern country for the first time …. I'm confident that through football, people will see our country and region in a positive light. Negative stereotypes will be dispelled and—thanks to football—we will bridge the gap between East and West. (Hassan Al-Thawadi, interview at Sports Diplomacy: A vision for the future, 30 November 2018)

Evidentially, for the Supreme Committee for Delivery and Legacy, there appears to be the crucial and clear intention to use the World Cup to overcome any 'negative stereotypes' that exist of the Middle East and, in doing so, to position Qatar, its culture and its people in a 'positive light'. Why might such a desire exist amongst Qataris, and how exactly can a major sports event—and other sporting endeavours—help to (re)create a more positive image of a country? This chapter seeks to answer these questions. It does so by briefly exploring why states seek to paint a positive image of themselves on the international stage, and how this can equate to the acquisition of (small state) power. This is achieved by focusing on the work of Joseph Nye, and his conceptualization of 'soft power', in the next section. Following this, we then turn our attention in this chapter to Qatar's World Cup strategy, and shed light on how the tournament seeks to acquire the state power regionally and globally, as well as how its broader investment in sport also seeks to help it achieve the objectives set out in its Qatar National Vision 2030, the blueprint for future development.

POWER IN INTERNATIONAL RELATIONS

At the broadest level, 'power' can be defined as the ability to make, receive or resist some form of change in order to get what one wants. Elsewhere, it has been suggested that power is arguably 'the single most important organizing concept in social and political theory' (Ball, 1992, p. 14). It has been, and continues to be, one of the most discussed concepts in political science, sociology and IR, generating extended and, at times, heated debate. Indeed, we may suggest, as others have done, that power is to political analysis what energy is to physics, or money to economics (see Nye, 2011). Despite this, scholars have largely remained divided on what exactly power is and how it can and should be defined.

As discussed in Chap. 1, such a divide on how power should be defined stems from competing (neorealist, neoliberalist and constructivist) perspectives inherent in IR, and, more specifically, their subsequent treatment of the very constitution of what power is and how it actually manifests in practice. For some, such as Robert Dahl, for instance, power quite simply refers to the ability of person A to prevail over person B by making person B 'do something that B would not otherwise do' (Dahl, 1957, p. 201). In this regard, power takes shape when an actor gets what they want by *directly forcing* others to consciously change their actions or behaviours in ways that are contrary to their preferences during times of observable conflict. For others, such as Peter Bachrach and Morton Baratz (1975), power also has a more hidden element: indeed, while the forceful changing of conscious behaviours during times of observable conflict is certainly part of power acquisition, power can also be gained *indirectly*, such as when A gets what they want via their ability to *influence the environment* or 'rules of the game' in which conflicts take place, to the advantage of A and disadvantage of B. Consequently, while conflicts of power can certainly be played out in the open, so too can they take place 'behind the scenes'. Furthermore, others, such as Steven Lukes (2004), have pointed out that power does not purely exist at times of (overt or covert) conflict, but can also be gained in non-conflictual situations, such as when A is able to *influence or shape the preferences* of B, so that both A and B end up wanting and getting the same thing. In this sense, while actors can get what they want through direct or indirect coercion, so too can power be non-coercive, when exercised through the seductive shaping of norms and preferences (see: Hay, 1997).

The above contrasting accounts of power have come to be known as the 'faces of power' debate. Combined, they argue that power can be exercised in three ways: through *direct force*, via *indirect manipulation* and/or by *shaping norms and preferences*. Building on the faces of power debate is the American political scientist Joseph Nye. As opposed to focusing solely on how we might define power, Nye rather seeks to shed light on the power *options* available to actors—states, non-state organizations, transnational corporations, and so on—in their bid to make, receive or resist change. Importantly, for Nye (2011), the constitution of what 'power' is, is highly dependent on specific human relationships, which, more importantly, vary in different situations and settings. Indeed, while the saying 'money is power' may ring true for many, this would not be considered so amongst the indigenous tribes of Brazil's Amazon basin, for instance, whose communities are based not on the accumulation of financial wealth, but rather reflect a more hunter-gatherer type of society; and, while more forceful forms of power may be employed to get what one wants in some settings, a coercive strategy is not an effective solution in all interactions and contexts. In recognizing this, Nye (2011) puts forward what he calls a 'policy oriented' power approach, one that emphasizes *how* actors can effectively get what they want in varying scenarios. In doing so, Nye coins the concepts of 'hard' and 'soft' powers.

'Hard power' is 'the ability to get desired outcomes through coercion and payment' (Nye, 2011, p. 16). Here, states, for instance, may achieve outcomes through force or economic (dis)incentive. Indeed, as we saw in Chap. 1, realist accounts of power would align with hard power forms, when, for example, leaders employ military assets to physically engage, weaken and/or destroy others, as demonstrated by Russia's military coup and ultimate annexation of the Ukrainian owned peninsula of Crimea, in 2014 (see: *Foreign Affairs*, 18 April 2016). However, such assets may also be used to back up threats in 'coercive diplomacy', as was the case in 2003, when ex-Libyan prime minister Muammar Gaddafi dismantled Libya's weapons of mass destruction programme after America's commitment towards forceful change was showcased with the invasion of Afghanistan in 2001, and in Iraq two years later (see: Stevens, 2017).

Alongside military means, states may also endeavour to get what they want in hard power terms through the use of monetary (dis)incentives (Nye, 2011). There are two ways this may be achieved. First is through economic *incentives*, such as cross-border tariff reductions, favourable market access, investment guarantees (including the guarantee to financially invest in the organization and staging of a mega-event) or the provision of financial support. An example of the latter includes the 'Belt and Road' initiative, a $900 billion project launched by China in 2013, which finances key infrastructure development in countries across Asia, Europe and Africa, and, in doing so, effectively widens trade routes to and from Beijing (see: *Forbes*, 22 December 2017). Another example is China's building of sports stadiums in Africa, known as 'stadium diplomacy', to facilitate access to ruling elites and emerging markets (Dubinsky, 2021). A further way hard power is gained is through economic *disincentives*, in the form of sanctions, embargoes, the suspension of aid or unfavourable taxation (Nye, 2011). An illustrative example here includes the economic sanctions imposed on Burmese security forces by the United States in 2018 for atrocities relating to evidence of ethnic cleansing against

Rohingya Muslims, as well as general 'widespread human rights abuses' (see: *The New York Times*, 17 August 2018). Sanctions such as these—as well as diplomatic and/or sporting sanctions, embargoes and boycotts—act as forms of material and symbolic punishment, with the ultimate goal to forcibly change the behaviour of others.

'Soft power', in contrast, is the 'ability to obtain the outcomes one wants through attraction rather than coercion or payment' (Nye, 2008a, p. 94). This form of power stems from qualities such as an attractive culture, appealing values, policies and institutions, or acclaimed accomplishments. The Republic of Peru, for example, despite having relatively mediocre military and economic assets, nonetheless, continues to benefit from increasing international tourism gains, thanks to the country's iconic cultural historical attractions, such as Machu Picchu (*World Travel and Tourism Council Report*, 2017). Elsewhere, Belgium has successfully carved out a key position for itself in international politics, thanks largely to its vital role in the founding and housing of major transnational organizations, such as the European Union (EU) and North Atlantic Treaty Organization (NATO). And finally, we point to a country such as Italy—dubbed a 'cultural superpower', the state is known for its 'global omnipresence of Italian cuisine and its iconic, internationally renowned luxury brands' (*Soft Power 30*, 2019). In cases such as these, states seek to get what they want not through coercion, but rather via adapting international agendas and influencing trends and tastes in order to align the preferences of others to their own.

Crucially, for Nye, is that, although hard power remains important in international affairs, it is soft power that states of all sizes and political hues need to take greater advantage of in the twenty-first century. This is due to two, interlinked developments that have taken place in international politics in recent decades. First, as we saw in Chap. 1, there has been a general movement away from the use of traditional harder forms of power (such as military deployment), which, for Nye, has resulted in the soft power quality of attraction becoming a more important, yet scarcer, resource for modern-day actors. As communications technologies have advanced, and the amount of data transmitted across the globe has grown, individuals and societies have become bombarded with more and more information about others' identities, ideas and visions. For Nye (2002, p. 67), this leads to a 'paradox of plenty', which in turn results in the 'poverty of attention'; in other words, with the increasing volume of information on hand, it becomes progressively more important for actors to echo notions of attractiveness and appeal, yet increasingly harder to showcase these traits in and amongst the background of informational 'white noise' (ibid.). The consequence is that, in the 'information society' of today, state and non-state individuals, groups and organizations not only feel the need to 'identify' themselves on the global stage, but must continuously look for new ways to distinguish their attraction and relevance from the ever-expanding flow of information in circulation (Nye, 2008).

Second, thanks to wider globalization trends, and specifically advances in information technologies, issues formerly regarded as the sole prerogatives of states have become shared by a growing variety of non-state actors (Keohane & Nye, 2003). With greater access to worldwide communicative technologies, more actors now occupy the ability to gather, shape and disseminate information to mass onlookers, leading to the political stage becoming shared by a broader, more diverse audience which now includes: international non-governmental organizations, transnational corporations, global media networks as well as other non-state actors, such as terrorist groups, internet hackers and religious movements. Crucially, this has not led to states and politicians no longer being the dominant actors in world politics; rather, non-state actors have simply added a layer on top of traditional global and national state politics through their ability to more easily, clearly and loudly raise their own concerns and expose immoral practices, all of which political leaders become increasingly pressured to take into account and/or directly confront (see also: Hocking, 2005).

The result of these twin developments is that, in the modern epoch, international politics has, in large part, become defined by the greater need for reputation promotion, display and management. Garnering an effective, positive image does nonetheless require a great deal of innovation from state leaders. This is because the modern-day nation state is, in large part, characterized as one of 'entrepreneurism'—that is, a state that proactively seeks to spur on innovation and economic income by deliberately and successfully taking advantage of external markets for domestic growth (see: Mazzucato, 2011). In truly encapsulating 'globalization-for-state-purposes', the contemporary entrepreneurial state does not just simply provide the 'conditions for innovation to flourish', but rather occupies the position as a leading agent in the pursuit of new markets, investment opportunities and growth-enhancing solutions (ibid., p. 18). Through this, the entrepreneurial state is also the 'competition state', one who competes with other states for global competitive advantages (see: Cerny, 1997). How successful one is within this competitive environment is dependent on a number of factors, one of which is how attractive one is in the eyes of others—as a place to live, work, visit and/or do business with. It is because of this, for those who seek to wield influence in international affairs, that one's ability to come up with innovative strategies in the highly competitive pursuit of soft power projection and control becomes crucial (see: Brannagan and Giulianotti, 2018).

For small states, soft power is a particularly vital facet to their global entrepreneurial ambitions. As we have seen, this is largely due to their relative lack of material power, specifically with regard to military might and population size. Indeed, as Chong (2010, p. 385) rightly notes on this, 'the informational power of getting others to want what one wants through attraction instead of coercion defies sovereignty-bound ways of comprehending power'. Thus, for small states such as Qatar, whose military capabilities are limited, the pursuit of soft power acts as one avenue through which to wield influence on the world stage, and to compete with its larger peers. Crucially however, for small states seeking to wield soft power, evidence suggests that they endeavour to do so by channelling their efforts on a limited range of what we might call 'niche markets' or 'niche areas'—such as tourism (Dubai), financial services (Switzerland), manufacturing (Mauritius) or humanitarian efforts (Norway). In many cases, this is due to small states' limitations around available human resources, labour supply chains and economies of scale (see: Armstrong and Read, 2006; Punnett and Morrison, 2006). Nonetheless, the desire to be innovative can also act as a further motivation to search for a niche area—as small states seek to carve out for themselves a 'space' within the international community, they look to do so by employing a targeted, distinctive approach, and thus avoid entering niches that other small or neighbouring states have already largely occupied for themselves (see: Peterson, 2006).

As we saw in Chap. 2, three of Qatar's niche areas can be said to lie in the state's exportation of oil and liquefied natural gas, its mediation work across the Middle East and North African region, and its promotion of a global media network, Al Jazeera. In the next section, we argue that a fourth niche market lies in the state's investment in global sport, and particularly its acquisition of the 2022 World Cup, which acts as the 'jewel in the crown' to its competitive pursuit of soft power.

THE 2022 FIFA WORLD CUP AND QATAR'S GLOBAL SPORTS STRATEGY

Qatar's sporting endeavours provide us with a notable case study on the ways in which hard power can be strategically used for soft power gains. Indeed, while Qatar has limited military capabilities of its own, important to remember is that, thanks to its sale of oil and natural gas, the state does occupy a level of wealth that most (small) states do not. In a number of ways, this places Qatar in a more favourable position than other countries when it comes to soft power deployment—Qatar can of course dedicate far greater sums of wealth and investment to its soft power push, and can, in certain instances where permitted, outbid others for key soft power assets. In doing so, in the realm of global sport, we argue that Qatar's niche soft power strategy rests on three key pillars: *the hosting of sports events; overseas sports investments; and leveraging domestic excellence*. We deal with each in turn.

Hosting Sports Events

We argue that the foremost pillar of Qatar's global sports strategy centres on the staging of sports events. Table 3.1 lists what we might call the more 'sporadic' sports events the state has hosted since 1976 (five years after Qatar gained independence). By 'sporadic' events, we refer to those events that are not automatically staged annually but take place every few years on a rotational basis, are secured through a bidding process and are individually awarded by various regional or international sports governing body, such as the Asian Football Confederation, World Athletics (formerly the International Association of Athletics Federations), the International School Sport Federation (ISF) or FIFA. Thus, Table 3.1 excludes those events that Qatar has, or will, stage annually on a consistent basis, such as the Qatar Tennis Open, which has been staged yearly since 1993, the International Handball Federation Super Globe, which Qatar staged in 2002, and again from 2010 to 2018, and the grand prix of the Formula One circuit, which the state will stage for the first time in 2021, and then from 2023 to 2033. In reviewing Table 3.1, we can suggest that Qatar is therefore what we might call a 'serial user' of sporadic major sports events—that is, a country that demonstrates a consistent track record of pursuing the staging of such events in a variety of sports, large and small, over a sustained period of time (for more on this, see: Black, 2017).

Table 3.1   List of sports events hosted in Qatar

Event	Hosted
Arabian Gulf Cup	1976
AFC Asian Football Cup	1988
Arabian Gulf Cup	1992
Asian Handball Championships	2004
ITTF World Table Tennis Championships	2004
Arabian Gulf Cup	2004
Asian Basketball Championships	2005
World Weightlifting Championships	2005
West Asian Games	2005
Asian Sailing Championships	2006
Asian Games	2006
Asian Indoor Athletics Championships	2008
Asian Fencing Championships	2009
ISF World Gymnasiade	2009
IAAF World Indoor Championships	2010
ISAF World Junior Sailing Championships	2010
AFC Asian Football Cup	2011
Pan Arab Games	2011
ASC Asian Shooting Championships	2012
FINA Short Course World Championships	2014
INF World Handball Championships	2015
AIBA World Amateur Boxing Championships	2015
UCI World Cycling Championships	2016
Asian Indoor Athletics Championships	2016
FIG Artistic World Gymnastics Championships	2018
IAAF World Championships	2019
Arabian Gulf Cup	2019
ASC Asian Shooting Championships	2019
FIFA Club World Cup	2019
FIFA Club World Cup	2020 (postponed to 2021)
FIFA Arab Cup	2021
FIFA World Cup	2022
FINA World Aquatics Championships	2023

Indeed, between 2000 and 2023, for instance, Qatar will have hosted a total of 30 of these more sporadic regional or international sports events over a 23-year period.

Why, then, might the staging of multiple sports events be so appealing to a small state such as Qatar? In sporting terms, we may argue that Qatar's more recent hosting of a multitude of 'large' and 'small' events may well be explained by what we might call a 'building up to' strategy—that is, building up to bid for or stage a 'first-order'[1] sports event, in this case the 2022 World Cup. As mentioned in the introduction, Qatar has a limited history of competing at major global sports events—it has never competed in a World Cup, and has only collected at handful of medals at the Summer Olympic Games, which it only started to attend in 1984. Nonetheless, for states such as Qatar, one avenue through which to make up for this lack of athletic participation is to acquire experience of staging a number of smaller events. On the one hand, the hosting of multiple events fosters a vital internal 'process of ongoing learning and growing organizational sophistication' for the host country, both prior to bidding for and hosting a major first-order event (see: Black, 2017, p. 220). On the other hand, it crucially also allows the host to develop a portfolio and reputation as a successful organizer and deliverer of numerous events, which, in turn, can then be leveraged as part of any future attempt to showcase one's readiness and capacity to host future events. Consequently, we may hypothesize that Qatar's staging of multiple sports events—particularly from 2004 onwards—may in part have been tied to its preparation to bid for the 2022 World Cup, the bidding process of which started in 2009 and concluded in 2010.

In political terms, we argue that Qatar's appetite for staging multiple sports events lies in the state's desire to secure what Nye (2011) calls sources of 'strategic communication'. Sources of strategic communication refer to resources that enable state leaders to disseminate a series of widely heard, reputation-promoting messages over a sustained period of time. Obtaining and effectively wielding such resources requires a high degree of planning, innovation and, most notably, competition, as states come to compete with one another for such scarce communications platforms that can help them stand out from the 'white noise' of the global information society, and thus can provide a significant competitive advantage when it comes to projecting soft power. Examples of such resources include the housing and control of a successful global media network, such as Al Jazeera, or, more relevantly, the staging of an international (sports) event. In the case of the latter, we may contend that something like a World Cup acts as a strategic communications recourse of the very highest calibre. Indeed, not only do events of this magnitude put their hosts in the global limelight for a sustained period of time, from the bidding process to the final whistle (12 years, in Qatar's case), but they are also one of the few resources on the planet that attract the attention of international audiences numbering in the billions—the last World Cup, played in Russia in 2018, for instance, generated a television audience of 3.572 billion, equivalent to 51.4% of the entire global population aged four years and over (FIFA, 21 December 2018).

For Qatar, we contend that the 2022 World Cup as a strategic communications resource helps the state achieve three objectives. The first is the innovative attempt to overcome one of the greatest hurdles faced by small sates: their invisibility on the world stage. Indeed, for highly recognized states such as China, Germany and the United Kingdom, promoting their existence is of little concern, and image projection is thus rather focused towards *improving or adding* to one's (inter)national soft power (see: Leonard and Small, 2003). Small states, however, are commonly 'characterized by a lack of information' and, thus, in order to acquire influence abroad, must first overcome their invisibility by capturing the attention of international audiences (Bátora, 2005, p. 6). This issue is compounded by the fact that small states are also continuously mindful of 'the need to differentiate themselves from their [larger] neighbours who are often culturally similar' (Houlihan & Zheng, 2015, p. 334). Such similarity acts as a particular problem for small states in their quest to raise awareness of their existence: note, for instance, how Hong Kong has eagerly sought to detach itself symbolically from Chinese foreign policy, decision-making and authority (Ho & Bairner, 2013); while Singapore has sought ways to emblematically disengage the state from South-East Asian rule (Leifer, 2000); and, as we saw in Chap. 2, how Qatar has sought to carve out for itself an independent foreign policy, one that helps it break with notions that it is simply a 'minor regional actor in the shadow of Saudi Arabia' (see: Khatib, 2014, p. 1).

In continuously seeking for new ways to promote awareness of the state's independence, Qatar attempts to achieve what Chong (2010, p. 386) calls 'audience socialization': that is, increasing visibility and separating oneself from larger neighbours by educating global audiences on one's existence, individuality and right to sovereign rule. In shedding light on how forms of audience socialization might be achieved, Lakatos (2017, p. 59) notes that success in this regard rests on innovative and imaginative solutions, whereby, for maximum efficiency, small states need to focus their energies in specific areas that generate 'the best returns and the widest international recognition'. In searching for a suitable avenue through which to obtain such optimal recognition, Qatar's leadership views the 2022 World Cup as an unrivalled resource in this regard. Indeed, the

Qatar National Development Strategy 2011–2016 (2011, pp. 19–196)—the first in a series of roadmaps to assist the state achieve the Qatar National Vision by the year 2030—acknowledges how 'Qatar has enjoyed unprecedented global recognition' through sport, with events such as the 2022 World Cup in particular greatly enhancing 'the nation's regional and international image'.

Evidence of such enhancement can arguably be supported by looking at the FutureBrand Country Brand Index, an annually produced list which measures countries from across the world in terms of 'country brand' and international perception. In 2012, for the first time ever, Qatar made it into the Index's 'future 15' list—finishing 4th out of 15, the Index noted that Qatar was able 'to elevate its global role following its winning bid for the 2022 World Cup' (FutureBrand Country Brand Index, 2012–2013, p. 47). Since 2014, Qatar has consistently remained in the top 30 of the FutureBrand Country Brand Index list, a marked improvement on its position of 72 in 2010 (prior to being awarded the rights to the 2022 World Cup) (see: FutureBrand Country Brand Index, 2019). More recently, in the 2021 Best Countries ranking by U.S. News, Qatar was placed at 32 (U.S. News, 2021); and according to the Global Soft Power Index published by Brand Finance, Qatar jumped from rank 30 in 2020 to position 26 in the 2021 index (Brand Finance, 2021, pp. 3, 18).

Nonetheless, when it comes specifically to sport, Nassif (2020) argues that 'if Qatar is a powerhouse in the organization of mega-sport events, the same cannot be said about the performance of its athletes in international competitions'. He refers in his article to the Global Sports Impact (GSI) Nations Index, established by the company Sportcal, which measures countries' performances in organizing global sport events and ranks Qatar in the 2019 report 17th in the world. In the 'Ranking of Sports Cities', established by Burson Cohn & Wolfe to evaluate the performance of cities in hosting sporting events, Doha has however consistently made the top 50 since 2012. This is, according to Nassif, 'impressive, considering there are an estimated 10,000 cities around the world' (Nassif, 2020). Yet, in the World Ranking of Countries in Elite Sport (WRCES) index, which measures the performance of countries in those sports recognized by the Global Association of International Sports Federations (GAISF), Qatar has made the top 80 only twice since the first edition of this index, finishing 67th in 2015 and 80th in 2019. According to Nassif (ibid.), a notable reason why Qatar has performed so poorly here is due to the fact that, while it does compete in many male categories of sport, it has yet to make serious inroads in terms of female participation, an issue we discuss further in Chap. 5.

Second, alongside seeking to raise awareness of its existence, and to further break from under the shadow of its larger, culturally similar neighbour, Saudi Arabia, the staging of a major event such as the 2022 World Cup serves an additional, long-term purpose: to demonstrate what Qatar has to offer to those beyond its borders. Having captured the attention of international audiences, the 2022 World Cup also provides the state with a stage through which it can showcase its relevance, usefulness and attractiveness to others—be that in terms of investment opportunities, education and knowledge exchange, or humanitarian causes. For small states such as Qatar, this is crucial, as raising awareness of one's significance to others is vital to their security—indeed, as Chong (2010, p. 385) notes, 'the art of survival for small states includes attempts to enlarge their *importance* to the international community [emphasis added]'. Endeavouring to do so via the staging of a major sport event resonates with what is known as 'virtual enlargement'—that is, in making up for their physical size, the deliberate attempt of a small state to enlarge its importance on the world stage and further safeguard its survival by aligning what it has to offer with the interests and desires of external leaders, groups and communities (see also: Cooper & Shaw, 2009).

A common virtual enlargement strategy of small states is the diffusion of one's culture, which, in the majority of cases, is linked to attempts to foster material gains in tourism. Note, for instance, how the Bahamas, Dubai and Singapore have enlarged their presence and significance on the international stage through successes in this regard. In doing so, crucial for a relatively successful post-oil economy such as Dubai—Qatar's GCC counterpart—has been to overcome what has been termed as the 'neighbourhood effect' (Steiner, 2010, p. 729; see also: Brannagan & Grix, 2014). This locates how states in close proximity to those who regularly experience instances of conflict and civil turmoil come to have their images severely damaged by notions of instability and insecurity, even if they themselves have never directly witnessed any domestic unrest. In the majority of cases, this comes to severely damage their tourism intake. It has been frequently shown, for instance, that tourists occupy negative stereotypes of entire regions based on regular media reports of just a few national, isolated illustrations of hostility (Sönmez, 1998). This has been particularly so since 9/11 and the resulting conflicts in Afghanistan and Iraq, whereby 'terrorism' has largely been interpreted as a specific problem of 'Arab' countries, thus significantly impacting tourism numbers across the Middle East and North Africa[2] (Daher, 2007; Steiner, 2007). Added to this have been instances of civil protest across the region, stating with the Arab Spring in 2011, and more recently in Lebanon, when between 2019 and 2021 a series of demonstrations took place in opposition to the government's perceived sectarian rule and the country's stagnant economy (*BBC*, 29 March 2021).

Consequently, for Qatar, we can argue that a third way that the 2022 World Cup assists the state is in its attempt to overcome broad-brush, negative stereotypes of the Middle East—as highlighted by Hassan Al-Thawadi in the introduction to this chapter. This looks to be done by using the spotlight generated by the World Cup to show international audiences that the state is not only an attractive place to visit but also a safe and stable one. Key to note here, is that, in 2021, according to the Global Peace Index (2021), Qatar was listed as the 29th most peaceful country in the world, and the most peaceful Arab country, ahead of key tourist destinations such as the United Kingdom (33rd), the UAE (52nd) and France (55th). Similarly, in the 2021 edition of Global Finance's safest countries in the world ranking, Qatar was, after Iceland and the United Arab Emirates, ranked the third safest country in the world.

Leading the way in this regard is the National Tourism Sector Strategy 2030 (2014, p. 3), which is the state's strategic blueprint for turning Qatar into an 'unavoidable destination on the world tourism map' by the year 2030. Crucially, the strategy highlights how, on the one hand, the staging of sports events seek to be used to entice 'sport enthusiasts [who] can expect to enjoy the experience of a lifetime in Qatar' (National Tourism Sector Strategy Q&A, n.d, p. 13), while, on the other hand, and more broadly, tournaments such as the 2022 World Cup look to 'introduce Qatar to more people around the world … helping them discover what the country has to offer and further tempting them to visit' (ibid., p. 17). Consequently, Qatar looks to use events such as the World Cup to *introduce* potential tourists to the state's various leisure and cultural amenities, such as its museums and other heritage sites, or its plethora of high-end restaurants, shops and hotels. In this sense, Qatar joins the long list of states who have previously sought to use sports events for tourism branding: take the 2014 World Cup and 2018 Winter Olympics, for instance, which were in part hosted with the hope of encouraging a greater number of tourists to visit Brazil and South Korea, respectively (see: Baumann & Matheson, 2018; Wood & Meng, 2020).

Crucially, increases in tourism would go some way towards helping the state confront one of its central concerns: 'diversifying the economy and reducing Qatar's dependence on its hydrocarbon resources' (National Tourism Sector Strategy, 2014, p. 3). Indeed, as discussed in Chap. 2, Qatar's oil and gas sector contributes to 70% of the state's total revenues, 85% of its export earnings and 60% of its gross domestic product. Consequently, encouraging tourism through the hosting of sports events acts as one solution for the state in this regard. The need for the state to find innovative ways to open up new tourism markets is further compounded by Qatar's recent inability to compete with its neighbours for this crucial economic resource. Indeed, in 2019—the year before the outbreak of the Covid-19 pandemic, and its associated impact on international tourism—Qatar welcomed a mere 2.1 million tourists to its shores (see: United Nations, World Tourism Barometer, 2019). In comparison, in the same year, Saudi Arabia welcomed 17.5 million, the UAE 16.7 million, and Oman 2.5 million—even Qatar's smaller neighbour, Bahrain, recorded 3.8 million visitors (see: ibid.). Of note is that Qatar's low tourism numbers here are likely the part-result of the Saudi-led blockade of the state that took place from 2017 to 2021. Although the blockade never truly came close to any forms of real hostility nor violence, this incident has nonetheless not helped to promote tourism to Qatar. Thus, not only will the 2022 World Cup need to assist Qatar rid itself of any broader Middle Eastern stereotypes, but it will also need to show that relations with its immediate neighbours have pacified (a topic we discuss further in Chap. 5).

A final point to mention here is that, as previous research has constantly reminded us (see, in particular: Solberg & Preuss, 2007), short-term tourism economic benefits are, of course, relative to how much states spend on organizing sports events. Presently, Qatar is, on average, dedicating $500 million a week towards the construction of tournament-related infrastructure, and has set itself a total World Cup budget of $191 billion (*The Guardian*, 12 December 2012). Consequently, it is unlikely the state will profit in financial terms solely from event tourism itself, particularly given ongoing uncertainties around the state of international tourism in a 'post'-Covid-19 world (see also: Grix et al., 2021). However, unlike well-known states such as Brazil and South Korea, who consistently exert moderate tourism numbers, and thus seek to use sports events to generate tourism 'spikes'[3] by reminding audiences what they have to offer, we must remember that, for Qatar, the focus here is on improving tourism in the much longer term. Indeed, as we have seen in this section, the 2022 World Cup—and other international sports events—seeks to be used to *introduce* international audiences to what the state has to offer in cultural terms, with the hope that this will start to pay dividends by the year 2030 and beyond. In short, for Qatar, the World Cup is thus a crucial part of the state's longer-term plan, one which extends well beyond 2022.

We argue that, as part of this 'long-term plan', the 2022 World Cup plays a central role; however, the state's other sporting investments and endeavours come to strongly complement what Qatar seeks to achieve through the World Cup. The Qatar Sports Sector Strategy is the state's blueprint document for identifying how sport will contribute to Qatar's future development. In doing so, it specifies that:

> Hosting of the FIFA 2022 World Cup will accelerate the development of the objectives of Qatar National Vision 2030, which aim at transforming Qatar into an advanced country by 2030 ... At the international level, sports events ... help raise Qatar's regional and global profile .... International sport [more broadly] is also a powerful tool for international engagement and diplomacy ... [and] can also be a significant economic force in itself through activities such as sports events, sports-related services, sports tourism and the media ... Success in sports has become an inspiration for the whole society and contributes to an energized, confident and modernising nation. (Qatar Sports Sector Strategy 2011–2016, pp. 4–10)

In picking up on this, Qatar's Second National Development Strategy 2018–2022 (2018, p. 260)—the follow-up roadmap to the Qatar National Development Strategy 2011–2016—identifies sport and sports events as being crucial to enhancing the state's 'regional and international cooperation and communication to reflect the civilized image of the country', as well as 'the sector's ability to contribute to the diversification of the economic base and national income sources, in addition to activating the role of the private sector'; it further contends that broader areas such as 'sports media activity' and 'achieving sport excellence' are to play a notable role in 'building Qatar's future as a global sport hub' (ibid., pp. 251–253).

Thus, while securing the rights to the 2022 World Cup may well be Qatar's greatest achievement in sport (to date), we can argue with some certainty that it is part of a broader state strategy, one that looks to take full advantage of the sports sector beyond simply the hosting of sports events. This is perhaps not surprising. Indeed, when seeking to situate themselves as leaders of niche markets, small states endeavour to have 'maximum impact' on a specific sector, and do so by acquiring full knowledge of the entire niche market (see: Smith, 1999). Furthermore, we can suggest that such a strategy also reflects a form of 'bundling', referring to the 'practice of marketing two or more products and/or services in a single "package"' (Guiltinan, 1987, p. 74)—in the case of Qatar, such bundling occurs by piggybacking off the symbolic and material opportunities that the 2022 World Cup provides, leading up to, and after, the tournament and, in doing so, supporting the development of state companies such as Qatar Airways and linked sub-industries within the niche (sports media, elite athlete development, sports humanitarianism etc.). It is towards an examination of these sub-industries that we now turn.

Overseas Sports Investments

As mentioned, the reaming two pillars of Qatar's global sports strategy look to take advantage of and complement its staging of the 2022 World Cup. The first of these centres on investment in key overseas markets. One form through which this is achieved is via the state's investment in various sports properties. An example of this can be found in Qatari Diar's 2011 purchase—in collaboration with British property developer Delancey Estates—of the London 2012 Olympic Athletes' Village, for a fee of £557 million (*The Guardian*, 12 August 2011). Now known as 'East Village', Qatar Diar—the real estate arm of the Qatar Investment Authority—has played a key role in converting the former-Athletes' Village into a state-of-the-art residential neighbourhood, inclusive of luxury residential homes, bars, restaurants, gyms and gardened parks (see Qatari Diar, n.d.). Then there is of course the state-owned Qatar Sports Investment's purchase in 2011 of French Ligue 1 club, Paris Saint-Germain, for an estimated fee of €100 million (*Reuters*, 6 March 2012). Since Qatar's takeover of Paris Saint-Germain, the club has gone on to break several transfer records in its pursuit of some of the world's most renowned football talent. Most notable here has been the 2017 acquisition of Brazilian star, Neymar Jr., for a world record fee of €222 million, as well as the 2018 purchase of French forward, Kylian Mbappé, for a fee of €180 million (the second most expensive fee ever recorded in world football, and the largest ever paid for a teenager). Such extravagant spending has radically transformed Paris Saint-Germain into one of Europe's financial elite: it currently records the seventh highest annual revenue in world club football (see: Deloitte Football Money League, 2021), with its total worth rising from €100 million in 2011, to just over €2 billion in 2021, making it the globe's ninth most valuable professional football club (see: *Forbes*, 2021). Such financial muscle has led to PSG arguably pulling off one the greatest symbolic coups for Qatar—the ability to fund the extravagant wage demands of arguably the greatest footballer ever, Lionel Messi, who signed for PSG from Barcelona in August 2021.

An additional investment avenue lies in Qatar's attempt to attach the state's name to prestigious sports clubs and events. This is achieved chiefly through the medium of sports sponsorships (on this, see also: Chadwick et al., 2020). Table 3.2 provides a list of Qatar's major overseas investments in this regard. From this, we can clearly see that it has been Qatar Airways—the state-owned flag carrier of Qatar—that has been the most prominent in overseas sponsorships of this nature. Key highlights include when, upon taking over from the Qatar Foundation, the airline became the first-ever commercial sponsor of the FC Barcelona shirt from 2013 to 2017, in a deal worth £25 million per annum (*The Independent*, 9 April 2013). Also of note here is Qatar Airways position as an 'Official Airline Partner' of FIFA, as well as its certified sponsorship of the 2018 and 2022 FIFA World Cups (see: FIFA, 7 May 2017). Then, in 2018, the airline became the shirt sponsor of Italian Serie A side, AS Roma, with Qatar Airways paying €40 million for an initial deal up until the 2020/2021 season (*Reuters*, 23 April 2018). And most recently, Qatar Airways was one of the main sponsors of the UEFA Euro 2020 Championships (played in summer 2021)—during each of the tournament's games, Qatar Airway's name and logo could be seen on the pitch-side advertising banners, along with the message 'see you in Qatar 2022'.

Another prominent sponsor in Table 3.2 is the Qatari telecommunications provider, Ooredoo, which, along with the Qatar National Bank, Qatar Airways and the Qatar Tourism Authority, is one of a number of 'premium partners' of Qatari-owned Paris Saint Germain (see: PSG.fr, 'partners', n.d.); of note is also Ooredoo's sponsorship of the Leo Messi Foundation, the international educational and healthcare charity set up by the PSG and Argentinian forward Lionel Messi (see: Ooredoo, 'Lionel Messi', n.d.). Finally, of significance here is Qatar's investment in various overseas prestigious horse racing events, such as the Qatar Investments and Projects Development Holding Company's (Qipco) sponsorship of the esteemed Royal Ascot—the first-ever commercial deal in the tournament's 303-year history (*Financial Times*, 16 June 2014)—as well as its

Table 3.2 List of Qatar's major overseas sports sponsorship agreements, past and present

Qatari organization	Sponsored organization/event	Date
Qatar Airways	FC Barcelona	2013–2017
	Sydney Swans	2016–
	FIFA Official Airline Partner	2017–
	2018 and 2022 World Cups	2017–2022
	Formula E Championship	2017–
	Boca Juniors	2018–
	AS Roma	2018–
	2018 Asian Games	2018
	FC Bayern Munich	2018–
	FIFA CONMEBOL	2018–
	K.A.S. Eupen	2019–
	Golf Australia	2019–
	NBA Brooklyn Nets	2019–
	Paris Saint Germain	2020–
	Euro 2020	2021
Qatar Foundation	FC Barcelona	2010–2013
Ooredoo	Paris Saint-Germain	2013–
	Lionel Messi Foundation	2013–
	Real Madrid CF	2015–2017
Qatar Tourism Authority	Paris Saint-Germain	2012–
Qatar National Bank	Paris Saint-Germain	2012–
Qatar Racing and Equestrian Club (QREC)	Prix de l'Arc de Triomphe	2008–
	Goodwood Festival	2014–
Qatar Investments and Projects	Royal Ascot	2014–
Holding Company (Qipco)	British Champions Series	2015–

£50 million sponsorship agreement with the British Champions' Series, the largest ever commercial deal in British racing history (*BBC*, 11 June 2015).

A further resource lies in Qatar's acquisition of overseas television rights. Notable here is Doha-based, former-Al Jazeera subsidiary, beIN Sports. Now an independent media network in its own right, and run by QSI and PSG Chairman, Nasser al-Khelaifi, since its establishment in 2003, beIN has sought to challenge multiple established media corporations in acquiring the rights to sports competitions all over the world. In 2010, beIN competed with Canal Plus to secure several rights to broadcast across France live games from Ligue 1, Ligue 2, UEFA Champions League, UEFA Europa League, the English FA Cup and La Liga (cf.

UEFA, 17 February 2012); in the United States, beIN airs live football from English, Spanish, French and Italian leagues, as well as covering U.S.A World Cup qualifying games (*The New York Times*, 30 August 2012). On sports mega-events, in 2011 beIN (then known as 'Al Jazeera Sport') secured the Middle East and North African broadcasting rights to the 2018 and 2022 FIFA World Cups; in 2015, beIN then won the Middle East and North African rights to broadcast the 2018 and 2022 Winter Olympic Games, and the 2020 and 2024 Summer Olympic Games (*IOC*, 27 July 2015). Moreover, in 2019, beIN acquired the Middle East and North Africa rights to the 2019 and 2020 FIFA Club World Cups (see: beIN, 28 November 2019). Fronted by well-known sports pundits, such as ex-Sky Sports' Richard Keys and Andy Grey, beIN currently broadcasts a total of 60 channels to over 43 countries, and has over 55 million pay TV subscribers worldwide (*Financial Times*, 22 April 2020).

Combined, Qatar's overseas sports investments feed into its staging of the 2022 World Cup in a number of ways. Its acquisition of sporting properties, and its sponsorship of high-profile teams and events, act as additional assets in the state's drive to globally raise awareness of its existence. Indeed, while such pursuits do not attract the kind of international attention as that of a major sport event, they do nonetheless complement the 2022 World Cup by acting as constant signals of the state's foreign policy independence. In doing so, such pursuits also help remind others of Qatar's 'entrepreneurial' nature and intent. Chong (2010) argues that proactively showcasing one is 'open for business' is vital for small states, as both short- and long-term inward foreign investment is largely based on how successful such states are in reminding others not only of their presence, but, more importantly, of their economic attractiveness. One way this is achieved is through engagement with high-profile overseas ventures—such as investment in one of football's 'big-five' commercial leagues—which loudly demonstrate how the investor state can positively influence others' domestic economies (Mazzucato, 2011). By actively pursuing new international markets, we can suggest that Qatar symbolically flexes its financial muscles and, in doing so, gains soft power by enticing those who seek to take advantage of the financial opportunities on offer—note, for example, how political figures, such as ex London mayor and current UK prime minister, Boris Johnson, have previously attempted to seduce Qatari officials into investing in Britain by claiming, 'we can't afford to ignore our dynamic friends in the East' (*Huffington Post*, 26 June 2013), while UK and German companies have previously fallen over themselves in their pursuit of winning 2022 World Cup-related infrastructure projects in Doha. Like in the case of its liquefied natural gas exports, through this, Qatar also further shores up its security, as external markets become depend on the state's financial investment.

Consequently, Qatar joins some of its regional counterparts in their desire to use sport for global recognition and security, and to attract and influence overseas markets: take, for example, the Abu Dhabi United Group's £200 million purchase of English Premier League club, Manchester City, in 2008 (*Financial Times*, 2 September 2008); over the years, the City Football Group (CFG) developed the ambition 'to build the first truly global football organisation', with Manchester City's sister club New York City FC and other franchises in countries such as Australia, Japan, Spain and Uruguay (*Financial Times*, 8 December 2017). And then there is Dubai-based Emirates Airline's £100 million stadium naming rights and shirt sponsorship agreement with Arsenal FC in 2004, a deal that was renewed in 2012 for £150 million, with the shirt agreement then again extended in 2018 for a further £200 million (see: *BBC*, 19 February 2018); and more recently is Emirates' deal to become the main shirt sponsor of French Ligue 1 club, Olympique Lyon, from the 2020/21 to the 2024/2025 season (*Emirates*, 6 February 2020).

Such overseas sporting pursuits do, of course, also feed into the desire of these small states to overcome the financial vulnerabilities that accompany such a heavy reliance on natural resources wealth. Indeed, we may argue that the harvesting of overseas investments of this nature act as an example of Qatar's desire to 'support the development of entrepreneurship and innovation' in its bid to foster in a more 'diversified economy' (Qatar National Vision 2030, pp. 24–27). Take the state-owned Qatar Airways, for instance, which has emerged to become one of the world's leading airlines, with over 200 aircraft flying to 150 destinations across five continents, and annual revenues of US$13.2 billion (Qatar Airways, 18 September 2019). During the Covid-19 pandemic, Qatar Airways dethroned Emirates as the world's largest long-haul airline (*The Wall Street* Journal, 25 April 2021). For the airline company, sport is essential to its continued expansion, with its 'sponsorship of some of the world's greatest [sporting] club sides' offering Qatar Airways an unparalleled avenue through which to ensure its 'brand is seen in more countries than ever' (Qatar Airways Annual Report, 2019, p. 24). In this sense, alongside the 2022 World Cup, global sports sponsorships play a key role in supporting the state in its attempt to grow its non-hydrocarbon-based industries. For Vincent (2021), who has worked on the significance of Qatar Airways and Fly Emirates to small-state foreign policy in the Gulf, argues that 'the strength of the Qatar Airways brand is thus a key element of the projection of Qatari soft power'.

Furthermore, the rapidly expanding reach of the global sport media network, beIN, provides Qatar with a compelling platform through which to subtly disseminate its soft power message en masse. Within the highly networked world of today, control over the distribution of information becomes a form of power in itself, and, by looking to cement Qatar's position as a significant 'hub' within broader sports networks, BeIN offers the state the potential to take control over the flow not only of its own messages, but also those of others' (cf. Castells, 1996; Barney, 2004). Indeed, in the same way Al Jazeera has emerged to become a highly effective tool for Qatar to 'regain control over the messages transmitted to global audiences', through its live sports coverage and analysis (in the United States, Europe and across the Middle East and North Africa), so too does beIN offer the state the opportunity to further solidify its position as a 'key player in the current [global] information exchange market' (Samuel-Azran, 2013, p. 1294). Qatar's controlling position in this regard was demonstrated in 2020, when Saudi Arabia's attempt to purchase Newcastle United FC was blocked by the Premier League, in part due to Saudi's domestic ban on beIN, one of the Premier League's key broadcasters; it wasn't until Saudi lifted its national ban on beIN broadcasts in 2021 that the Premier League finally gave the green light for the purchase of Newcastle United to be completed (see: *The Independent*, 6 October 2021). Additionally, as mentioned, beIN has also secured the Middle East and North Africa broadcast rights for the 2022 World Cup, and thus will come to play a key role in shaping how Qatar is portrayed across the region leading up to, and during, the tournament.

Leveraging Domestic Excellence

The third and final pillar of Qatar's global sports strategy centres on what we call 'leveraging domestic excellence'—referring to the conscious effort to globally promote one's talent and expertise in specific areas. One area here for Qatar would certainly be the showcasing of its expertise in the staging of sport events, with the 2022 World Cup acting as the greatest demonstration in this regard—that is, if the tournament takes place without any obvious organizational and/or other issues. Complementing its

sports event hosting expertise is the state's proficiency in athlete development and rehabilitation. Key in this regard is the Aspire Zone. Established
in 2003, the Aspire Zone is a state-of-the-art, 250-hectare sports complex,
with facilities that include one Olympic-sized swimming pool, a 50,000-all-
seater football stadium, two five-star hotels and the world's largest indoor
multipurpose dome. In recent years, Aspire has attracted some of world's
leading athletes and teams, who have chosen the complex as their preferred training destination. Examples include in 2013, for instance, when
Premier League club Manchester United FC chose Aspire as its destination of choice for winter training, and in 2020, when German Bundasliga
champions, FC Bayern Munich, attended their tenth winter training camp
at Aspire (*FC Bayern*, 3 January 2020). Key here is also the Aspire-based
Aspetar—the only FIFA Medical Centre of Excellence in the Middle East,
and the first 'specialised orthopaedic and sports medicine hospital in the
Gulf region' (Aspetar, n.d.). Established in 2007, Aspetar has quickly
developed into a leading global centre for athletic medical care, attracting
some of the world's most prominent professional athletes for treatment
and rehabilitation, such as the following: Spanish tennis star, Rafael Nadal;
British long-distance runner, Mo Farah; PSG and Brazilian forward,
Neymar Jr.; French and FC Barcelona winger, Ousmane Dembélé; and
Borussia Dortmund and Norwegian striker, Erling Haaland.

Then there is the Aspire Dome's elite talent development programme,
the Aspire Academy. Established in 2004, the Academy's underlying man-
date is to create, manage and maximize talent pathways to turn young
athletes into tomorrow's champions (see: Brannagan, 2017). The key tar-
get group here are of course Qataris themselves. The Aspire Academy not
only houses leading facilities but also world-class coaches and sport scien-
tists who are sourced from across the globe in order to nurture and develop
any young Qatari athlete who shows promise. Those Qataris who have
come through the Academy's ranks to reach international success include
Mutaz Barshim, the Qatari high jumper who took gold at the Tokyo 2020
Olympic Games, and Nada Arkaji, female professional swimmer and the
first woman to represent Qatar at the Olympics (in 2012); additionally, in
2019 Qatar won its first ever AFC Asian Cup, with a team largely comprised of Aspire Academy graduates (see: *Forbes*, 6 February 2019).

Leading on from this is Qatar's endeavours in various 'sports humani-
tarian' projects. Alongside developing Qatari athletic talent, the Aspire
Academy, for example, also welcomes non-Qataris. In 2006, the Aspire
Academy launched a programme titled 'Football Dreams' that lasted until

2016 and has been described as 'the most ambitious scouting programme in sporting history' (*The Economist*, 10 March 2018). During its existence, the programme scouted more than 3.5 million 13-year-old boys in 17 African, Asian and Latin American countries (Aspire, 2021). Those who excelled were invited back to Aspire on a full scholarship, which covered everything from training expenses, to education and accommodation costs (Brannagan, 2017). According to the Aspire website, the motivation of the programme was 'to support developing countries in combination with helping local Aspire talents in their development' (Aspire, 2021). The journalist Sebastian Abbot wrote a book about the programme titled *The Away Game: The epic search for soccer's next football star.* Following the ambitious project, and specifically following the development of three boys who joined the programme named Ibrahima, Bernard and Diawandou, Abbot argues that, apart from humanitarian goals, a major objective of the programme was to provide local Qatari talent with competition to help them grow into world-class footballers (Abbot, 2018).

According to Abbot, early evidence suggests that the programme may have failed to identify the next Lionel Messi or Cristiano Ronaldo, as was originally expected when Football Dreams was launched (Abbot, 2018). However, the programme had some success stories of players who made it to top European football clubs, usually after first playing for K.A.S. Eupen, a Belgium First Division A professional club that was purchased by the Aspire Academy in 2012 to act as a feeder club, particularly for its non-Qatari football graduates (Aspire, 11 December 2019). Diawandou Diagne, after playing two seasons in Eupen, was signed by FC Barcelona in 2014. In 2021, he played for an Indian professional football club. For fellow Aspire graduate Henry Onyekuru, Eupen became a stepping stone to English Premier League club Everton in 2017. In 2021, he was under contract with French club AS Monaco and played for the Nigerian national team. Moussa Wagué made it in 2019, after graduating from Aspire and playing for Eupen, to FC Barcelona and became a Senegalese national team player. However, all the above-mentioned players have, to date, largely been sent out on loan, and have thus only made a few appearances with the top clubs that originally signed them.

Furthermore, in the area of sports humanitarianism is the not-for-profit International Centre for Sports Security (ICSS). Established in 2010, the Centre, in seeking to become a 'global hub of expertise', was set up with the clear objective 'to improve security, safety and integrity in sport by addressing real issues and providing world-leading services, skills, networks and knowledge' (ICSS Securing Sport Report, n.d., p. 3). The ICSS currently offers its expertise to a host of professional sports bodies and leagues across the world, and, in 2012, it became an official member of the United Nations Global Compact, the largest voluntary corporate responsibility initiative in the world (*ICSS*, 18 June 2012).

A final area in this regard is the investment in, and development of, the state's highest level domestic professional football tournament, the Qatar Stars League. A key strategy of the League and its respective clubs centres on signing some of the most well-known footballers worldwide. Key examples include: ex-FC Barcelona midfielder, and current Manchester City FC manager, Josep 'Pep' Guardiola, who played for Qatari club Al-Alhi SC from 2003 to 2005 (see: Brannagan, 2017); ex-Real Madrid CF and FC Schalke 04 forward, Raúl González, who in 2012 spent two years playing for Al Sadd SC (see: *Gulf Times*, 26 June 2014); former FC Barcelona captain and Spain midfielder, Xavier 'Xavi' Hernández, who in 2015 signed and played for Al Sadd SC until 2019, upon which time he became the club's manager, a post he continued to occupy until November 2021, when he returned to Barcelona and became the head coach of the team (see: *Gulf News*, 6 November 2021); and, more recently, in 2020, when former Arsenal FC and CF Villarreal midfielder, Santi Cazorla, signed for Al Sadd SC and, in 2021, when former Bayern Munich player Javi Martinez joined Qatar Sports Club (*The Peninsula*, 20 July 2020; *Doha News*, 22 June 2021).

Together, the housing of world-class talent and knowledge helps Qatar cement its position as the dominant actor within this niche market, and it shows that, despite its size, it can effectively contribute to international issues and society. In doing so, Qatar gains forms of what we may term as 'expertise power'—that is, the symbolic power and real influence that comes with being an expert state in a highly sought-after area. Indeed, like Cuba in the field of medicine, or Finland in the industry of telecommunications, for Qatar, athlete development, rehabilitation and sports security, as well as the effective staging of sports events, act as vehicles through which the state seeks to become known as a 'go-to' destination for expertise, best-practice advice and progression. This occurs in the same way as those small states (such as Iceland or Norway) which have deliberately endeavoured to position themselves as 'norm entrepreneurs'—states which actively seek to reframe or remobilize established global understandings through the construction of new and innovative ideas and/or solutions to contemporary problems (see: Fuentes-Julio, 2020). When successful, norm entrepreneurs not only acquire admiration from those they benefit, but, perhaps more importantly, they also gain leadership, as others continue to rely on their expertise when faced with challenges. Qatar's desire to welcome and train athletes from other countries, and its dedication to sports humanitarian causes, also showcases its willingness to assist others, thus further establishing its standing as a 'good global citizen'.

World-leading on-hand sports expertise and facilities—such as those found at the Aspire Academy—do of course also help with Qatar's desire to become a regular and successful competitor at major international athletic events. Consistent engagement with global sport provides small states in particular with a unique opportunity: the hosting of sports events, membership to transnational governing bodies (such as FIFA or the IOC), and athletic competition not only offers these states the opportunity to showcase their cultural distinctiveness from neighbouring states and/or ex-colonial masters, but also provides them with equivalent symbolic status with their larger peers, through, for example, equal recognition of their statehood at opening and closing ceremonies (Houlihan, 2015; Houlihan and Zheng, 2015). Additionally, major global sports events also provide small states with one opportunity through which to get one over larger, more established states—note, for example, how Iceland's 2–1 win over England at the UEFA Euro 2016 tournament captured the admiration of football fans from around the world and, in doing so, helped elevate the former's international profile (see: Orttung & Kazakov, 2018). For Qatar, on-field 'success' during its hosting of the 2022 World Cup would also demonstrate its ability to effectively overcome a small state limitation, namely that it can be successful despite the fact that its small population relative to its peers means that it is at a disadvantage when it comes to national team selection.

Finally, the housing of top-level athletes also provides Qatar with a level of what is known as 'celebrity diplomacy', referring to the use of celebrities by states in their attempt to frame and sell specific causes, ideas or visions to international audiences (see: Cooper, 2008). Key here is how celebrities can help 'bridge' the gap between Western audiences and non-Western states (see: Tsaliki et al., 2011, p. 299)—a point of concern expressed by Hassan Al-Thawadi in the introduction to this chapter. Few celebrities from small, non-Western states are well known in the West, and thus, in seeking to overcome this, such states can set about recruiting globally renowned celebrities to act as 'national representatives' (see: Avraham,

2020)—note, for instance, how Qatar's line-up of 2022 World Cup 'global ambassadors' includes the likes of ex-FC Barcelona midfielder, Xavi Hernandez, former Brazilian World Cup winner and A.C. Milan defender, Cafu, and former Cameroon and FC Barcelona forward, Samuel Eto'o (Qatar2022.qa, n.d.). The cosying up to world-renowned sports athletes and teams is intended to provide Qatar's message with a level of added value and credibility—indeed, its affiliation with multiple sporting stars, such as Paris Saint-Germain's Neymar Jr. and Lionel Messi, and European teams, such as Germany's FC Bayern Munich, not only helps Qatar connect with global audiences, but these sporting celebrities and brands also provide a level of symbolic endorsement in the state's attempt to position itself as a western-friendly, cooperative, safe and forward-looking Middle Eastern country.

CONCLUSION

This chapter set out to understand Qatar's World Cup strategy, and shed light on how the tournament seeks to acquire the state power, as well as how its broader investment in sport looks to assist with the objectives set out in its Qatar National Vision 2030. Through focusing on Nye's concept of soft power, we have seen in this chapter how small states can gain influence via proactively engaging in a process of what we might call 'strategic social construction'—that is, the attempt to (re)produce certain values, ideas, meanings and images. In doing so, small states can 'virtually enlarge' their presence within the international system—demonstrated by the examples of Dubai (in tourism) and Norway (in humanitarian efforts).

Qatar's global sport strategy arguably acts as one example of the ways through which subjectivism and materialism factors come to interact on the international stage. In this chapter, we have argued that Qatar's use of global sport can be said to be the state's fourth 'niche area', alongside its exportation of oil and (liquefied) natural gas, its regional mediation work and its investment in, and promotion of, global media network, Al Jazeera. Furthermore, we have argued that the state's overall sports strategy is underpinned by three main pillars: *the hosting of sports events; overseas sports investments; and leveraging domestic excellence.* Upon reviewing the state's intentions through sport, we can suggest that Qatar's use of global sport seeks to achieve two overarching outcomes. The first of these overarching outcomes is subjective, but is nonetheless underpinned by significant material investment, linked to the state's desire to raise awareness of its existence and, more importantly, symbolically cement its right to sovereign independence. As we have discussed in this chapter, a common anxiety amongst small states is the need to overcome their invisibility, and for Qatar, so too is the need to emerge from the political and cultural shadow of its larger neighbour, Saudi Arabia. In looking to overcome these hurdles, we have argued in this chapter that the state's (economic) investment in global sport, and its staging of sport events, seek to be used, in part, to enter into a process of 'audience socialization'—that is, to introduce and educate global audiences on who and where Qatar is and, in doing so, showcase that the state is an independent actor in its own right.

The second overarching theme here is materialist, but is nonetheless heavily dependent on subjective factors, linked to Qatar's desire to diversify its national economy, and safeguard its security. As we have seen in this chapter, and supported by the added credibility that comes with one's association with well-known athletes, pundits and other sporting celebrities, Qatar's staging of major tournaments—such as the 2022 World Cup—helps drive forward the narrative that the state is a safe and attractive place to visit, while its sponsorship of a multitude of major sports clubs and events helps increase relevant international audiences' brand familiarity with the likes of Qatar Airways, Ooredoo and Qipco; and its housing of world-class sports facilities and expertise help position the state as a welcoming, helpful and useful actor. Combined, Qatar's endeavours in sport act as a medium through which the state looks to globally position itself as a friendly, cooperative, proactive, international law respecting and forward-looking entrepreneurial state that is not only ripe for investment opportunities, but that, despite is size, it so too can be a leading and effective actor within international society. Connecting with global audiences in this way, it is hoped, will go some way towards moving the state away from its heavy reliance on hydrocarbon resources and extending the range of external actors who rely on Qatar's input and investment, and thus come to have a vested interest in its survival.

Taken together, we would agree with Peterson (2006, p. 732) that the state's above endeavours here have, in part, 'been deliberately designed to put Qatar on the map'. However, as opposed to simply raising international awareness of the state, we also see here authority's desire and attempt to go a step further and actually wield power and influence on the global stage. Consequently, backed by its abundance of natural resource wealth (hard power), we can suggest Qatar's leadership demonstrate the belief that globalization can indeed be harvested for the benefit of the local/national. Through this, Qatar joins others such as Singapore or Hong Kong, which have shown a great deal of 'creative agency' and innovation by consciously being proactive in taking advantage of what the global information society has to offer, and, in doing so, actively come to challenge the long-held realist construction of what 'small' states are able to achieve in and amongst the international system (cf. Cooper & Shaw, 2009, pp. 2–4; Braveboy-Wagner, 2010). In short, thanks to the highly interconnected and technologically advanced network society of today, the case of Qatar and global sport reveals that globalization has the potential to enhance the power of small states, not decline it (cf. Nye, 2011). This is not to suggest of course that effectively engaging with 'globalization-for-state-purposes' does not come with a multitude of risks for (small) states, something we now turn our attention to in Chap. 4.

NOTES

1. Referring to the two most global of sports events: the FIFA World Cup and the Summer Olympic Games; this is in contrast to 'second-order' events, denoting those smaller and, in many cases, more-regional sports events—such as a Winter Olympic Games, European Championships and Asian Games
2. In 2011, the Pew Research Centre conducted 15,000 interviews across 15 countries, and found over half non-Muslims living in the United States and Western Europe held the general stereotype of Arab communities as predominantly 'fanatical' and/or 'violent'.
3. Important to note is that, more generally, supposed tourism gains from sports event hosting can be drastically overstated: the 2002 FIFA World Cup in Japan and South Korea, for example, proved to be wildly optimistic, with Japan attracting only 30,000 more visitors than the year before the Games, and South Korea reporting the same number as the previous year (see: Horne & Manzenreiter, 2004).

REFERENCES

Abbot, S. (2018). *The away game: The Epic search for Soccer's next superstar*. Norton.
Armstrong, H., & Read, R. (2006). Geographical 'handicaps' and small states: Some implications for the Pacific from a global perspective. *Asia Pacific Viewpoint, 47*(1), 79–92.
Aspetar. (n.d.) About Aspetar [online]. Available at: https://www.aspetar.com/about.aspx?lang=en (Accessed 17.09.21)

Aspire. (2019, December 11). Aspire Football dreams graduate Wague in solid CL debut for Barca, 11 December [online]. Retrieved January 18, 2021, from https://www.aspire.qa/Media/News/aspire-football-dreams-graduate-wague-in-solid-cl-debut-for-barca

Aspire. (2021). Football Dreams [online]. Retrieved April 12, 2021, from https://www.aspire.qa/football/football-dreams

Avraham, E. (2020). Nation branding and marketing strategies for combatting tourism crises and stereotypes toward destinations. *Journal of Business Research, 116,* 711–720.

Bachrach, P., & Baratz, M. S. (1975). Power and its two faces revisited: A reply to Geoffrey Debnam. *American Political Science Review, 69*(3), 900–904.

Ball, T. (1992). New faces of power, in T.E. Waternberg (ed.), *Rethinking Power.* Albany: State University of New York Press.

Barney, D. (2004). *The network society.* Polity.

Bátora, J. (2005). *Public diplomacy in small and medium-sized states: Norway and Canada.* Netherlands Institute of International Relations.

Baumann, R., & Matheson, V. (2018). Mega-events and tourism: The case of Brazil. *Contemporary Economic Policy, 36*(2), 292–301.

BBC. (2015, June 11). British Champions Series secures record sponsorship deal [online]. Retrieved September 12, 2021, from http://beta.bbc.co.uk/sport/0/horse-racing/33090512?print=true

BBC. (2018, February 19). Arsenal and Emirates in £200m shirt sponsorship extension [online]. Retrieved March 12, 2021, from https://www.bbc.co.uk/news/business-43113951

BBC. (2021, March 29). Lebanon 'could sink like Titanic' without new government. Retrieved April 11, 2021, from https://www.bbc.co.uk/news/world-middle-east-56570407

beIN. (2019, November 28). beIN Sports agrees exclusive broadcast rights deal [online]. Retrieved May 05, 2021, from https://www.beinmediagroup.com/article/bein-sports-agrees-exclusive-broadcast-rights-deal-for-the-next-two-editions-of-fifa-club-world-cup/

Black, D. R. (2017). Managing the mega-event 'habit': Canada as serial user. *International Journal of Sport Policy and Politics, 9*(2), 219–235.

Brand Finance. (2021). Global soft power index [online]. Retrieved March 07, 2021, from https://brandfinance.com/press-releases/global-soft-power-index-2021-15-nations-from-mena-feature

Brannagan, P. M. (2017). *The state of Qatar and global sport: A case study of globalization, the nation-state and soft power* (Doctoral dissertation, Loughborough University).

Brannagan, P. M., & Giulianotti, R. (2018). The soft power–soft disempowerment nexus: The case of Qatar. *International Affairs, 94*(5), 1139–1157.

Brannagan, P. M., & Grix, J. (2014). Qatar's soft power gamble: The FIFA World Cup 2022. *E-International Relations*. Retrieved February 09, 2021, from https://www.e-ir.info/2014/01/18/qatars-soft-power-gamble-the-fifa-world-cup-2022/

Braveboy-Wagner, J. (2010). Opportunities and limitations of the exercise of foreign policy power by a very small state: The case of Trinidad and Tobago. *Cambridge Review of International Affairs, 23*(3), 407–427.

Castells, M. (1996). *The rise of the network society, the information age: Economy, society and culture* (Vol. I). Blackwell.

Cerny, P. G. (1997). Paradoxes of the competition state: The dynamics of political globalization. *Government and Opposition, 32*(2), 251–274.

Chadwick, S., Widdop, P., & Burton, N. (2020). Soft power sports sponsorship–A social network analysis of a new sponsorship form. *Journal of Political Marketing*, 1–22.

Chong, A. (2010). Small state soft power strategies: Virtual enlargement in the cases of the Vatican City State and Singapore. *Cambridge Review of International Affairs, 23*(3), 383–405.

Cooper, A. F. (2008). Beyond one image fits all: Bono and the complexity of celebrity diplomacy. *Global Governance, 14*, 265.

Cooper, A. F., & Shaw, T. (2009). *The diplomacies of small states*. Palgrave Macmillan.

Daher, R. (Ed.). (2007). *Tourism in the Middle East: Continuity, change, and transformation*. Channel View.

Dahl, R. A. (1957). The concept of power. *Behavioral Science, 2*(3), 201–215.

Deloitte Football Money League. (2021). Retrieved September 09, 2021, from https://www2.deloitte.com/uk/en/pages/sports-business-group/articles/deloitte-football-money-league.html

Doha Goals (n.d.) 2013 [online]. Available at: https://www.qfa.qa/doha-goals-2013-in-december/ (Accessed 19.03.21)

Doha News. (2021, June 22). Spanish football star Javi Martinez set to join Qatar SC [online]. Retrieved June 22, 2021, from https://www.dohanews.co/spanish-football-star-javi-martinez-set-to-join-qatar-sc/

Dubinsky, I. (2021). China's stadium diplomacy in Africa. *Journal of Global Sport Management, 1*–19. https://doi.org/10.1080/24704067.2021.1885101

Emirates. (2020, February 06). Emirates and Olympique Lyonnais announce new partnership [online]. Retrieved March 19, 2021, from https://www.emirates.com/media-centre/emirates-and-olympique-lyonnais-announce-new-partnership/

FC Bayern. (2020, January 03). Bayern head to Doha training camp with 26-man squad [online]. Retrieved November 10, 2021, from https://fcbayern.com/en/news/2020/01/doha/bayern-travel-to-doha-training-camp-with-26-man-squad

FIFA. (2017, May 7). Qatar Airways announced as official partner of FIFA until 2022. Retrieved September 16, 2021, from https://www.fifa.com/tournaments/mens/worldcup/qatar2022/media-releases/qatar-airways-official-partner-airline-fifa-2882728

FIFA. (2018, December 21). More than half the world watched record-breaking 2018 World Cup [online]. Retrieved Decmeber 03, 2020, from https://www.fifa.com/tournaments/mens/worldcup/2018russia/media-releases/more-than-half-the-world-watched-record-breaking-2018-world-cup

Financial Times. (2008, September 02). Qatari connection casts long shadow over Barclays [online]. Retrieved February 11, 2015, from https://www.ft.com/content/dadda8fa-0d58-11e7-a88c-50ba212dce4d

Financial Times. (2014, June 16). Royal Ascot breaks tradition with Qatari sponsorship [online]. Retrieved May 17, 2015, from https://www.ft.com/content/c18faca4-f55a-11e3-afd3-00144feabdc0

Financial Times. (2017, December 08). Manchester City and the 'Disneyfication' of football [online]. Retrieved May 13, 2021, from https://www.ft.com/content/e1961ea2-d6c5-11e7-a303-9060cb1e5f44

Financial Times. (2020, April 22). Qatar's beIN demands Premier League block Saudi takeover of Newcastle [online]. Retrieved May 14, 2021, from https://www.ft.com/content/bfcd005c-4506-432c-8535-57402407b486.

Forbes. (2017, Decmeber 22). Belt and Road: China's strategy to capture supply chains from Guangzhou to Greece [online]. Retrieved January 09, 2021, from https://www.forbes.com/sites/riskmap/2017/12/21/belt-and-road-chinas-strategy-to-capture-supply-chains-from-guangzhou-to-greece/?sh=55bf292c6237

Forbes. (2019, February 06). Qatar's Asian Cup win was a fairy tale; now it faces the reality of 2022 [online]. Retrieved March 12, 2021, from https://www.forbes.com/sites/steveprice/2019/02/06/qatars-asian-cup-win-was-a-fairytale-now-it-faces-the-reality-of-2022/?sh=429065b13150

Forbes. (2021). Paris Saint Germain [online]. Retrieved September 17, 2021, from https://www.forbes.com/teams/paris-saint-germain/?sh=621dcbfe51f4

Foreign Affairs. (2016, April 18). Why Putin took Crimea [online]. Retrieved February 23, 2021, from https://www.foreignaffairs.com/articles/ukraine/2016-04-18/why-russian-president-putin-took-crimea-from-ukraine

Fuentes-Julio, C. (2020). Norm entrepreneurs in foreign policy: How Chile became an international human rights promoter. *Journal of Human Rights, 19*(2), 256–274.

FutureBrand Country Brand Index. (2012–2013). [online] Retrieved March 17, 2021, from https://www.futurebrand.com/uploads/CBI_2012-Final.pdf

FutureBrand Country Brand Index. (2019). [online]. Retrieved March 10, 2021, from https://www.futurebrand.com/uploads/FCI/FutureBrand-Country-Index-2019.pdf

Global Peace Index. (2021). [online]. Retrieved July 11, 2021, from https://www.visionofhumanity.org/wp-content/uploads/2021/06/GPI-2021-web-1.pdf

Grix, J., Brannagan, P. M., Grimes, H., & Neville, R. (2021). The impact of Covid-19 on sport. *International Journal of Sport Policy and Politics, 13*(1), 1–12.

Guiltinan, J. P. (1987). The price bundling of services: A normative framework. *Journal of Marketing, 51*(2), 74–85.

Gulf News. (2014, June 26). Al Sadd part ways with Raul [online]. Retrieved February 06, 2021, from https://www.gulf-times.com/story/398076/Al-Sadd-part-ways-with-Raul

Gulf News. (2021, November 06). Xavi faces 'biggest challenge of career' as Barcelona coach [online]. Retrieved April 12, 2021, from https://www.gulf-times.com/story/703952

Hassan Al-Thawadi. (2013). Interview at Doha GOALS Forum, December 11.

Hassan Al-Thawadi. (2018). Interview at Sports Diplomacy: A vision for the future, November 30.

Hay, C. (1997). State of the art: Divided by a common language: Political theory and the concept of power. *Politics, 17*(1), 45–52.

Ho, G., & Bairner, A. (2013). One country, two systems, three flags: Imagining Olympic nationalism in Hong Kong and Macao. *International Review for the Sociology of Sport, 48*(3), 349–365.

Hocking, B. (2005). Rethinking the 'New' public diplomacy. In J. Melissen (Ed.), *The new public diplomacy: Soft power in international relations.* Palgrave Macmillan.

Horne, J. D., & Manzenreiter, W. (2004). Accounting for megaevents: forecast and actual impacts of the 2002 Football World Cup Finals on the host countries Japan/Korea. *International review for the sociology of sport, 39*(2), 187–203.

Houlihan, B. (2015). Political science, sociology and the study of sport. In R. Giulianotti (Ed.), *Routledge handbook of the sociology of sport.* Routledge.

Houlihan, B., & Zheng, J. (2015). Small states: Sport and politics at the margin. *International Journal of Sport Policy and Politics, 7*(3), 329–344.

Huffington Post. (2013, June 26). London Mayor should get his facts straight on Qatar [online]. Retrieved May 25, 2021, from http://www.huffingtonpost.co.uk/nicholas-mcgeehan/london-mayor-should-get-h_b_3163127.html

ICSS. (2012, June 18). The International Centre for Sport Security joins the United Nations Global Compact [online]. Retrieved September 23, 2021, from http://www.theicss.org/wp-content/uploads/2012/06/ICSS033.12-ICSS-joins-UN-Global-Compact-English-Press-Release.pdf?lbisphpreq=1

ICSS. (n.d.). Securing Sport Report [online]. Retrieved May 02, 2021, from https://webcache.googleusercontent.com/search?q=cache:UfauEHr6XXIJ:h

ttps://members.ehf.eu/community/activities/download.ashx%3Freason%3D
ehfcanFile%26id%3D1834+&cd=15&hl=en&ct=clnk&gl=uk

IOC. (2015, July 27). IOC awards 2018–2024 broadcast rights in Middle East and North Africa [online]. Retrieved July 26, 2021, from https://www.olympic.org/news/ioc-awards-2018-2024-broadcast-rights-in-middle-east-and-north-africa

Keohane, R. O., & Nye, J. S. (2003). The concept of accountability in world politics and the use of force. *Michigan Journal of International Law, 24*(4), 1–21.

Khatib, L. (2014). Qatar and the Recalibration of Power in the Gulf [online]. Available at: https://www.jstor.org/stable/pdf/resrep12983.pdf?acceptTC=true&coverpage=false&addFooter=false (Accessed 03.02.21)

Lakatos, I. (2017). The potential role of small states and their Niche diplomacy at the UN and in the field of human rights, with special attention to Montenegro. *Pécs Journal of International and European Law, 58.*

Leifer, M. (2000). *Singapore's foreign policy: Coping with vulnerability.* Routledge.

Leonard, M., & Small, A. (2003). *Norwegian public diplomacy.* The Foreign Policy Centre.

Lukes, S. (2004). *Power: A radical view.* Macmillan International Higher Education.

Mazzucato, M. (2011). The entrepreneurial state. *Soundings, 49*(49), 131–142.

Nassif, N. (2020, December 01). How powerful has Qatar become in Elite Sport? [online]. Retrieved December 15, 2020, from https://cirs.qatar.georgetown.edu/how-powerful-has-qatar-become-elite-sport/

National Tourism Sector Strategy. (2014). [online]. Retrieved June 15, 2021, from https://www.visitqatar.qa/corporate/planning/strategy-2030

Nye, J. S. (2002). The information revolution and American soft power. *Asia Pacific Review, 9*(1), 60–76.

Nye, J. S. (2008). Public diplomacy and soft power. *The ANNALS of the American Academy of Political and Social Sciences, 616*(1), 94–109.

Nye, J. S. (2011). *The future of power.* Public Affairs.

Ooredoo. (n.d.) Lionel Messi [online]. Retrieved March 26, 2021, from https://www.ooredoo.com/en/who_we_are/sponsorship/our-brand-ambassador/

Orttung, R., & Kazakov, V. (2018). Winter Olympics/World Cup. *Russian Analytical Digest (RAD), 216.*

Peterson, J. E. (2006). Qatar and the world: Branding for a micro-state. *The Middle East Journal, 60*(4), 732–748.

PSG.fr. (n.d.). Partners [online]. Retrieved July 14, 2021, from https://en.psg.fr/club/sponsors

Punnett, B. J., & Morrison, A. (2006). Niche markets and small Caribbean producers: A match made in heaven? *Journal of Small Business & Entrepreneurship, 19*(4), 341–353.

Qatar 2022. (n.d.). Stadiums [online]. Retrieved June 17, 2021, from https://www.qatar2022.qa/en/stadiums

Qatar Airways. (2019, September 18). Annual report highlights [online]. Retrieved February 13, 2021, from https://www.qatarairways.com/en/press-releases/2019/September/2019AnnualReport.html

Qatar Airways Annual Report. (2019). [online]. Retrieved March 17, 2021, from https://www.qatarairways.com/content/dam/documents/annual-reports/2019/ENG_Annual_Report_2019_V2.pdf

Qatar National Development Strategy 2011–2016. (2011). [online]. Retrieved May 11, 2021, from http://www.mdps.gov.qa/en/knowledge/HomePagePublications/Qatar_NDS_reprint_complete_lowres_16May.pdf

Qatar's Second National Development Strategy 2018–2022. (2018). [online]. Retrieved March 06, 2021, from https://www.psa.gov.qa/en/knowledge/Documents/NDS2Final.pdf

Qatari Diar. (n.d.) East Village [online]. Retrieved March 09, 2021, from https://www.qataridiar.com/English/OurProjects/Pages/East-Village.aspx

Reuters. (2018, April 23). AS Roma, Qatar Airway multi-year shirt sponsorship worth 40 mln euros [online]. Retrieved January 17, 2021, from https://www.reuters.com/article/soccer-italy-as-roma-qatar-airways-idUSI6N1RO00W

Samuel-Azran, T. (2013). Al-Jazeera, Qatar, and new tactics in state-sponsored media diplomacy. *American Behavioral Scientist, 57*(9), 1293–1311.

Smith, A. D. (1999). Ethnic election and national destiny: Some religious origins of nationalist ideals. *Nations and Nationalism, 5*(3), 331–355.

Soft Power 30. (2019). [online]. Retrieved March 08, 2021, from https://soft-power30.com/wp-content/uploads/2019/10/The-Soft-Power-30-Report-2019-1.pdf

Solberg, H. A., & Preuss, H. (2007). Major sport events and long-term tourism impacts. *Journal of sport Management, 21*(2), 213.

Sönmez, S. F. (1998). Tourism, terrorism, and political instability. *Annals of Tourism Research, 25*(2), 416–456.

Steiner, C. (2007). Political instability, transnational tourist companies and destination recovery in the Middle East after 9/11. *Tourism and Hospitality Planning & Development, 4*(3), 169–190.

Steiner, C. (2010). An overestimated relationship? Violent political unrest and tourism foreign direct investment in the Middle East. *International Journal of Tourism Research, 12*(6), 726–738.

Stevens, C. A. (2017). The Libyan debate: Coercive diplomacy reconsidered. *Diplomacy & Statecraft, 28*(2), 320–343.

The Economist. (2018, March 10). An epic search for football's next superstars [online]. Retrieved July 13, 2021, from https://www.economist.com/books-and-arts/2018/03/10/an-epic-search-for-footballs-next-superstars

The Guardian. (2011, August 12). Olympic Village snapped up by Qatari ruling family for £557m [online]. Retrieved July 16, 2021, from https://www.the-guardian.com/sport/2011/aug/12/olympic-village-qatari-ruling-family

The Guardian. (2012, December 12). Qatar promises fans to take the heat out of 2022 World Cup [online]. Retrieved May 12, 2021, from https://www.theguardian.com/football/2012/dec/12/qatar-cool-2022-world-cup

The Independent. (2021, October 06). Newcastle: Saudi-backed takeoever nears completion after broadcast dispute settled [online]. Retrieved November 01, 2021, from https://www.independent.co.uk/sport/football/newcastle-takeover-saudi-arabia-broadcast-b1933612.html

The New York Times. (2018, August 17). U.S. imposes sanctions on Myanmar military over Rohingya [online]. Retrieved July 07, 2021, from https://www.nytimes.com/2018/08/17/us/politics/myanmar-sanctions-rohingya.html

The Peninsula. (2020, July 20). Spanish star Cazorla hails Xavi as signs on at Qatar's Al-Sadd: Club [online]. Retrieved January 17, 2021, from https://thepeninsulaqatar.com/article/07/08/2020/Spanish-star-Cazorla-hails-Xavi-as-signs-on-at-Qatar-s-Al-Sadd-club

The Wall Street Journal. (2021, April 25). How Qatar Airways, with its Covid-19 playbook, dethroned Emirates as biggest long-haul airline [online]. Retrieved July 19, 2021, from https://www.wsj.com/articles/how-qatar-airways-with-its-pandemic-playbook-dethroned-emirates-as-biggest-long-haul-airline-11619348400

Tsaliki, L., Huliaras, A., & Frangonikolopoulos, C. A. (Eds.). (2011). *Transnational celebrity activism in global politics changing the world?* Intellect.

U.S. News. (2021). Overall Best Countries Ranking 2021 Rankings [online]. Retrieved October 15, 2021, from https://www.usnews.com/news/best-countries/overall-rankings

United Nations, World Tourism Barometer. (2019). [online]. Retrieved May 02, 2021, from https://www.unwto.org/world-tourism-barometer-2019-nov

Vincent, N. (2021, May 16). Qatar Airways' football sponsorships as a foreign policy strategy [online]. Retrieved May 27, 2021, from https://cirs.qatar.georgetown.edu/qatar-airways-football-sponsorships-as-a-foreign-policy-strategy/

Wood, J., & Meng, S. (2020). The economic impacts of the 2018 Winter Olympics. *Tourism Economics.* https://doi.org/10.1177/1354816620921577

World Travel and Tourism Council Report. (2017). Coping with success [online]. Retrieved March 08, 2021, from https://wttc.org/Portals/0/Documents/Reports/2017/Coping%20With%20Success%20-%20Managing%20Overcrowding%20in%20Tourism%20Destinations%202017.pdf?ver=2021-02-26-192645-677

CHAPTER 4

The Controversial Games: Responses to Qatar's 2022 World Cup

Abstract This chapter discusses the negative scrutiny Qatar has received since being awarded the 2022 World Cup, and, in doing so, centres on the ways in which certain international actors have come to respond to the state's use of sport and sports events for soft power. It does so by first focusing on how the competitive pursuit of soft power plays out between state and non-state actors and locates how the latter—particularly international non-governmental organizations and the global media—seek to gain their own soft power through strategies that simultaneously 'disempower' others. In doing so, the chapter argues that whilst the staging of a major sports event can provide the host state with an opportunity to (re) shape their image on the world stage, so too do such events provide non-state actors with the opportunity to significantly damage state's reputations. In showing this process in action in the context of the 2022 World Cup, we argue that the negative scrutiny levied towards Qatar has centred on three keys areas: *Qatar's human rights record; accusations of bribery and corruption; and Qatar as a sports events destination.* In discussing each of these three areas, we also locate the ways in which such negativity has come to damage the state's attempts at international soft power acquisition.

Keywords Global politics • Soft disempowerment • Media politics • Non-state actors

P. M. Brannagan, D. Reiche, *Qatar and the 2022 FIFA World Cup*, https://doi.org/10.1007/978-3-030-96822-9_4

In December 2018, one of the authors was interviewed for a media article that was published a few weeks later by the British online newspaper *The Independent* (see: *The Independent*, 19 December 2018). The title of the article read '*Qatar 2022: A reputation irrevocably damaged, what has a minor Gulf state to gain from hosting the World Cup?*' The article sought to shed light on two key points. The first was to understand why Qatar sought to stage one of the world's largest events, which it correctly identified as the state's desire to 'achieve its primary goal of accumulating soft power' (as we saw in Chap. 3). The second, and most notable, was to explore whether the state was likely to ever achieve such an objective given the significant negative scrutiny it had received since being awarded the tournament in 2010. Indeed, in locating how the World Cup had come to raise international awareness of Qatar's 'inhumane' treatment of migrant workers and accusations of bribery and corruption, amongst other things, the article advocated the following:

> The 2022 World Cup has already become perhaps the most controversial sports mega-event since the 1936 Berlin Olympics in Nazi Germany…Some of the tournament's organisers initially thought the adverse attention was a necessary consequence of hosting the World Cup…yet Qatar's image has been so badly damaged that you wonder what it now hopes to gain from hosting the tournament…Only time will tell the tournament's true legacy, and what implications it has for the image of the country and the wider region. What we do know is that by the time [the] 2022 World Cup is over, Qatar will no longer be invisible. (*The Independent*, 19 December 2018)

Other media outlets have similarly offered comparable analysis. Indeed, as mentioned in Chap. 1, both the British broadsheet, *The Telegraph*, and U.S. news network, *CNN*, have previously labelled the 2022 World Cup as 'the most controversial ever' sports event (see: *The Telegraph*, 24 February 2015b; *CNN*, 27 May 2015). More recently, in March 2021, British newspaper, *The Times*, contended the following:

> it seems the world of football has woken up to the fact that the most controversial World Cup in history will be taking place in less than two years' time, and that since Qatar won the FIFA vote in December 2010 many of the important issues surrounding the tournament have not been addressed properly. (*The Times*, 30 March 2021)

In this chapter, we discuss the negative scrutiny Qatar has received since being awarded the 2022 World Cup, and, in doing so, centre on the ways in which certain international actors have come to respond to the state's use of sport and sports events for soft power. We do so by first focusing on how the competitive pursuit of soft power plays out between state and non-state actors and locate how the latter—particularly international non-governmental organizations and the global media—seek to gain their own soft power through strategies that simultaneously 'disempower' others. In doing so, we argue in this chapter that whilst the staging of a major sports event can provide the host state with an opportunity to (re)shape their image on the world stage, so too do such events provide non-state actors with the opportunity to significantly damage state's reputations. In showing this process in action in the context of the 2022 World Cup, we argue that the negative scrutiny levied towards Qatar has centred on three keys areas: *Qatar's human rights record; accusations of bribery and corruption; and Qatar as a sports events destination.* In discussing each of these three areas, we also locate the ways in which such negativity has come to damage the state's attempts at international soft power acquisition.

STATE AND NON-STATE ACTORS IN INTERNATIONAL RELATIONS

As described in Chaps. 1 and 3, one of the most defining features of contemporary capitalist societies has been, and continues to be, advances in information technology and global communications. Indeed, while the transatlantic telegraph cable of 1866 reduced the transmission time between London and New York by over a week, and the telephone increased the velocity of information interchange to just a few minutes, the invention of the internet has permitted instantaneous, real-time exchanges across distant geographic locations. The capacity for people to receive great quantities of communicative data immediately and, more importantly, cheaply has led many to suggest the human race has entered into its third industrial revolution, one characterized by information-led, highly technological 'networked' societies (see: Webster, 2002).

Living in such technologically dominated times comes with significant consequences to our daily lives. The ability to instantaneously connect with an ever-growing number of peoples in far-away lands has drastically affected the way we come to act within, and view the world, as an interconnected place. With greater connectivity comes our increasing exposure to distant tragedies such as epidemics, wars and natural disasters, foreign products and trends such as foods, fashions and music, and recurrent reference to 'global' economics, health and justice. This has resulted in the information revolution—and wider globalization trends—having a substantial impact on what Mills (1959) termed individuals' 'sociological imaginations', fostering, in particular, a shift in the way publics, politicians, activists, journalists and the like come to define their position and role within the world (see: Breton & Lambert, 2003).

As we saw in the previous chapter, for state leaders, advances in information technology and communications have also had a fundamental impact on how power is acquired on the international stage. Notable in this regard is how, in the modern epoch, global politics has, in large part, become defined by the greater need for reputation promotion, display and management, leading states to compete with one another for soft power assets and gains. In the case of Qatar, we have seen how one type of soft power 'asset' is the acquisition and staging of a major event, such as the 2022 World Cup. A global event such as this provides Qatar with what Nye (2011) calls 'strategic communication', referring to a mechanism through which the state can attempt to cut through the white noise of the global information society and disseminate a series of widely heard, reputation-promoting messages over a sustained period of time. In doing so, such events can offer their hosts a significant competitive advantage in the quest for soft power. This is not to suggest, of course, that states always act alone in their pursuit of power. Indeed, states may, and do, act collectively in ways that mutually increase their influence and power: note, for example, as mentioned in Chap. 1, how small states often pool together in order to get what they want through voicing collective concerns at international gatherings (a strategy known as 'balancing'); or how states of all sizes get behind various trade agreements, military alliances and other bilateral and multilateral treaties that are of mutual benefit.

A further consequence—also discussed in Chap. 3—of advances in information technologies, is that issues formerly regarded as the sole prerogatives of states have today become shared by a growing variety of non-state actors. When we speak of 'non-state actors', we are referring to the group of international actors who 'are in principle autonomous from the structure and machinery of the state, and of the governmental and intergovernmental bodies below and above [the sovereign state]' (Josselin & Wallace, 2001, p. 3). Such actors include the following: the growing array[1] of 'international non-governmental organizations' (henceforth 'INGOs'), such as Amnesty International, Save the Children, Oxfam, Greenpeace and Human Rights Watch; 'global media networks', such as the *BBC, CCN, Fox News, The Guardian* and *the New York Times*; 'transnational corporations', such as Apple, Microsoft, Amazon, Coca-Cola and McDonalds; 'global celebrities', such as well-known actors, sports stars, social media influencers and renowned campaigners, such as the environmental activist Greta Thunberg; and finally, the range of what we might call 'focused counterculture groups', such as various terrorist cells, new religious movements and internet hackers, all of whom take issue with specific (and usually established) cultural practices. Importantly, our chosen definition of non-state actors above highlights how these actors are *in principle* autonomous from state control. This is because, while the above-mentioned organizations, individuals and groups are 'theoretically' independent from state intervention, the relationship between state and non-state actors is always 'muddied by the complexities of practice' (ibid., p. 2)—take, for example, the way certain media groups back specific political parties, and, of note too, is how wealthy individuals and groups provide financial support to particular political campaigns, usually in exchange for the upholding of market-friendly policies.

Crucially is that, thanks to the internet, it is arguably non-state actors who have benefitted most from advances in information technologies. On the one hand, such actors have sought to use the digital era to more effectively identify and uncover the (in)actions and practices of others—take the example of WikiLeaks, the international non-profit, activist organization who has on multiple occasions accessed and published classified documents in a bid to expose the secretive goings-on of political leaders from across the globe. While, on the other hand, so too have these non-state actors taken significant advantage of internet-based communication tools (social media, webpages) to get their messages across to the widest possible audiences—note, for instance, how in the month of August 2020 alone, the 'bbc.co.uk' website received a total of 627.47 million visits, while 'cnn.com' witnessed 754.71 million (see: Similarweb.com, 2020). The result is that, with more actors gaining operational control over the gathering, shaping and dissemination of information, within this competitive international environment, states do not come to simply compete with one another for soft power gains and losses, but also with this extended array of non-state actors (see: Nye, 2011).

A potent weapon within this competitive battle is the ability to publicly and convincingly challenge one's soft power. In many cases, this is achieved through directly raising questions over the credibility and trustworthiness of states' power attempts. This occurs for two reasons. First, identifying and highlighting the flaws of state leaders and policymakers helps non-state actors bolster their own soft power by positioning themselves as crucial members of international, contemporary society. Important to remember is that the very existence of many non-states actors, particularly INGOs and the global media, is highly dependent on the perceived positive and progressive impact they have on modern societies. Indeed, as Barnett and Finnemore (2004, pp. 1–2) note, most INGOs, for example, come to see themselves as a type of international 'civilian police' and, in doing so, seek to get involved in almost every issue imaginable, be that related to human rights, animal welfare, environmentalism or finance and trade; similarly, as others have noted, so too do the global media actively look to symbolically position themselves as 'vital' members of international communities who are, above all else, motivated by the desire to serve the 'public interest' and act as humanity's 'global conscience' (Bell, 1973, p. 283; cf. Robertson, 2015). In this sense, non-state actors come to see themselves as representing various international *community* interests, while the state, in opposition, is seen first-and-foremost to promote its own *self-interest* (see: Barnett & Finnemore, 2004).

Second, highlighting the flaws of others not only helps to increase the soft power of various non-state actors, but within this competitive game, it also simultaneously destroys the soft power of states. The destruction of soft power has previously been labelled by Brannagan and Giulianotti (2018, p. 1152) as 'soft disempowerment', which they refer to as to 'actions, inactions and/or policies of states that ultimately upset, offend or alienate others, leading to a loss of credibility and attractiveness'. Brannagan and Giulianotti argue that states' soft power is most in danger from various non-state actors at times when the latter choose to disseminate information which challenges, contradicts and ultimately discredits states' soft power strategies and messages. This is because the more illegitimate and/or distasteful behaviour a state is associated with, the more global audiences come to interrogate, challenge and/or reject its efforts to be seen as attractive. This, in turn, means it becomes much harder for a state's soft power attempts to transfer into desired outcomes in the minds of targeted onlookers (potential tourists, investors, policymakers etc.) (for more on this, see: ibid.)

When choosing how to discredit state's soft power, non-state actors search out those incidents that occupy the greatest degree of controversy or 'scandal'—the latter referring to 'an event in which the public revelation of an alleged private breach of a law or a norm results in significant social disapproval or debate and, usually, reputational damage' (West, 2008, p. 6). For non-states actors such as INGOs and the media, scandalous portrayals not only offer the most scathing blow to states' credibility, trustworthiness and ultimately their soft power, but they also generate significant public interest, and can thus easily be used in their attempt to position themselves as serving key altruistic goals (see: Street, 2005). Important to note however is that such portrayals do not make their way into the public domain naturally, but are rather selectively chosen—indeed, there are too many issues in the world to investigate and report on, and thus INGOs and the media alike must decide what to disseminate, and, perhaps more notably, what not to disseminate (see: Rowe, 2000; Stoldt et al., 2012). Furthermore, usually in collaboration with one another, INGOs and the media also come to frame certain issues in ways that not only fit their own preferences and mandates, but which help to shame, pressure and ultimately regulate states into some form of reactive change (see: Street, 2005; Barnett & Finnemore, 2004).

Through the framing and dissemination of some issues and not others, non-state actors thus come to play a crucial role in the social construction of international society. Indeed, as Barnett and Finnemore (2004, p. 6) note, in many cases, these non-states actors are powerful not because they possess certain material resources, but primarily 'because they use their authority to orient action and create social reality'. Barnett and Finnemore call this 'social construction power', which seeks to encapsulate how certain non-state actors, by drawing on their knowledge and/or authority on certain issues—human rights, environmentalism, civil strife, etc.—do not just come to pressure states into action, but they also come to constitute and define norms of 'acceptable' or 'unacceptable', 'legitimate' or 'illegitimate' actions and behaviours. By framing specific issues, these non-state actors give meaning to domestic, regional and international issues, create new categories of actors, set priorities and outline modes of responsive action. By doing so, non-state actors help 'shape both how the world is constituted and our agendas for acting in it' (ibid., p. 7; see also: Kaid, 2004).

Thus, in this sense, we may speak of IR as a game of 'competitive strategic social construction', one where states not only compete with each other for soft power, but where so too do they compete with non-state actors in the construction of competing ideas, identities, agendas and actions. Indeed, as Nye (2014, p. 2) himself advocates, in the global information age, 'victory' does not solely depend on 'whose army wins, but on whose story wins'. IR is, therefore, in large part, the battle over the minds of global publics, as how people think comes to determine the norms and values on which domestic and international societies are constructed (see: Castells, 2007). It is because of this that the 'battlefield' for this competitive contest takes place in the field of global communications—it is here where the world is constructed, where minds are shaped and where power is forged, contested and destroyed (Castells, 2013). In the next section, we shed light on how Qatar's soft power attempts through the 2022 World Cup have come to be challenged, disputed and destroyed by other's opposing narratives.

THE 2022 FIFA WORLD CUP

In the search for controversial, scandalous stories that can easily be framed, major sports event—such as a World Cup or Olympic Games—provide non-state actors with a prime opportunity. In the same way, these events offer state leaders what Nye (2011) calls 'strategic communication', so too do they afford non-state actors a pivotal platform to satisfy their own interests. Crucial in this regard is the way non-state actors look to use the international publicity surrounding these events to shine a spotlight on a state's sociopolitical issues and (in)actions. In doing so, non-state actors come to raise questions over whether the host is morally and/or practically deserving of the event itself. Note, for example, how prior to the 2012 European Football Championships the British media and organizations such as the gay rights charity, Stonewall, heavily critiqued UEFA's decision to award the tournament to countries such as Ukraine and Poland, which, particularly through football, are known to voice specific racist and homophobic beliefs. Labelling the Jewish country as an 'Apartheid State', Pro-Palestinian groups also heavily criticized UEFA's decision to host the Unter-21 Football European Championship in 2013 in Israel (*CNN*, 6 June 2013). We may add to this the reporting on Brazil's staging of the 2014 World Cup, which largely fixated on the growing dissatisfaction by locals over the state's mismanagement of public resources, leading to growing rates of poverty (Grix et al., 2019a). And, finally, where calls were made to strip Russia of the 2018 World Cup due to its involvement in the annexation of Crimea, as well as the evidential high levels of racist and anti-LGBT sentiment inherent in Russian football and wider society (see: Grix et al., 2019b).

Crucial to mention, however, is that what is considered to be a 'negative' action is, of course, relative. Indeed, just like soft power, and the inherent subjectivity involved in constituting 'attractive' behaviours, so too is the manifestation of unattractive (in)actions dependent on contextual and subjective (moral, ethical, cultural) assessments. Consequently, if and where a state's credibility and legitimacy is lost, much depends on audiences' perceptions (see: Nye, 2011). Notwithstanding such perceptual variations, we argue that certain responses to the 2022 World Cup have come to challenge, discredit and, ultimately, damage Qatar's international image in three foremost forms, related to: *Qatar's human rights record; accusations of bribery and corruption; and Qatar as a sports events destination*. We deal with each in turn.

Qatar's Human Rights Record

The first form through which Qatar's image has been damaged is via critique of its human rights record. In the most recent report of the Cato Institute's Human Freedom Index (2020), which assesses states on their level of personal, human and economic domestic freedoms, Qatar ranked 129th out of a total of 162 countries. Qatar's low ranking, according to the report, was due to the state's relative lack of civil justice and freedom of movement, as well as its strict laws around women's rights and same-sex marriage (see: Human Freedom Index, 2020, p. 296). Similarly, the 2020 Democracy Index, produced by the Economist Intelligence Unit, a research subsidiary of *The Economist Group*, ranked Qatar in 126th position out a total of 167 countries. The Democracy Index evaluates and ranks states based on their pluralism, civil liberties and political culture (see: The Democracy Index, 2020).

In the context of the 2022 World Cup, most notable in this regard has been critique of Qatar's adherence to the kafala sponsorship system, an age-old Arab practice that took shape during the British occupation of the Gulf, and one that looked to offer a 'legal and state-based system for governing foreign labor' (Gardner, 2011, p. 8). Although kafala originated from the informal Bedouin principles of ensuring the safety and protection of foreign guests, over time, as a much greater number of expatriate workers entered the Gulf, age-old codes of Arab hospitality have been converted into a formal system of control, introduced 'to provide the central governments of the GCC countries with the means of regulating labour flow into their respective countries' (Bajracharya & Sijapati, 2012, p. 3). Such control and regulation has come in the form of the dissemination of strict non-citizenship, short-term residency visas and temporary work permits and, most notably, the requirement of a native employment sponsor—known as a 'kafil'—who takes full responsibility for their worker(s). Key here is that, by conditioning the long-term residency prospects for expatriates and by passing over all legal and social responsibility to the kafil, GCC governments have largely absolved themselves from providing foreign workers with any kind of labour protection, as well as denying them the right to participate as full members of society (Parreñas, 2010). It is only because of this that, despite being the numerical minority in their countries, native populations have ensured their continued political and social supremacy, whereby, for expatriates, 'the threat of deportation works as a distinct form of state control' (Pande, 2013, pp. 463–437).

For GCC states such as Qatar, the kafala sponsorship system has become of paramount importance during times of mass-infrastructure development—such as in preparation for a World Cup—when an influx of blue-collar expatriate workers are required. Alongside acting as a system of state control, the kafala system has also significantly added to the very high standard of living for many nationals across the GCC, particularly those located high up within the business sector. This is because, in states such as Qatar, as expatriate workers have come to rely completely on their kafil in legal, social and economic terms, kafala has fostered a pro-elite and pro-business system 'that effectively serves to create and sustain a legally vulnerable—and hence, relatively tractable and "cheap"—reserve of labor' (De Genova & Nathalie, 2010, p. 300). It is due to this that many sponsors confiscate their workers' passports upon arrival in the Gulf, justifying such an act as a necessity to ensure their financial investment is protected and to maintain control over this highly vulnerable and low-cost group of workers—workers who are lawfully, contractually and politically powerless to demand higher salaries and/or improvements to working and living conditions. This favourable situation for employers has meant that national governments across the GCC, including in Qatar, have come under little internal pressure to make any rapid changes to this age-old system—note, for example, how, in a 2014 survey, 58% of Qataris felt kafala 'should be kept about the same', 30% believed the system should be 'changed to make foreign workers more dependent on their sponsors' and only 7% said the system should be totally 'eliminated' (see: SESRI, 2014, p. 18).

For some international onlookers, however, the kafala system has acted as a lightning rod through which to highlight Qatar's human rights issues at home. In 2014, for instance, British newspaper, *The Guardian*, published a series of articles detailing how many of Qatar's South Asian workers—many of whom worked on World Cup-related construction projects—faced daily cases of exploitation as a result of the kafala system, including instances of mental abuse; dangerous working and living conditions; and a lack of pay, food and free drinking water (see: *The Guardian*, 25 September 2013b; *The Guardian*, 29 July 2014e). Such conditions have equated, investigations claimed, to a form of 'modern-day slavery', and have led to 'thousands' of workers dying on World Cup-related construction sites across Qatar (*Huffington Post*, 3 June 2015). These accusations, in turn, prompted a number of INGOs to work alongside the media in their criticism of Qatar's 'slave-like' kafala system. Human Rights Watch, for example, labelled Qatar a 'crucible of exploitation and misery' (*Huffington Post*, 26 June 2013); Bert Schouwenburg, International Officer of the UK's GMB trade union, called the kafala system in Qatar the 'worst and most extreme exploitation of workers anywhere in the world' (*The Guardian*, 29 July 2014e); and former Amnesty International Secretary General, Salil Shetty, sternly condemned Qatar, citing how 'it is simply inexcusable in one of the richest countries in the world that so many migrant workers are being ruthlessly exploited' (*The Guardian*, 17 November 2013a).

Although the simple presence of kafala in Qatar has been highly scrutinized, it is arguably the state's evidential lack of urgency to abolish the sponsorship system completely which has fostered some of the most scathing criticism. Indeed, although the state has made several changes to improve the kafala system since being awarded the World Cup in 2010, it was not until 2020 that the system was radically overhauled, as we discuss below. One such minor change that occurred prior to 2020 came in 2013, when the Qatar Foundation (QF) introduced its Migrant Workers' Charter, which, it claimed, reflected its strong belief that 'dignified living and working conditions are absolutely essential to unlocking human potential and indispensable to QF's mission of raising the quality of life for all workers in Qatar' (Qatar Foundation, 30 April 2014). In seeking to raise the 'quality of life' for workers, the Qatar Foundation said it would ensure that all contractors and their subcontractors adhered to its

Mandatory Standards for Migrant Workers, which were written in to all awarding contracts to make sure a set of formal standards were followed which 'guarantee the rights of workers at all stages of the migration cycle' with respect to 'recruitment, living, and working conditions, as well as the general treatment of workers engaged in construction and other projects' (Qatar Foundation, 24 April 2013). Also in 2013, the Supreme Committee for Delivery and Legacy then adopted and implemented a version of the Qatar Foundation's Charter in order to ensure all workers engaged with World Cup projects 'enjoy health, safety [and] equality in terms of rights irrespective of belief, nationality ethnicity and religion, access to accurate information regarding workers' rights, and safer living conditions' (*Doha News*, 26 April 2013). The World Cup organizers claimed that such changes would bring 'enhanced, sustainable and meaningful progress for workers across the country' (Supreme Committee for Delivery and Legacy, 'Workers' Welfare Standards', n.d.).

The introduction of the Qatar Foundation and Supreme Committee for Delivery and Legacy charters, although fostering minor improvements for some workers, were ultimately criticized by certain international members for not going far enough. *The Guardian* (14 May 2015c), for example, argued that the introduction of the charters were simply 'chipping away around the edges on welfare rather than engaging on any of the major issues'. In similar fashion, Sharron Burrow, general secretary of the International Trade Union Confederation (ITUC), labelled the mere implementation of workers' welfare charters as a feeble 'reaction to public pressure', claiming that 'Qatar has to change its laws, nothing else will do' (ITUC, 11 February 2014). Others, such as Nicholas McGeehan from Human Rights Watch, likewise argued how the introduction of non-judicial charters only protected a 'small fraction of Qatar's migrant workers', and thus called upon the Qatari government to 'apply these standards to the whole migrant worker population'.

In response, in 2016 Qatar introduced new and actual 'laws' that it claimed would have positive implications for all workers across the state. The new set of labour laws included the creation of state-run grievance committees, which all workers could appeal to if employers denied them permission to switch employer or leave the country, and initiated fines of up to QAR25,000 riyals (US$6850) on businesses that confiscated employees' passports (*Al Jazeera*, 14 December 2016). In commenting on these new laws, Qatar's then minister of labour, Issa bin Saad al-Jafali al-Nuaimi, for example, argued how the changes replaced 'the kafala system with a modernised contract-based system that safeguards worker rights and increases job flexibility' (*The Guardian*, 13 December 2016). In short, these news labour laws, Qatar claimed, guaranteed 'greater flexibility, freedom and protection for workers', which, ultimately, 'abolished its kafala system' (ibid.; *Human Rights Watch*, 12 January 2017).

Several INGOs, nonetheless, disagreed that kafala had been drastically altered (let alone abolished), citing the fact that, while the 2016 law stated that expats who finish fixed contracts would no longer need permission from their sponsor to change jobs or leave the country, they would still need authorization from the Qatari government (see: *Doha News*, 22 May 2016). It is because of this that many INGOs argued that the 2016 law did little to change the situation of migrant workers in Qatar: James Lynch from Amnesty International, for example, contended 'this new law may get rid of the word 'sponsorship' but it leaves the same basic system intact' (*BBC*, 13 December 2016), while Human Rights Watch (12 January 2017) concluded that Qatar's new laws have 'left its fundamentally exploitative characteristics in place'.

In shedding light on one reason why the state has been slow to implement substantial changes to kafala, Millward (2017) pinpoints how responsibility for working conditions and deaths of blue-collar workers in Qatar has largely been passed between the network of key stakeholders in this respect. Indeed, as Millward correctly locates, since Qatar's awarding of the 2022 World Cup in 2010, the state's representatives have essentially passed off accountability on workers' rights to the various international construction contractors, subcontractors and relevant authorities from workers' home countries. In turn, international contractors and subcontractors have principally blamed each other for worker fatalities, as well as justified their practices as complying with 'Qatari labour law', which has come to fashion an environment where such malpractices are 'harmful but not "illegal" in state judicial terms' (ibid., p. 765). Finally, football's world governing body, FIFA, has similarly attributed guilt towards Qatari authorities, who it claims are responsible for the governing of laws and policies inside their own sovereign territory. As Millward (2017, p. 12) rightly argues here, FIFA's lack of desire to strongly press Qatar over its human rights abuses stems from the fact that its major sponsors have, in large part, 'been cautiously disapproving of [the] poor treatment of migrant workers but have fallen short of exerting their influence'. Indeed, although in 2014 Fly Emirates decided not to renew its sponsorship agreement with FIFA, its reasons for doing so were related not to Qatar's migrant workers, but to ongoing claims of corruption surrounding the 2018 and 2022 World Cup bidding process (an issue we discus below) (*Sky News*, 3 November 2014); and, as we saw in the last chapter, upon Emirates' sponsorship departure, Qatar Airways quickly filled this void, becoming FIFA's Official Airline partner in 2017.

The lack of direct pressure from both below (Qatari citizens) and above (FIFA) meant that it was not until 2020—and later in 2021—that Qatar introduced a set of key laws that marked, according to the International Labour Organization, 'a new era' for the Qatari labour market. This reform process started at the end of 2017 when Qatar and the International Labour Organization (ILO) entered into a partnership to support the state' planned labour reforms. As a result, ILO's Project Office for the State of Qatar was established in Doha in April 2018. In marking the series of a number of forthcoming major reforms, on 30 August 2020 the requirement of an exit permit for expatriate workers to leave the country was abolished, and, under this new law, workers are no longer required to seek permission to change jobs. Furthermore, the introduction of a minimum wage became mandatory for all newly signed contracts from 30 August 2020, and was extended to all employment agreements on 20 March 2021. The minimum wage applies to all workers of all nationalities in all sectors, including domestic workers. The latter is relevant since domestic workers in many Middle Eastern countries are exempt from protection under the general labour laws. The Qatari minimum wage consists of three pillars: a minimum monthly basic wage of 1000 Qatari riyals (US$274) and allowances of at least 300 riyals (US$82) for food and 500 riyals (US$137) for housing (when these amenities are not provided for workers by their employers). According to the ILO, more than 400,000 workers (20% of the private sector workforce) will benefit directly from the new law: 'This wage increase will also improve the lives of a large number of family members in the workers' countries of origin who rely on the remittances sent every month', said Max Tuñón from the ILO Project Office in Qatar (ILO, 19 March 2021a). The Qatari government also introduced severe sanctions for non-compliance with the above reforms.

Additionally, in May 2021, the Qatari government set out new rules that immediately became effective to better protect workers from heat stress. Workers can no longer work outside between 10.00 am and 3.30 pm from 1 June to 15 September. This regulation extended former rules for work exemptions during summertime—previous legislation from 2007 prohibited work in outdoor workspaces from 11.30 am to 3.00 pm between 15 June and 31 August. The Supreme Committee for Delivery and Legacy was one of the driving forces for the new rules: in cooperation with the Qatari Labor Ministry and the ILO, it had commissioned in 2019 the FAME Lab from the University of Thessaly, Greece, to do, according to the ILO, 'the world's largest study into heat stress' (26 May 2021). As part of these new rules, 'all work must [also] stop if the wet-bulb globe temperature (WBGT)[2] rises beyond 32.1 °C in a particular workplace' (ILO, 26 May 2021b). The new measures also introduced require that annual health checks be carried out for all workers.

Commenting on the new set of laws and reforms, *The Guardian* (1 September 2020) claimed that such changes 'will largely bring an end to the *kafala*—or sponsorship—system, under which workers are unable to change jobs without their employer's permission, a practice that leaves many vulnerable to exploitation and in some cases forced labour'. In an interview in March 2021, Houtan Homayounpour, head of the ILO, called the reforms 'revolutionary' and a set of 'historic achievements'. He said the main accomplishment of the reforms is that 'the power imbalance between worker and employer has been addressed to a large extent' (Homayounpour, 2021). The U.S. Embassy in Qatar highlighted Qatar's role as a regional reformer. It announced its support by tweeting about 'Qatar's new minimum wage legislation', emphasizing that it is 'the first of its kind in the region' (U.S. Embassy in Qatar, 10 March 2021). This was supported by Sharan Burrow of the ITUC, who remarked: 'The ITUC stands ready to support the Government of Qatar in the implementation of this historic move, to ensure all workers are aware of the new rules and benefit from them. Other countries in the region should follow Qatar's example' (ILO, 2020); in 2021, she further commented, 'We welcome this new legislation and commend the Government of Qatar for its continued efforts to protect workers' health and safety at work' (ILO, 2021b).

Qatar's (eventual) reforming of the kafala system provides us with one example of what Beck (2006, p. 342) calls 'global domestic politics', referring to the process through which international organizations seek to pressure national governments into action, change and transparency, by raising key questions over their ethical and moral credibility via the global publication and dissemination of various media articles, investigative reports and/or league tables. Through this, INGOs and other non-state actors gain soft power when states admit their mistakes and make appropriate changes in response. Furthermore, for the state under global scrutiny, sometimes admitting fault and making amends can be the best (and only course) of action—indeed, in the case of Qatar, Ulrichsen (2020, p. 104) notes how the labour reforms have allowed Qatar to positively distinguish itself from its GCC neighbours who still have the kafala system in place, with the state also gaining positive headlines in the Western press and 'cautious praise of international human rights organizations'.

This is not to suggest of course that Qatar's image has not been negatively impacted by scrutiny of the kafala system and by how long it has taken the state to implement meaningful change. Indeed, although the human rights standards INGOs promote largely derive from a liberal, Western interpretation, Qatar's 'violations' here do nonetheless come to damage the state's desire to position itself as a friendly, 'good global citizen'. While the state's various humanitarian acts (sporting and otherwise) look to echo notions of benevolence and cooperation, the consistent reporting of its human rights abuses comes to potentially cement the state in the minds of certain audiences as a 'bad' and self-centred actor, who, through its lack of care for the well-being and safety of others, exhibits what is widely considered to be 'inappropriate behaviour', thus distancing itself from the 'club' of 'responsible' states—the majority of whom make up the international governmental organizations that Qatar seeks support and protection from (see also: Risse & Sikkink, 1999; Baylis & Smith, 2005). Furthermore, although Qatar looks to position itself as the torchbearer of civil freedoms across the Middle East, most notably through Al Jazeera's active and well-publicized criticisms of foreign undemocratic and repressive systems, the fact that at home the state has been slow to provide its expatriate workers with basic rights means that—as we have seen—Qatar itself regularly scores low on various international democracy indexes. In both cases, the result is that the state comes to be seen as a 'hypocritical actor', one that does not fully practise what it preaches. In doing so, the state loses credibility, admiration and respect in the minds of those its wishes to court through its soft power endeavours.

Accusations of Bribery and Corruption

The second form through which Qatar's image has been damaged is via critique over the state's awarding of the 2022 World Cup, which has been shrouded in accusations of bribery and corruption. Initially broadcast to the world in 2014 by UK-based newspaper, *The Sunday Times*, it is claimed that Qatar unfairly acquired the rights to host the 2022 World Cup via a series of undisclosed payments-in-kind to various political and sporting officials (*Sunday Times*, 1 June 2014b). Notable here has been the purported role of Qatari-born, former Asian Football Confederation president and ex-FIFA Executive Committee member, Mohammed bin Hammam, who, it is claimed, used multiple slush funds to pay in excess of £3 million to FIFA officials to ensure Qatar won the rights to the World Cup (*The Sunday Times*, 24 November 2014a; 19 April 2015). It has also been reported that bin Hammam entered into mutual agreements with Russian president, Vladimir Putin, to taint the voting process for the 2018 and 2022 World Cups, and brokered attractive gas deals between Thailand and Qatar to ensure the former's vote (*The Sunday Times*, 19 April 2015). The British newspaper also claimed to have 'proof' that Bin Hamman paid £250,000 to former FIFA Executive Committee member, Reynald Temarii, and $1.6 million to former FIFA vice president, Jack Warner (*The Sunday Times*, 1 June 2014b).

In late 2014, these allegations prompted FIFA to conduct its own investigation into claims of corruption. Although FIFA's ethics committee eventually cleared Qatar after it was ruled that 'very limited scope' bidding rules were breached (cf. *The Guardian*, 13 November 2014), suspicion has continued, largely due to the 2014 resignation of FIFA's Ethics Committee Chairman, Michael Garcia, who claimed the governing body's investigation into the 2018 and 2022 World Cup bids included 'numerous materially incomplete and erroneous representations of facts' (*The Telegraph*, 17 December 2014). This in turn compelled various FIFA sponsors and football officials to voice their own concerns on the matter. While commentating on the allegations made against the state, ex-German Football Association president, Theo Zwanziger, previously labelled Qatar a 'cancer on world football' (*Doha News*, 13 June 2015b); and FIFA's main sponsors, Adidas, Coca-Cola, Sony, Visa and Hyandai/Kia, all publicly registered their discomfort with the 'poor image' the 2022 World Cup bid had brought onto the world of football, and their subsequent association with the sport (*BBC*, 9 June 2014b)—as we saw in the last section, in 2014 Fly Emirates also decided not to renew its sponsorship agreement with FIFA due to ongoing claims of corruption surrounding the 2018 and 2022 World Cup bidding process.

Growing out of the allegations levied against Qatar (and Russia), in 2015, U.S. prosecutors opened a federal case against FIFA for charges of corruption (see: *Department of Justice*, 27 May 2015). In May 2015, for example, the U.S. Department of Justice indicted 14 current and former FIFA executives and associates on charges of wire fraud, money laundering, bribery and racketeering. Then, in December 2015, 16 further FIFA officials were charged. Among them was former Brazil football federation chief, Ricardo Teixeira, who was accused of being 'involved in criminal schemes involving well over $200m in bribes and kickbacks' (see: *BBC*, 21 December 2015a). In between these two waves of indictments, and under the pressure of the ongoing corruption allegations levied against FIFA—as well as the negativity surrounding FIFA's decision to award the 2022 World Cup to a country with the human rights record of Qatar—in June 2015, long-standing FIFA president, Joseph 'Sepp' Blatter, announced his decision to resign, stating that he would remain in office until a successor had been appointed (*The New York Times*, 2 June 2015). However, in September 2015, Swiss prosecutors opened their own investigation into charges that Sepp Blatter had made a series of illegal payments to UEFA President Michel Platini. On the back of this, FIFA's main sponsors—VISA, Coca-Cola, Budweiser and McDonalds—all publicly called for Blatter's immediate removal from office, and, in turn, the world governing body banned Blatter and Platini from all football activities for eight years (see: *The Guardian*, 21 December 2015a). In 2016, current FIFA president, Gianni Infantino, was appointed, thus effectively ending Blatter's long-term reign. Upon reflecting on the downfall of the long-serving president, some have argued that it was arguably FIFA's awarding of the 2022 World Cup to Qatar that 'marked the beginning of the end for Blatter' (*Forbes*, 2 June 2015).

Furthermore, and more recently, in 2019, *The Sunday Times*—and other media sources—claimed that they had in their possession files that showed that Qatar's media network, Al Jazeera, had secretly offered FIFA $400 million 21 days prior to the state's awarding of the 2022 World Cup in December 2010. Of the $400 million offered to FIFA, $300 million was in relation to Al Jazeera's (later known as beIN) successful negotiation of the Middle East and North Africa broadcasting rights to the 2018 and 2022 World Cups, which, as we saw in Chap. 3, the television network was awarded in 2011. Crucially, however, according to *The Sunday Times* (10 March 2019), is that the remaining $100 million sought to act as a 'success fee', and was only to be paid to FIFA 'if Qatar was successful in the World Cup ballot in 2010'. Picked up by *The Guardian* (10 March 2019), it was claimed that the *Sunday Times*' files clearly showed that a contractual agreement between Qatar and FIFA had been drawn up, one which stated that 'in the event that the 2022 competition is awarded to the state of Qatar, al-Jazeera shall, in addition to the…[television] rights fee, pay to

Fifa into the designated account the monetary amount of $100m'. To some, such as the UK's former chairman of the Digital, Culture, Media and Sport Committee, Damian Collins, the *Sunday Times*' files were further evidence of Qatar acting 'in clear breach of the rules' (ibid.).

In responding to claims of bribery and corruption in connection to the 2022 World Cup bidding process, Qatari officials have outright denied that they were ever involved in any illegal or inappropriate activities, and have pointed to a lack of evidence that rules were ever breached. In 2011, when rumours first started that Qatar might have bribed FIFA officials, Hassan Al Thawadi, Secretary General of the Qatar Supreme Committee for Delivery and Legacy, stated, 'there is no evidence behind any of these claims, not a sliver…At the moment there is not a sliver of evidence we did anything wrong' (*The Guardian*, 11 July 2011). Then, in 2014, former Emir, Sheikh Hamad, called the bribery claims 'wild accusations' (*The Guardian*, 20 June 2014b), while the official statement of the Qatar Supreme Committee for Delivery and Legacy has been that such claims are 'baseless and riddled with innuendo' (*The Guardian*, 15 June 2014d).

One possible example of what the Qataris might be referring to as 'baseless' reporting is *The Sunday Times' claim that it had obtained 'millions of secret documents' which it alleged were 'proof'* that former FIFA Executive Committee member Mohammed bin Hammam directly paid in excess of £3 million to football officials across the globe in exchange for support for Qatar's bid for the 2022 World Cup (1 June 2014). This story built on a claim previously made by Phaedra Almajid, the former iInternational media specialist for the Qatar Supreme Committee for Delivery and Legacy, who, in 2011, admitted that she'd personally witnessed the Qatar bid team offer African FIFA Executives bribes in excess of $1.5 million (*BBC*, 11 July 2011). Given this mounting 'evidence' against Qatar, *The Sunday Times* then confirmed Interpol had officially called for a criminal investigation into the 2022 World Cup bid (15 June 2015). However, *The Sunday Times*' 'millions of documents' have never been made public, and thus their existence arguably never verified, while the paper's *Interpol claim was immediately refuted by the INGO itself, who labelled the story a 'false report'* (*Interpol*, 15 June 2015); *and only months after her accusations,* Almajid retracted her statement, claiming she was motivated by anger and wanted to 'hurt' Qatar and 'exact revenge after losing her campaign job' (*BBC*, 11 July 2011).

A further example where we might suggest the media scrutiny levied towards Qatar has not been entirely accurate is *The Washington Post*'s somewhat infamous story entitled '*The Toll of Human Casualties in Qatar*', which incorrectly claimed the 'fact' that more than 1000 workers had died on 2022 World Cup projects, even though actual tournament construction had at the time yet to become fully underway (see: *Doha News*, 10 October 2014). The *Washington Post*'s article prompted the Qatari government to respond by claiming that the 'facts' presented were 'completely untrue' and that 'not a single worker's life had been lost' on any World Cup construction site (*Doha News*, 3 June 2015). In admitting it had reported incorrectly, *The Washington Post* was forced to edit its original story to read:

> Correction: An earlier version of this post, and accompanying graphic, created the impression that more than 1000 migrant workers in Qatar had died working on 2022 World Cup infrastructure. The post should have made clearer that the figures involved all migrant deaths in Qatar. A report by Qatar's government found 964 deaths of migrants from India, Nepal and Bangladesh in 2012 and 2013. Other groups have cited a higher number over a longer period of time. A lengthy statement by Qatar's government said "not a single worker's life has been lost" in connection with the World Cup construction, while an account by The Guardian linked some deaths to the construction. Ultimately, we are unable to verify how many deaths, if any, are related to World Cup construction. This post and the graphic have been revised to provide a more accurate picture of what's known and not known. (*The Washington Post*, 27 May 2015)

The above reference to *The Guardian* is in connection to an article published on 23 December 2014, which claimed that the 'death toll among Qatar's 2022 World Cup workers' equated to 'a rate of one every two days', despite the fact that the state's World Cup construction projects had barely started prior to 2015 (see: *Doha News*, 10 October 2014). It is instances of such inaccuracy that Qatari officials, such as Hussain Al Mulla, Undersecretary of the Qatar Ministry of Labour and Social affairs, have used to underpin their assessment of the media's coverage of the 2022 World Cup as 'malicious, fabricated and false foreign press reports' (*Doha News*, 8 October 2013).

In investigating further the opinions of Qatari policy-makers vis-à-vis the reasons why the 2022 World Cup has been so heavily scrutinized by certain media groups, Brannagan (2017) found that the local perspective was largely considered to be the result of what was referred to as 'sour gapes'. That is, in recognizing how the overwhelming majority of mediated stories about the 2022 World Cup had come from British and United States' media networks and newspapers, the notion here was that the media's reporting on Qatar was the result of jealousy, created by the fact the United States and England were beaten by Russia and Qatar to the rights to stage the 2018 and 2022 World Cups, respectively. Such a standpoint resembles the perspective that the global media come to largely serve the foreign policy interests of their native country, a notion which has been widely discussed in academic circles (see: Andersen, 2006). Most notable in this regard has been work by Herman and Chomsky (2010), whose research has argued how the media come to align stories to the interests of the dominant economic and political elites within society, and thus act as *the* most potent vehicle in the control and management of public opinion (ibid.). Herman and Chomsky's core rationale here is that the media—like all social institutions—are highly reliant on their structural surroundings, most particularly corporate sponsors, who provide key advertising revenues, and national governments, who regulate their practices, provide key information and highly reputable sources and, at times, offer public funding. In short, rather than seeing the media as free, liberal actors concerned only for societies' well-being, they are instead considered to be highly contained and controlled by multiple economic and political self-interests. Gans (1980, p. 149) argues that such a perspective helps us locate why journalists tend to focus on foreign nations that are of interest to one's own country and/or government[3]—not only are stories about these foreign nations already highly topical, thus generating significant public interest back home,[4] but they also deter criticism from one's own national government by drawing attention towards 'others'' problems.

Offering up an alternative perspective, we point to the length of time Qatar has spent in the 'pre-event' stage, which is when the most scathing media attacks tend to take place for sport event hosts. This is because, during the event, international focus tends to turn away from the hosts' sociopolitical and practical issues, and towards the athletic competition; in the post-event phase, international focus usually then turns to the next event host. Thus, it is in the pre-event phase where non-states actors, including the global media, make full use of the attention of international audiences. Qatar's extended length of time in the 'pre-event' stage has been the result of FIFA's unique decision to award the 2018 and 2022 World Cups in 2010. With the exception of the 1978 and 1982 World Cup finals, which were awarded in 1966, FIFA has predominantly concluded voting proceedings roughly within a six-seven-year period. FIFA's rationale for choosing the 2018 and 2022 World Cups so far in advance—a policy since scrapped—was that it would provide host countries and FIFA's partners with more time to plan and organize future World Cups, which was considered by football's world governing body to be 'better' for all concerned (cf. *FIFA*, 30 May 2008). Nonetheless, important to note is that this extended period of time also presents non-state actors with a greater opportunity through which to build their own 'strategic communication' and, in doing so, construct and develop a set of widely heard critical themes through which to disempower the host state. The consequence is that, by the time 2022 comes around, Qatar would have spent twice as long than the majority of other sport event hosts in the highly negative and scrutinized pre-event stage, leading to the press it arguably receives being 'harsher than that levelled at other countries hosting World Cups or Olympics' (*Doha News*, 5 July 2015c).

Furthermore, in this pre-event stage, once a nation is considered 'newsworthy', two developments are most likely to occur. The first is that the balance of attention given to a certain nation by one media source has the knock-on effect of attracting focus from several others sources, leading to similarity in the reporting of events by competing media organizations, which, in turn, results in a greater level of negativity for the host state to confront (cf. Golan & Wanta, 2003). Second, and leading on from this, the incessant coverage of stories about a specific country also comes to have momentous consequences for how that country is regarded by global audiences. Indeed, a plethora of studies have located how constant negative reporting of a country comes to have 'significant influence of our perceptions' of that country and its peoples (McCombs & Reynolds, 2009, p. 1; see also: Zhang & Meadows, 2012). This is particularly so when few individuals have direct experience of the state under scrutiny, and thus their sole source of knowledge of said nation derives from this relentless negativity (Wanta et al., 2004).

Given this, accusations of bribery and corruption surrounding the 2022 World Cup have come to negatively impact Qatar's soft power in multiple ways. Although the state seeks to position itself through is soft power (sporting and otherwise) endeavours as an efficient, innovative and successful actor, such accusations have come to undermine the state's integrity by positioning Qataris in the minds of certain audiences as self-centred and deceitful peoples who resort to cheating in order to achieve victory. The result is that, as opposed to talk of Qatar's achievements—such as being the only Middle Eastern state to be entrusted with staging a first-order SME—being met by others with admiration and praise, they are instead potentially met with a sincere amount of suspicion. Indeed, as one commentator correctly summarized, 'part of the reason for its [Qatar's] World Cup bid was to raise its profile in the eyes of international audiences. So far, it has done so for all the wrong reasons' (*The Guardian*, 1 June 2014f). Through this, Qatar comes to suffer from a 'crisis of legitimacy', resonating notions of untrustworthiness and egocentricity, which, in turn, comes to considerably damage its credibility in the minds of certain audiences and political leaders (Nye, 2011; Castells, 2013).

Qatar as a Sports Event Destination

The third and final form through which Qatar's image has been damaged is through questions being raised over its suitability to act as a sports events destination of choice. One example here relates to concerns raised by certain audiences over Qatar's lack of sporting—and particularly football—heritage and competence. FIFA's decision to award the 2022 World Cup to a state such as Qatar that lacks the kind of existing facilities needed to stage an effective tournament has been severely questioned. Upon Qatar's winning of the 2022 World Cup rights, *The Independent* (2 December 2010), for example, published an article titled 'Shock as Qatar win vote for 2022 World Cup', citing concerns over a 'lack of [football] infrastructure', and the fact that Qatar had 'never before hosted a major global sporting event'. In response, Qatar has constructed from scratch seven new stadiums for the World Cup (Ras Abu Aboud Stadium, Education City Stadium, Lusail Stadium, Al Janoub Stadium, Ahmad Bin Ali Stadium, Al Thumama Stadium and Al Bayt Stadium), as well as carried out major renovation works on its existing national stadium, the Khalifa International Stadium, which was originally built in 1976 (see: Qatar 2022, 'Stadiums', n.d.). According to Hassan Al Thawadi, Secretary General of the Qatar Supreme Committee for Delivery and Legacy, Qatar's total World Cup stadium construction costs will amount to 'between $8 billion to $10 billion' (*Arabian Business*, 22 May 2016). This is in comparison to the $1.3 billion South Africa spent on stadium costs for the 2010 World Cup, the $3.5 billion Brazil spent on 2014 World Cup stadia and the $3.8 billion Russia spent on venue construction and refurbishment for the 2018 World Cup (see: IMS, 14 June 2018; see also: Grix et al., 2019c).

Alongside sports infrastructure, some have also pointed to Qatar's lack of international athletic prowess, and the fact the country has never qualified for a World Cup finals, and has only collected a handful of medals at the Olympic Games. Although in the long term the state seeks to make up for its lack of sporting talent through its Aspire Academy (as we saw in Chap. 3), in the immediate term Qatar has been criticized for its heavy investment in the naturalizing of athletes from other countries. Examples include Kenyan-born Stephen Cherono, who won gold for Qatar in steeplechase at both the 2003 and 2005 IAAF World Championships under the Qatari name Saif Saaeed Shaheen (*BBC*, 8 April 2015b). Then there was the Qatari Men's Handball team, who made it to the final of the 2015 World Handball Championships (hosted in Qatar) with a squad that overwhelmingly comprised of naturalized athletes, mainly from Spain, France, Cuba, Bosnia and Montenegro (*DW*, 4 February 2015). According to a case study by Reiche and Tinaz (2019, p. 156), 24 out of 35 Qatari athletes at the 2016 Summer Olympics Games (65%) were foreign-born. Krug (2019), however, argues in his book *Journeys on a Football Carpet*, on Qatari football history specifically, that the game has become an integral part of Qatar's national DNA. The Qatari Football Association (QFA) was established in 1960 and joined FIFA in 1970, two years before the country became independent. The Qatari men's football team made it to the final of the FIFA World Youth Championship in Australia in 1981 and qualified both for the football tournaments of the 1984 Los Angeles and the 1992 Barcelona Summer Olympic Games. In 2019, Qatar won the AFC Asian Cup for the first time.

Furthermore, some have suggested that Qatari citizens themselves lack the kind of sporting interest and appetite found elsewhere, demonstrated most evidently by their lack of desire to attend live sporting events. The Qatar Stars League's inability to attract a remotely sufficient number of live spectators to its competitive games was experienced first-hand by one of the investigators, who attended a match in 2013 between Al Arabi SC and Al Gharafa SC at the Grand Hamad Stadium, which, although has a total capacity of 13,000, attracted no more than 100 people to the game. More recently, Qatar's 2019 hosting of the IAAF World Athletics Championships recorded the lowest number of spectators 'ever' in the tournament's history, resulting in athletes 'parading in front of empty stands', and leading to 'international outcry over the lack of spectators at athletics' most prestigious event outside the Olympics' (*CNN*, 1 October 2019). In an attempt to cover up its citizen's lack of evidential live sporting desire, it has been reported that state authorities have been forced to pay expatriate workers £3.50 per head to pose as 'fake sports fans' at Qatar's staging of various sports events, in a bid to make empty stadiums appear full, including during its hosting of the 2014 FIVB Men's Volleyball World Cup (see: *The Guardian*, 17 December 2014c).

Qatar hosted the FIFA Club World Cup editions in 2019 and 2020 (the latter postponed to February 2021 because of COVID-19), which showcased the ability to learn from previous failures in organizing sporting events. Secretary General of the Supreme Committee, H. E. Hassan Al Thawadi admitted after the 2019 FIFA Club World Cup: 'We are not currently 100 percent ready to host the World Cup… The Club World Cup is a pilot tournament aimed at experimenting [with] various preparations and operational plans before hosting the World Cup in 2022' (*The Peninsula*, 22 December 2019). However, Qatar showed that it could successfully manage an event at the FIFA Club World Cup 2020 (in February 2021). One of the authors attended matches at the tournament. He went without any difficulties by metro to the matches in the Education City and Al-Rayyan stadiums. Spectators had to do a COVID-19 rapid test before the match, which was offered free of charge. Notably, the fans of the Egyptian team Al Ahly (mainly comprised of the prominent Egyptian diaspora in Doha due to the travel restrictions at that time) contributed to a great atmosphere. One of the authors also attended the inauguration of the Al Thumama stadium for the Qatari Cup Final in October 2021, the fifth stadium to be completed out of the eight World Cup stadiums. There were about 40,000 people present in the stadium to witness the final, and both the organization of the event and the atmosphere were excellent.

Qatar's sport event suitability has been further thrown into question through the perception by some that the state acts as a 'high-risk' World Cup destination. One example where this stance has manifest is through concerns expressed over Qatar's climate. As mentioned in Chap. 1, in the hottest months of June, July and August, temperatures in Qatar can reach more than 40°C. This has led some to raise concerns over the feasibility of a summer World Cup, and the subsequent dangers posed to players and fans (see: *The Sun*, 22 July 2011). FIFA's own chief medical officer, Professor Jiri Dvorak, for example, proclaimed a July–August World Cup in Qatar would equate to a 'highly critical risk' to those expected to travel to the state in 2022 (*The Guardian*, 3 November 2014a). In 2015, such concerns resulted in FIFA moving the 2022 World Cup to the cooler months of November and December (*The New York Times*, 19 March

2015). This then culminated in the European Professional Football Leagues—and in particular the English Premier League—as well as the IOC strongly opposing such a move, claiming a winter World Cup would severely disrupt the international sporting calendar (cf. *The Guardian*, 3 November 2014a; *The Telegraph*, 19 March 2015a). There was however less complaint from states such as the United States, the Scandinavia countries and the Baltic nations, all of whom play their seasons from spring to fall, and, consequently, their national leagues won't be affected by a winter World Cup. The European Professional Football Leagues, nonetheless, did finally accepted FIFA's decision to move the 2022 World Cup to winter after the governing body trebled its payments to clubs for the 2018 and 2022 World Cups (*The Guardian*, 20 March 2015b). Additionally, the IOC's complaints ceased after FIFA promised the tournament would not clash with the programming of the 2022 Beijing Winter Olympic Games.

Additionally, alongside concerns expressed over the state's summer climate, anxieties have also been articulated with regard to the potential terrorism threat and crowd control issues the 2022 World Cup poses. Both these points were picked up by FIFA's own risk assessment officer, who, in reviewing Qatar's original bid for the tournament, proclaimed the state should be seen as a 'high security risk', due to its proximity to countries housing terrorist groups, as well as its plan to locate eight stadiums within a 55 km radius of one another, which will equate, it has been claimed, to 'major crowd management and traffic problems' during the tournament (*BBC*, 14 June 2014a; *The Sunday Times*, 15 June 2014c). On the former, in 2014, it was reported that the terrorist group Islamic State urged FIFA not to hold the World Cup in Qatar, claiming football constituted to 'a deviation from Islam' (see: *Huffington Post*, 9 July 2014a); a year later, the Islamic State of Iraq and the Levant (ISIL) then publicly threatened hostile force during the 2022 World Cup if the tournament was not relocated to a non-Muslim state (see: *Doha News*, 16 November 2015a). Nonetheless, as we saw in Chap. 3, in 2021, Qatar was listed as the 29th most peaceful country in the world by the Global Peace Index 2021 report. Furthermore, the University of Maryland's Global Terrorism Database also found that between 1982 and 2012 Qatar suffered only 6 terrorist attacks compared to the 431 which tragically occurred in the United Kingdom throughout the same period (cf. *Huffington Post*, 24 August 2014b). Nevertheless, important to bear in mind is that the hosting of major global events can make relatively safe countries more prone to attack due to their capacity to 'quickly make a powerful statement' for fundamentalist-motivated individuals and/or groups (Goldbatt & Hu, 2005, p. 141)—note, for instance, the examples of Munich 1972 and Atlanta 1996.

These more sports-specific issues around Qatar's suitability as an effective and safe sports event host undermine the state's soft power in two crucial ways. The state's strategy to invest its natural resource wealth to make up for its shortcomings as a sports event host—including its lack of sporting infrastructure, viewer interest and athletic prowess—comes to arguably overshadow its success as the first Middle Eastern country to acquire a World Cup, and in doing so, draws increased attention to its desire and ability to simply gloss over the cracks through extravagant tactics that draw on its financial prosperity. Nye (2008) himself advocates that those who overcompensate on their hard power for self-interested gains significantly prohibit and undercut the manifestation of soft power, and thus Qatar's acquisition of the 2022 World Cup has, if anything, reminded certain audiences of its fortunate position as opposed to its skill and accomplishment. Furthermore, as opposed to presenting itself to various tourists as a safe location, the state's acquisition of the tournament has debatably rather positioned the state as a 'high-risk' location. Since the state's acquisition of the World Cup in 2010, the global heightened awareness of Qatar's soaring summer climate and in particular its perceived 'close proximity' to terrorist groups arguably overshadows the state's attempts to present itself as a welcome, benign and attractive destination, and thus its desire to escape the stereotypical problem of the neighbourhood effect.

Conclusion

Upon reflecting on the scrutiny Qatar has received in connection to the 2022 World Cup, we are reminded that both soft power and the hosting of a sports mega-events are mixed blessings, ones that simultaneously create new opportunities *and* challenges. As Nye (2011) himself locates, due to its social constructive nature, soft power is a dance that requires partners, and thus one's image is always in the hands of others' interpretations of one's (in)actions. Crucially, here, is that, as we have seen in this chapter, the acquisition of a sports event, although providing unique opportunities to get their host's message across to international audiences, can also come to severely undercut a states' soft power attempts through their propensity to invite scrutiny. These events thus act as key forms of 'strategic communication' for INGOs and the media in their desire to police, resist and discipline states and, in doing so, to significantly challenge and distort their soft power attempts. It is because of this that Cull (2008, p. 137) correctly notes that, in a 'world of the Internet and global satellite news', for those who acquire and host major sports events, a state comes to be 'known as it is, not as it wishes to be'.

In this chapter, we have suggested that the scrutiny Qatar has received (so far) has revolved around three forms: *Qatar's human rights record; accusations of bribery and corruption; and Qatar as a sports events destination*. Through this, two developments have overall occurred. The first is that, although largely presenting Qatar to the world in more negative terms, the scrutiny surrounding the 2022 World Cup has certainly raised awareness of the state's global existence, and, in doing so, has allowed it to somewhat stand out from its neighbours, although not in the way it intended. Indeed, as mentioned by *The Independent* (19 December 2018) in the introduction to this chapter, when all is said and done, one outcome we can be sure of is that 'Qatar will no longer be invisible' on the world stage. In this sense, for Qatar, as for other hosts of sports events, the 2022 World Cup has indeed acted as a key 'delivery system for consciousness raising' (Barney, 2004, p. 126).

This is of course not to suggest that simply being known by international audiences is the same as wielding forms of influence, leadership nor power. In the case of Qatar, it has indeed become known in ways that simultaneously hinder its soft power attempts. As we have seen in this chapter, Qatar's human rights record and abuses have come to damage the state's desire to position itself as a friendly, 'good global citizen' with humanitarian desires. Rather, the state has come to be seen in this sense as a 'hypocritical actor', one whose own domestic policies do not align with its international intentions. This has been particularly so with regard to the state's slow and sluggish attempts to meaningfully dismantle the kalafa sponsorship system, something that did not take place until 2020. However, important to mention here is that the fact that Qatar is now one of the few states in the region to have made positive changes in this respect, means that the state may well carve out for itself a position as a future Arab leader for a more progressive, liberal take on the human rights of expatriate workers.

Furthermore, accusations of bribery and corruption come to undermine the state's integrity by positioning Qataris in the minds of certain audiences as self-centred and deceitful peoples who resort to cheating in order to achieve victory. Through this, Qatar comes to suffer from a 'crisis of legitimacy', forcing audiences to more vigorously question the credibility of its soft power. Finally, the state's strategy to extravagantly invest its natural resource wealth in order to make up for its shortcomings raises questions about its true sporting accomplishments, while concerns over its 'high-risk' potential as a sport event host overshadows the state's attempts to present itself to the world as a welcome, safe and attractive destination. In the next chapter, we identify and discuss the opportunities and challenges Qatar faces leading up to, and after, its staging of the 2022 World Cup, as well as the areas where further political and social change is needed.

Notes

1. Indeed, while in 1960 there were estimated to be roughly 2000 'international non-governmental organizations' in existence worldwide, by 2005 this number had increased to 28,000 (see: Turner, 2010, p. 82).
2. The WBGT index takes into consideration ambient temperature, humidity, solar radiation and wind speed.
3. Herman and Chomsky (1988) provide the example here of the Cold War, where the U.S. media dichotomized the world into one of Communist and anti-Communist powers, continuously condemning the former and championing the latter; we may also include here the U.S. media's coverage of the 2003–2011 Iraq War, which was criticized by then director general of the BBC, Greg Dyke, who accused American broadcasters of being 'unquestionably patriotic' and 'so lacking in impartiality that it threatened the credibility of America's electronic media' (Timms, 2003).
4. The 2003 U.S. invasion of Iraq serves as an example here, when Fox News was widely accused of abandoning all forms of media objectivity in its offering of a blatant pro-war account in a bid to boost ratings and audience figures across America (cf. Jackson & Stanfield, 2004).

References

Al Jazeera. (2016, December 14). Qatar introduces changes to labour laws [online]. Retrieved April 12, 2021, from https://www.aljazeera.com/economy/2016/12/14/qatar-introduces-changes-to-labour-law

Andersen, R. (2006). *A century of media, a century of war*. Peter Lang.

Arabian Business. (2016, May 22). Qatar's World Cup stadiums to cost $10bn, official says. Retrieved June 17, 2021, from https://www.arabianbusiness.com/qatar-s-world-cup-stadiums-cost-10bn-official-says-632410.html

Bajracharya, R., & Sijapati, B. (2012). *The Kafala system and its implications for Nepali domestic workers.* Center for the Study of Labour Mobility [online]. Retrieved February 09, 2021, from http://www.ceslam.org/files/Policy%20 Brief%201_The%20Kafala%20System%20and%20Its%20Implications%20 for%20Nepali%20Domestic%20Workers.pdf

Barnett, M., & Finnemore, M. (2004). *Rules for the World: International Organizations in Global Politics.* Cornell University Press.

Barney, D. (2004). *The network society.* Polity.

Baylis, J., & Smith, S. (2005). *The globalization of world politics: An introduction to international relations.* Oxford University Press.

BBC. (2011, July 11). Qatar 2022 World Cup bid 'did nothing wrong' [online]. Retrieved March 17, 2021, from http://www.bbc.co.uk/sport/football/14112036

BBC. (2014a, June 14). Qatar 2022 World Cup a 'high security risk', report claimed [online]. Retrieved February 18, 2021, from https://www.bbc.co.uk/sport/football/27852582

BBC. (2014b, June 09). World Cup 2014 sponsors face whole new ball game [online]. Retrieved September 12, 2021, from https://www.bbc.co.uk/news/business-27667473

BBC. (2015a, December 21). Fifa corruption crisis: Key questions answered [online]. Retrieved March 13, 2021, from https://www.bbc.co.uk/news/world-europe-32897066

BBC. (2015b, April 08). How will Qatar build a good team for the 2022 World Cup? [online]. Retrieved July 23, 2021, from http://www.bbc.co.uk/sport/football/32147203

BBC. (2016, December 13). Qatar abolished controversial 'kafala' labour system [online]. Retrieved February 15, 2021, from http://www.bbc.co.uk/news/world-middle-east-38298393

Beck, U. (2006). Living in the world risk society: A hobhouse memorial public lecture given on Wednesday 15 February 2006 at the London school of economics. *Economy and Society, 35*(3), 329–345.

Bell, D. (1973). *The coming of post-industrial society: A venture in social forecasting.* Basic Books.

Brannagan, P. M. (2017). *The state of Qatar and global sport: A case study of globalization, the nation-state and soft power* (Doctoral dissertation, Loughborough University).

Brannagan, P. M., & Giulianotti, R. (2018). The soft power–soft disempowerment nexus: The case of Qatar. *International Affairs, 94*(5), 1139–1157.

Breton, G., & Lambert, M. (2003). *Universities and globalization: Private linkages, public trust.* UNESCO/Université Laval/Economica.

Castells, M. (2007). Communication, power and counter-power in the network society. *International journal of Communication, 1*(1), 29.

Castells, M. (2013). *Communication Power* (2nd ed.). Oxford University Press.

CNN. (2013, June 06). Should soccer boycott Israel's European Championship? [online]. Retrieved July 10, 2021, from https://edition.cnn.com/2013/06/06/sport/football/israel-sarsak-uefa-u21-football/index.html

CNN. (2015, May 27). FIFA in crisis: The men who have been charged [online]. Retrieved July 25, 2021, from http://edition.cnn.com/2015/05/27/football/fifa-arrests-webb-warner-marin/

CNN. (2019, October 01). Where are the crowds at the World Athletics Championships? [online]. Retrieved September 07, 2021, from https://edition.cnn.com/2019/10/01/sport/world-athletics-championships-low-crowds-doha-spt-intl/index.html

Cull, N. J. (2008). The public diplomacy of the modern olympic games and China's soft power strategy. In M. E. Price & D. Dayan (Eds.), *Owning the olympics: Narratives of the New China*. University of Michigan Press.

De Genova, N., & Nathalie, P. (2010). *The deportation regime: Sovereignty, space, and the freedom of movement*. Duke University Press.

Department of Justice. (2015, May 27). Nine FIFA officials and five corporate exectutives indicated for racketeering conspiracy and corruption [online]. Retrieved March 06, 2021, from https://www.justice.gov/opa/pr/nine-fifa-officials-and-five-corporate-executives-indicted-racketeering-conspiracy-and

Doha News. (2013, April 26). To tackle labor rights violations, QF, 2022 Supreme Committee ratify workers' charters [online]. Retrieved July 12, 2015, from https://dohanews.co/to-tackle-labor-rights-violations-qf-2022-supreme/

Doha News. (2014, May 18). Blatter ruffles feathers after calling Qatar's 'World Cup a 'mistake' [online]. Retrieved May 12, 2015, from https://dohanews.co/blatter-ruffles-feathers-calling-qatars-world-cup-mistake/

Doha News. (2015a, November 16). How safe is Qatar from an ISIS attack? Experts weigh in [online]. Retrieved May 06, 2021, from https://dohanews.co/how-safe-is-qatar-from-an-isis-attack-experts-weigh-in/

Doha News. (2015b, June 13). Qatar launches legal offensive against some critics [online]. Retrieved August 26, 2016, from https://dohanews.co/qatar-launches-legal-offensive-against-some-critics/

Doha News. (2015c, July 05). Qatar launches legal offensive against some critics [online]. Retrieved August 26, 2016, from https://dohanews.co/qatar-launches-legal-offensive-against-some-critics/

Doha News. (2016, May 22). Kafala reforms in Qatar still expected to take effect in December [online]. Retrieved September 15, 2021, from https://dohanews.co/kafala-reforms-in-qatar-still-expected-to-take-effect-in-december/

DW. (2015). Qatar: Buying their way to sporting success, 4 February, 2015 [online]. Available at: https://www.dw.com/en/qatar-buying-theirway-to-sporting-success/a-18233576 (Accessed 17.02.21)

FIFA. (2008, May 30). Joint decision on 2018 and 2022 [online]. Retrieved May 06, 2021, from http://www.fifa.com/worldcup/news/y=2008/m=5/news=joint-decision-2018-and-2022-783630.html

Forbes. (2015, June 02). Sepp Blatter resigning from FIFA will boost value of World Cup [online]. Retrieved February 15, 2021, from https://www.forbes.com/sites/mikeozanian/2015/06/02/sepp-blatter-resigning-from-fifa-will-boost-value-of-world-cup/?sh=5b8cba8f5970

Gans, H. J. (1980). *Deciding what's news*. Vintage Books.

Gardner, A. M. (2011). Gulf migration and the family. *Journal of Arabian Studies, 1*(1), 3–25.

Global Peace Index. (2021). [online]. Retrieved July 11, 2021, from https://www.visionofhumanity.org/wp-content/uploads/2021/06/GPI-2021-web-1.pdf

Golan, G., & Wanta, W. (2003). International elections on US network news: An examination of factors affecting newsworthiness. *Gazette (Leiden, Netherlands), 65*(1), 25–39.

Goldblatt, J., & Hu, C. (2005). Tourism, terrorism, and the new world for event leaders. *E-review of Tourism Research, 3*(6), 139–144.

Grix, J., Brannagan, P. M., & Lee, D. (2019a). *Entering the global arena: Emerging states, soft power strategies and sports mega-events*. Palgrave Macmillan.

Grix, J., Brannagan, P. M., & Lee, D. (2019b). Russia's unique soft power strategy. In *Entering the global arena: Emerging states, soft power strategies and sports mega-events*. Palgrave Macmillan.

Grix, J., Brannagan, P. M., & Lee, D. (2019c). South Africa and the 2010 FIFA World Cup. In *Entering the global arena: Emerging states, soft power strategies and sports mega-events*. Palgrave Macmillan.

Herman, E., & Chomsky, N. (1988). *Manufacturing consent: The political economy of mass media*. New York: Pantheon.

Herman, E. S., & Chomsky, N. (2010). *Manufacturing consent: The political economy of the mass media*. Random House.

Homayounpour. (2021). Labor market reforms and the World Cup 2022 [online]. Retrieved May 25, 2021, from https://soundcloud.com/cirsguq/episode-9-houtan-homayounpour

Huffington Post. (2013, June 26). London Mayor should get his facts straight on Qatar [online]. Retrieved May 25, 2021, from http://www.huffingtonpost.co.uk/nicholas-mcgeehan/london-mayor-should-get-h_b_3163127.html

Huffington Post. (2014a, July 09). Islamic State urges FIFA to deprive Qatar of the World Cup [online]. Retrieved February 15, 2021, from http://www.huffingtonpost.com/james-dorsey/islamic-state-urges-fifa_b_5569524.html

Huffington Post. (2014b, August 24). Shedding light on the threat of terrorism at Qatar's 2022 World Cup [online]. Retrieved June 29, 2021, from http://www.huffingtonpost.co.uk/quintan-wiktorowicz/qatar-world-cup-terrorism_b_5522455.html

Huffington Post. (2015, June 03). Qatar's World Cup death toll claim leaves migrant worker rights campaigners unimpressed [online]. Retrieved September 19, 2021, from http://www.huffingtonpost.co.uk/2015/06/03/qatar-world-cup-deaths_n_7500920.html

Human Freedom Index. (2020). [online]. Retrieved February 08, 2021, from https://www.cato.org/human-freedom-index/2020

Human Rights Watch. (2017, January 12). Qatar: Labour reforms leave abusive system intact [online]. Retrieved February 07, 2021, from https://www.hrw.org/news/2017/01/12/qatar-labor-reforms-leave-abusive-system-intact#

ILO. (2020, August 30). Dismantling the kafala system and introducing a minimum wage mark new era for Qatar labour market [online]. Retrieved November 11, 2021, from https://www.ilo.org/beirut/projects/qatar-office/WCMS_754391/lang%2D%2Den/index.htm

ILO. (2021a, March 19). Qatar's new minimum wage enters into force [online]. Retrieved November 10, 2021, from https://www.ilo.org/beirut/projects/qatar-office/WCMS_775981/lang%2D%2Den/index.htm?_sm_au_=iVV7VSrgFWgMV5tPvMFckK0232C0F

ILO. (2021b, May 27). New legislation in Qatar provides greater protection to workers from heat stress [online]. Retrieved November 10, 2021, from https://www.ilo.org/beirut/projects/qatar-office/WCMS_794475/lang%2D%2Den/index.htm

IMS. (2018, June 14). The World Cup effect: Requirements and costs of infrastructure [online]. Retrieved March 07, 2021, from https://resources.investormanagementservices.com/the-world-cup-effect/

Interpol. (2015). *Summary of Activities [online]*. Available at: https://www.interpol.int/content/download/10994/file/Summary%20of%20activities%20-%202014-2016.pdf

ITUC. (2014, February 11). Qatar World Cup workers' standards: No legal enforcement, no worker rights [online]. Retrieved March 05, 2021, from https://www.ituc-csi.org/qatar-world-cup-workers-standards

Jackson, P. T., & Stanfield, J. R. (2004). The role of the press in a democracy: Heterodox economics and the propaganda model. *Journal of Economic Issues, 38*(2), 475–482.

Josselin, D., & Wallace, W. (2001). Non-state actors in world politics: A framework. In *Non-state actors in world politics* (pp. 1–20). Palgrave Macmillan.

Kaid, L. L. (Ed.). (2004). *Handbook of political communication research*. Routledge.

Krug, M. (2019). *Journeys on a football carpet: An inside look at Qatar's football story and its transformation into the 2022 FIFA World Cup host*. Hamad bin Khalifa University Press.

McCombs, M., & Reynolds, A. (2009). How the news shapes our civic agenda. In J. Bryant & M. B. Oliver (Eds.), *Media effects: Advances in theory and research*. Routledge.

Mills, C. W. (1959). *The sociological imagination.* Pelican.

Millward, P. (2017). World Cup 2022 and Qatar's construction projects: Relational power in networks and relational responsibilities to migrant workers. *Current Sociology, 65*(5), 756–776.

Nye, J. S. (2008). Public diplomacy and soft power. *The ANNALS of the American Academy of Political and Social Sciences, 616*(1), 94–109.

Nye, J. S. (2011). *The future of power.* Public Affairs.

Nye, J. S. (2014). *The information revolution and soft power. Current History.*

Pande, A. (2013). "The paper that you have in your hand is my freedom": Migrant domestic work and the sponsorship (Kafala) system in Lebanon. *International Migration Review, 47*(2), 414–441.

Parreñas, R. S. (2010). The indentured mobility of migrant women: How gendered protectionist laws lead Filipina hostesses to forced sexual labour. *Journal of Workplace Rights, 15*(3), 327–344.

Qatar 2022. (n.d.). Stadiums [online]. Retrieved June 17, 2021, from https://www.qatar2022.qa/en/stadiums

Qatar Foundation. (2013, April 24). Qatar foundation implements welfare standards to guarantee workers' rights [online]. Retrieved June 10, 2021, from http://www.qf.org.qa/news/240

Qatar Foundation. (2014, April 30). QF supports workers recreation initiative [online]. Retrieved June 17, 2021, from http://www.qf.org.qa/content/the-foundation/issue-64/qf-supports-workers-recreation-initiative

Reiche, D., & Tinaz, C. (2019). Policies for naturalisation of foreign-born athletes: Qatar and Turkey in comparison. *International Journal of Sport Policy and Politics, 11*(1), 153–171.

Risse, T., & Sikkink, K. (1999). The socialization of international human rights norms into domestic practices: Introduction. *Cambridge Studies in International Relations, 66*, 1–38.

Robertson, A. (2015). *Media and politics in a globalizing world.* Polity Press.

Rowe, D. (2000). Global media events and the positioning of presence. *Media International Australia, 97*(1), 11–21.

SESRI (2014). Attitudes towards foriegn workers [online]. Available at: https://sesri.qu.edu.qa/static_file/qu/research/SESRI/documents/Publications/14/Qatari%20Attitudes%20Towards%20Foreign%20Workers.pdf (Accessed 17.09.21)

Sky News. (2014, November 03). Emirates ends FIFA World Cup sponsorship [online]. Retrieved March 09, 2021, from https://news.sky.com/story/emirates-ends-fifa-world-cup-sponsorship-10383904

Stoldt, G. C., Dittmore, S. W., & Branvold, S. E. (2012). *Sport public relations: Managing stakeholder communication.* Human kinetics.

Street, J. (2005). Politics lost, politics transformed, politics colonised? Theories of the impact of mass media. *Political Studies Review, 3*(1), 17–33.

Supreme Committee for Delivery and Legacy. (n.d.). Workers' welfare standards [online]. Retrieved June 02, 2021, from https://www.qatar2022.qa/sites/default/files/docs/Workers'-Welfare-Standards.pdf

The Democracy Index. (2020). [online]. Retrieved March 12, 2021, from https://www.eiu.com/n/campaigns/democracy-index-2020/

The Guardian. (2011, July 11). World Cup corruption claims fuelled by prejudice, says Qatar bid chief [online]. Retrieved May 12, 2021, from https://www.theguardian.com/football/2011/jul/11/world-cup-corruption-prejudice-qatar-bid

The Guardian. (2013a, November 17). Qatar 2022 World Cup workers 'treated like cattle', Amnesty report finds [online]. Retrieved June 29, 2021, from https://www.theguardian.com/world/2013/nov/17/qatar-world-cup-worker-amnesty-report

The Guardian. (2013b, September 25). Revealed: Qatar's World Cup 'slaves' [online]. Retrieved September 03, 2021, from https://www.theguardian.com/world/2013/sep/25/revealed-qatars-world-cup-slaves

The Guardian. (2014a, November 03). Fifa confirms 2022 World Cup in Qatar is likely to be held in winter [online]. Retrieved June 12, 2021, from https://www.theguardian.com/football/2014/nov/03/fifa-qatar-2022-world-cup-winter

The Guardian. (2014b, June 20). Qatar had the strongest bid for the 2022 Fifa World Cup. Here's why [online]. Retrieved March 21, 2021, from https://www.theguardian.com/commentisfree/2014/jun/20/why-qatar-had-strongest-bid-for-2022-fifa-world-cup

The Guardian. (2014c, December 17). Qatar hires migrant workers as 'fake sports fans' to fill up empty arenas [online]. Retrieved December 12, 2021, from https://www.theguardian.com/sport/2014/dec/17/qatar-migrant-workers-fake-sports-fans

The Guardian. (2014d, June 15). Qatar hits back at allegations of bribery over 2022 World Cup [online]. Retrieved November 16, 2015, from https://www.theguardian.com/football/2014/jun/15/qatar-world-cup-bid-2022

The Guardian. (2014e, July 29). Qatar World Cup stadium workers earn as little as 45p an hour [online]. Retrieved February 09, 2021, from https://www.theguardian.com/global-development/2014/jul/29/qatar-world-cup-stadium-workers-earn-45p-hour

The Guardian. (2014f, June 01). World Cup raising Qatar's profile for all the wrong reasons [online]. Retrieved June 17, 2021, from https://www.theguardian.com/football/2014/jun/01/2022-world-cup-qatar-fifa

The Guardian. (2015a, December 21). Sepp Blatter and Michel Platini banned from football for eight years by Fifa [onine]. Retrieved March 14, 2021, from https://www.theguardian.com/football/2015/dec/21/sepp-blatter-michel-platini-banned-from-football-fifa

The Guardian. (2015b, March 20). Fifa's Sepp Blatter says 2018 World Cup in Russia will stabilise region [online]. Retrieved May 19, 2021, from https://www.theguardian.com/football/2015/mar/20/fifa-sepp-blatter-2018-world-cup-russia-peace-region

The Guardian. (2015c, May 14). Qatar claims life improving for World Cup workers, but rights groups sceptical [online]. Retrieved August 11, 2021, from https://www.theguardian.com/world/2015/may/14/qatar-claims-life-improving-for-world-cup-workers-but-rights-groups-demur

The Guardian. (2016, December 13). Migrant workers in Qatar still at risk despite reforms, warns Amnesty [online]. Retrieved January 18, 2021, from https://www.theguardian.com/global-development/2016/dec/13/migrant-workers-in-qatar-still-at-risk-despite-reforms-warns-amnesty

The Guardian. (2019, March 10). Fifa facing urgent calls to investigate Qatar World Cup bid claims [online]. Retrieved February 17, 2021, from https://www.theguardian.com/football/2019/mar/10/qatar-fifa-world-cup-2022-damian-collins

The Guardian. (2020). New labour law ends Qatar's exploitative kafala system, 1st September [online]. Available at: https://www.theguardian.com/global-development/2020/sep/01/newemployment-law-effectively-ends-qatars-exploitative-kafala-system. (Accessed 09.05.21)

The Independent. (2010, December 02). Shock as Qatar win vote for 2022 World Cup [online]. Retrieved September 02, 2021, from http://www.independent.co.uk/sport/football/news-and-comment/shock-as-qatar-win-vote-for-2022-world-cup-2149429.html

The Independent. (2018, December 19). Qatar 2022: A reputation irrovocably damged, what has a minor Gulf state to gain from hosting the World Cup? [online]. Retrieved March 09, 2021, from https://www.independent.co.uk/sport/football/world-cup/qatar-world-cup-2022-host-bid-reputation-cost-soft-power-a8690366.html

The New York Times. (2015, June 02). Sepp Blatter decides to resign as FIFA President [online]. Retrieved February 14, 2021, from https://www.nytimes.com/2015/06/03/sports/soccer/sepp-blatter-to-resign-as-fifa-president.html

The Peninsula. (2019, December 22). Qatar presented one of most successful FIFA Club World Cup tournaments: SC [online]. Retrieved January 07, 2020, from https://thepeninsulaqatar.com/article/22/12/2019/Qatar-presented-one-of-most-successful-FIFA-Club-World-Cup-tournaments-SC

The Sun. (2011, July 22). Should Qatar host the 2022 World Cup? [online]. Retrieved April 18, 2021, from https://www.thesun.co.uk/archives/news/680064/should-qatar-host-the-2022-world-cup/

The Sunday Times. (2014a, November 24). England's secret file on 'Russia and Qatar World Cup vote fixing' [online]. Retrieved January 03, 2021, from

https://www.thetimes.co.uk/article/englands-secret-file-on-russia-and-qatar-world-cup-vote-fixing-pwhxb9zn03v
The Sunday Times. (2014b, June 01). Plot to buy the World Cup [online]. Retrieved December 14, 2021, from https://www.thetimes.co.uk/article/plot-to-buy-the-world-cup-lvxdg2v7l7w
The Sunday Times. (2014c, June 15). Security expert's warning: Tiny Qatar is wide open to attack [online]. Retrieved Febraury 17, 2021, from https://www.thetimes.co.uk/article/security-experts-warning-tiny-qatar-is-wide-open-to-attack-q6hv35pddbj
The Sunday Times. (2015, April 19). Fifa admits fixer helped Qatar cup bid [online]. Retrieved August 06, 2021, from https://www.thetimes.co.uk/article/fifa-admits-fixer-helped-qatar-cup-bid-f9xl3nxfxrx
The Sunday Times. (2019, March 10). Take it or leave it: Qatar's lucrative World Cup offer to FIFA [online]. Retrieved February 04, 2021, from https://www.thetimes.co.uk/article/take-it-or-leave-it-qatars-lucrative-world-cup-offer-to-fifa-qdj5fkxxm
The Telegraph. (2014, December 17). Fifa report into World Cup bid process 'misrepresented' says investigator Michael Garcia [online]. Retrieved May 13, 2021, from http://www.telegraph.co.uk/sport/football/world-cup/11228523/Fifa-has-misrepresented-my-report-says-investigator.html
The Telegraph. (2015a, March 19). World Cup 2022 final in Qatar will be on December 18 [online]. Retrieved May 26, 2021, from https://www.telegraph.co.uk/sport/football/world-cup/11483629/World-Cup-2022-final-in-Qatar-will-be-on-December-18.html
The Telegraph. (2015b, February 24). Qatar 2022 World Cup—the logistical nightmare before Christmas that will make Die Hard 2 look tame [online]. Retrieved March 27, 2021, from https://www.telegraph.co.uk/sport/football/world-cup/11432515/Qatar-2022-World-Cup-the-logistical-nightmare-before-Christmas-that-will-make-Die-Hard-2-look-tame.html
The Times. (2021, March 30). Qatar 2022: FA caught in dilemna over Qatar as protests show World Cup scandal still unresolved [online]. Retrieved August 14, 2021, from https://www.thetimes.co.uk/article/qatar-2022-player-protests-show-world-cup-scandal-still-unresolved-3x5lj55wj
The Washington Post. (2015, May 27). (UPDATED) The toll of human casualities in Qatar [online]. Retrieved June 05, 2021, from https://www.washingtonpost.com/news/wonk/wp/2015/05/27/a-body-count-in-qatar-illustrates-the-consequences-of-fifa-corruption/?utm_term=.35a00a25b997
Timms, D. (2003). Dyke Attacks unquestioning US media, The Guardian, 24 April [online]. Available at: https://www.theguardian.com/media/2003/apr/24/bbc.communicationsact (Accessed 15.01.21)
Turner, E. A. (2010). Why has the number of international non-governmental organizations exploded since 1960?. *Cliodynamics, 1*(1).

U.S. Embassy in Qatar @USEmbassyDoha. (2021, March 10). The U.S. Embassy values its partnership with @ADLSAQa and supports Qatar's new minimum wage legislation, the first of its kind in the region [online]. Retrieved March 10, 2021, from https://twitter.com/USEmbassyDoha/statu s/1369546352762437633?s=20

Ulrichsen, K. C. (2020). *Qatar and the gulf crisis: A study of resilience.* Oxford University Press.

Wanta, W., Golan, G., & Lee, C. (2004). Agenda setting and international news: Media influence on public perceptions of foreign nations. *Journalism & Mass Communication Quarterly, 81*(2), 364–377.

Webster, F. (2002). *Theories of the information society* (2nd ed.). Routledge.

West, M. D. (2008). *Secrets, sex, and spectacle.* Illionois: University of Chicago Press.

Zhang, C., & Meadows, C. W., III. (2012). International coverage, foreign policy, and national image: Exploring the complexities of media coverage, public opinion, and presidential agenda. *International Journal of Communication, 6,* 20.

CHAPTER 5

Qatar in 2022 and Beyond: Changes, Opportunities, Challenges

Abstract In this final, and concluding, chapter, we look ahead to Qatar's staging of the World Cup in 2022 and beyond. In doing so, this chapter identifies and discusses the opportunities and challenges Qatar faces. We argue that the following three areas will be vital for Qatar leading up to, and after, 2022: *delivering a successful World Cup; maintaining an independent foreign policy; and continuing with domestic reforms.* We deal with each in turn. The last section of this chapter looks to chart avenues for future research on Qatar and the 2022 World Cup.

Keywords Human rights • Gender politics • Kafala sponsorship system • Event organization

Up to this point, several key 'themes' have emerged from this text. In Chap. 1, we openly discussed our intention to analyse Qatar and the 2022 World Cup from a social constructivist position. In doing so, we argued for the need for international relations to be studied from a heterogeneous lens, one that appreciates the multiplicity and variation in state politics. Furthermore, due to advances in information and communications technologies, we argued that the need to maintain and manage a positive image and reputation has become of paramount importance for state leaders in the twenty-first century. This, in turn, has resulted in changes to the way power is and can be acquired and wielded on the international stage,

© The Author(s), under exclusive license to Springer Nature Switzerland AG 2022
P. M. Brannagan, D. Reiche, *Qatar and the 2022 FIFA World Cup*,
https://doi.org/10.1007/978-3-030-96822-9_5

allowing states whose power is less likely to be found through material resources to gain influence through more subjective means. Crucially, this is not to suggest that materialist interests do not matter; rather, we argued in Chap. 1 for the need to view material and subjective factors as constituting a mutual relationship, with the international state system being driven by *both* material factors (migration, trade, production, security etc.) and subjective patterning (ideologies, values, beliefs etc.). Adopting such a theoretical stance has allowed us to identify the full potential of small states' attempts at power acquisition, as well as the subsequent limitations and challenges that confront them.

Having set out our theoretical orientation to the study of IR, in Chap. 2 we then offered up a background to the State of Qatar. One obvious theme to emerge from this chapter was Qatar's continuous awareness of the need to safeguard its survival, which is a typical mindset for small states. For Qatar, a key survival strategy has been to 'bandwagon' the major powers of the day, starting with the British, then the Ottomans, the British again and, in more recent years, the United States. Such bandwagoning attempts have, nonetheless, been employed not just for survival for survival's sake, but to allow Qatar the means through which to retain a degree of control over its own fate, through the diplomatic tactic of hedging—that is, the ability to play powers off against one another, guard against 'mono-dependence' and occupy an influential position as an effective mediator. The need to retain some degree of control is underpinned by the continuous desire of Qataris to maintain an independent foreign policy and to uphold their right to act as a self-governing sovereign state, despite what their larger neighbour, Saudi Arabia, might think. It is here where Qatar seeks to employ a great deal of 'strategic social construction' through the state's active push in recent years to position itself as a regional and international hub in the areas of media, education, mediation, conflict negotiation, humanitarianism, culture and leisure. Through this, Qatar has become an influential actor in its own right and, in doing so, has wielded power via the (re)shaping of opinions, practices and norms. As we also saw in Chap. 2, Qatar's engagement with globalization and its (independent) foreign policy efforts have nonetheless also come to bring new challenges for the state to confront.

In Chap. 3, we then looked at how Qatar's investment in, and engagement with, sport and sports events has sought to be used by the state for strategic social construction. In doing so, we focused on Joseph Nye's concept of soft power, which helps to shed light on the ways in which states seek to position themselves as attractive and appealing on the world stage. In Chap. 3, we argued that Qatar's use of global sport can be said to be the state's fourth 'niche area', alongside its exportation of oil and (liquefied) natural gas, its regional mediation work and its investment in, and promotion of, global media network, Al Jazeera. Furthermore, we argued that the state's overall sports strategy is underpinned by three main pillars: *the hosting of sports events; overseas sports investments; and leveraging domestic excellence.* Through these pillars, Qatar not only seeks to raise awareness of its existence and right to sovereign independence but also looks to position itself in the eyes of others as a safe, friendly, cooperative, proactive, international law respecting and forward-looking entrepreneurial state that not only is ripe for investment opportunities, but also, despite its size, can be a leading and effective actor within international society. Such efforts do, of course, have materialist outcomes in mind, linked to tourism and the state's need to diversify its economy, as well as to shore up its security and survival, amongst other issues.

In Chap. 4, we saw that, like the way its broader foreign policy efforts have brought new challenges for the state to confront, simultaneously its exploits in sport and sports events have heralded novel problems that have come to hinder its soft power. In Chap. 4, we argued that the scrutiny Qatar has received on the back of the 2022 World Cup has revolved around three forms: *Qatar's human rights record; accusations of bribery and corruption; and Qatar as a sports events destination.* Qatar's human rights record and abuses have come to damage the state's desire to position itself as a friendly, 'good global citizen' with humanitarian desires, while accusations of bribery and corruption have come to undermine the state's integrity by positioning Qataris in the minds of certain audiences as self-centred and deceitful peoples who resort to cheating in order to achieve victory. Through this, Qatar comes to suffer from a 'crisis of legitimacy', forcing audiences to more vigorously question the credibility of its soft power. Furthermore, concerns over its 'high-risk' potential as a sport event host overshadows the state's attempts to present itself as a welcome, safe and attractive destination. Through such negativity, we were reminded in Chap. 4 that, for their hosts, sports mega-events are mixed blessings, ones that can simultaneously lead to soft power gains *and* losses.

In this final, and concluding, chapter, we look ahead to Qatar's staging of the World Cup in 2022 and beyond. In doing so, we look to identify and discuss the opportunities and challenges Qatar faces. We argue that the following three areas will be vital for Qatar leading up to, and after,

2022: *delivering a successful World Cup; maintaining an independent foreign policy; and continuing with domestic reforms.* We deal with each in turn. The last section of this chapter looks to chart avenues for future research on Qatar and the 2022 World Cup.

DELIVERING A SUCCESSFUL WORLD CUP

One opportunity and challenge facing Qatar is of course how successful the state will be in organizing and delivering the 2022 World Cup. A number of crucial points come into play here. First is that Qatar ensures it completes its extravagant range of infrastructure projects prior to the world's eyes fixating on the state in November 2022. The 2022 World Cup has come to largely shape Doha's infrastructure modernization since 2010. While some progress, such as the eight World Cup stadiums (seven newly built and one fully refurbished), can be explicitly related to the World Cup, other developments might have happened without the tournament coming to the state in 2022. However, as the Oxford Business Group noted in its analysis of Doha's infrastructure development, 'The 2022 FIFA World Cup has set a mid-term deadline for a number of high-profile projects' (Oxford Business Group, 2015). Examples here are the Doha Metro and Lusail City. As we have seen, Lusail is a 38 sq km new city that has been built from scratch. The Lusail National Stadium, a newly built 80,000-seater venue, will host the World Cup final in December 2022 and, in doing so, will look to globally market this new city, its residential and commercial neighbourhoods, 22 new hotels, golf course and its theme park. The plan is for the city to accommodate 450,000 people and become a major tourist attraction beyond 2022 (*The Independent*, 25 March 2021b). On the Doha Metro, 3 metro lines (Red, Green and Gold) and 37 stations were completed in September 2020, with the project deemed 'one of the most advanced and fastest driverless metro systems in the world' (*Designverse*, 25 September 2020). The metro will be the primary mode of transportation during the 2022 World Cup, directly connecting five of the eight World Cup stadiums to the Hamad International Airport, Qatar's central airport hub, recently named 'the best airport in the world' (*Goal*, 27 April 2021; *The Independent*, 10 August 2021a).

Linked to this is the need for Qatar to ensure it gets the more 'events management' side of the 2022 World Cup right, particularity given the state has previously experienced logistical issues when it comes to hosting sports events. In 2013, for example, many supporters were 'locked out' of the Khalifa International Stadium more than an hour before the Emir Cup final between Al Rayyan SC and Al Sadd SC, despite having paid for tickets months in advance (*Doha News*, 28 January 2015). In the same year, supporters from all over the world who had travelled to Qatar 'expressed mixed feelings' about the state's management and hosting of the international football friendly between Spain and Uruguay, after hundreds of people were left still queuing outside the stadium five minutes before kickoff, due to a lack of available parking (cf. *Doha News*, 18 May 2014). Then, during the state's staging of the 2011 AFC Asian Cup finals, almost 10,000 supporters with tickets were refused entry to the final for 'arriving late' after door's were prematurely closed early by the behest of the Qatari royal family's security detail, leaving kids and families being 'confronted by riot police and being told they weren't getting in' (*CNN*, 3 February 2011). And then there was Qatar's staging of the 2015 IHF World Men's Handball Championship, when organizers turned away ticketed fans hours before the start of Qatar's quarterfinal clash with Germany, claiming the venue was 'already full' (*Doha News*, 28 January 2015). Such issues—most notably related to the ticketing of, and entry to, various sports tournaments—have thus led to a situation where, more often than not, 'organizers of sporting events in Qatar have come under fire for poor organization' (*Doha News*, 18 May 2013b).

For Qatari event organizers, sticking to their intended infrastructure completion timelines, and ensuring they get the logistical side of hosting the 2022 World Cup right, will go some way towards limiting any further negative scrutiny from the international community. Indeed, one area where non-state actors such as the media strongly criticize event hosts relates to what Giffard and Rivenburgh (2000, p. 10) call *hosting abilities*—that is, a city or state's (in)ability to successfully organize and manage the challenges of staging a major event. As Giffard and Rivenburgh (ibid, p. 10) correctly locate, when hosts become 'overwhelmed' by the complexity of planning for, and staging, such major occasions, these events can have a significant negative impact on the image of domestic event organizers and, in doing so, 'can render a government politically vulnerable at home and abroad'. Furthermore, like all cities and states, if Qatar is able to successfully organize, plan and deliver the World Cup with minimal-to-no setbacks, the state would not only avoid the manifestation of further critique, but would also gain soft power, by showcasing to the world its ability to positively confront one of the 'biggest global planning challenges' and, in doing so, demonstrate its capacity to 'play with the big kids' on the world stage (ibid., p. 9).

One area that Qatar has somewhat limited control over when it comes to the 'success' of the World Cup relates nonetheless to how many non-Arab supporters will travel to Doha in 2022, and how this will subsequently impact the state's desire to use the tournament to foster long-term tourism gains. In 2021, football fans in European countries such as Norway and Denmark called for a boycott of the 2022 World Cup due to ongoing human rights abuses; and previously national football teams, such as Germany and the Netherlands, have been seen wearing shirts favouring human rights, in protest to FIFA's decision to push ahead with the World Cup in Qatar. In 2021, the Swedish national football team then cancelled its annual winter training camp in Qatar, citing the state's human rights record as its reasons for doing so (see: *Doha News*, 9 September 2021m). Also in 2021, a book by two German journalists on the Qatar World Cup came out with the demand for a boycott as its headline (see: Beyer & Schulze-Marmeling, 2021), reflecting a general attitude in Western European countries. It remains to be seen if such sentiments discourage fans from travelling to Qatar in 2022. For those who do attend the World Cup, a further issue lies in the appeal of the UAE, and whether fans decide to stay in neighbouring Abu Dhabi or Dubai, and just travel to Qatar for specific matches. Thus, as opposed to largely benefitting Qatar, it may well be the UAE that profits more from the 2022 World Cup in tourism terms, given places like Dubai are high up on many Westerners' bucket lists, and can offer some supporters a more appealing nightlife outside the tournament itself. According to the Global Destinations City Index (2019), Dubai is, after all, the fourth most visited city in the world.

Alongside the knock-on effect on tourism the 2022 World Cup may or may not have, a further point is how successful the tournament can be in changing the behaviours of Qataris themselves, particularly with regard to addressing issues with lifestyle diseases. As mentioned in Chap. 2, the World Health Organization (2017) estimates that 18.9% of Qataris have diabetes, 71.7% are 'overweight' and 35% are 'obese'. Such prevalence can be put down to high levels of wealth and affluence amongst Qataris, the rapid increase across Doha of Western-style, high-calorie fast-food outlets and a general lack of physical activity across the population. It is estimated, for instance, that 41.6% of all Qatari adults are 'physically inactive', while, 90.1% of adolescents are physically inactive (see: Global Health Observatory, 2017). Furthermore, the Qatar Olympic Committee initiated a study on women's participation in sports and physical activity, and concluded: 'The study found that just 15% of Qatari women aged 15 and above regularly participated in sport... Among Qatari women, the type of sport [or] physical activity most frequently [indulged in] are walking 58%, running 11%, aerobic exercise 14%, and swimming 6%' (Qatar Olympic Committee, 2011, p. 18). According to a government report on 'Sports in Qatari Society', women's sport in Qatar has, however, slightly increased over the last years: 'The number of male athletes registered at sports federations increased from 14,000 in 2010/2011 to 20,000 in 2015/2016, while the number of female players reached 2,000 in 2015/2016, twice the number for 2010/2011' (State of Qatar, 2017, p. 33).

Consequently, like organizers of most major sports events, for Qatari authorities, the hope is that the state's staging of the World Cup will encourage its citizenry to take sport more seriously and, in turn, to increase their participation in exercise and physical activity. A challenge for Qatar in this regard, however, is that previous research has shown that the staging of major sports events does little to inspire those to actually *take up* sport, but rather only encourages those *already* involved in sport to do more (see: Grix, 2016). Consequently, for Qataris, who predominantly prefer watching sport on television and via the internet than actively participating in some form of sport (see Table 5.1), the ability of the World Cup to have a positive effect on physical activity change is—given evidence from previous hosts—perhaps slim.

Table 5.1 Qatar Social and Economic Survey Research Institute's (2015, p. 5) findings on Qataris' regular sporting practices

Practices	Qataris (%)
Follow sport news on TV	47
Watch sport events on TV	41
Follow sport news through internet	27
Follow sport news through social media (Facebook, Twitter)	26
Follow sport news through newspapers	30
Actively participate in sports individually or in a group	30
Follow sport news on radio	21
Attend sports events	12
Volunteer for sport events	6

A further point here relates to how the 2022 World Cup will add to Qatar's soft power in environmental and humanitarian terms post-event. The 2022 World Cup might become one of the most environmentally friendly mega sporting events of all time. Indeed, Qatar has promised to deliver the first-ever carbon neutral World Cup. The eight stadiums certified by the Global Sustainability Assessment System are built in a radius of only 55 kms, thus limiting domestic travel—and thus pollution—by teams and fans. Furthermore, Qatar will ensure that fans can easily travel to matches by either the metro system or via 1100 electric buses, which will be incorporated into Doha's public transport system after the World Cup (*The Peninsula*, 25 April 2021a). This is all part of Qatar's plan to convert 25% of public transport to electric energy by 2022 and 100% by 2030 (*Doha News*, 9 June 2021l). Commenting on this, the British football historian David Goldblatt said in a public lecture, 'Qatar has set very high standards for environmental protection. I think the 2022 World Cup is going to set the standards for future World Cups. The ambition and commitment of Qatar towards the environment is very strong and very unique in global sports' (*Gulf Times*, 6 October 2020).

In contrast to the previous World Cups in South Africa (2010), Brazil (2014) and Russia (2018), Qatar also aims to avoid the existence of 'white elephants'—that is, stadiums built for a mega-sporting event that have no long-term use and cause enormous maintenance costs that remain financial burdens for decades to come. In the case of Qatar, for example, Education City Stadium will be reduced in capacity after the World Cup from 40,000 to 20,000 seats. In addition, the stadium's modular upper tier will be removed, with seats donated to those developing countries that lack their own sporting infrastructure. After the World Cup, the downsized stadium will then serve the local community, particularly students and faculty members at Education City. If the sustainability concept is implemented as announced, future organizers of mega-sporting events may well look to Qatar as the standard for stadium sustainability, and seek advice on the construction of similar concepts as a reference point in their post-event and legacy planning (Reiche, 2021).

Finally, if indeed Qatar successfully delivers the 2022 World Cup, then the state will likely be awarded further mega sporting events in the future. Qatar has already been selected to host the Asian Games in 2030, one of the largest mega-sporting events in Asia. Hosting other events on an annual basis in Doha will further contribute to Qatar's international prestige and possibly pressure the country to continue its reform agenda (a point we discuss further below). As we have seen, Qatar's hosting of mega-sporting events has been part of a small state survival strategy and a key component of an independent foreign policy that also serves intra-regional competition in a bid to challenge Saudi hegemony. However, for long-term stability, peace and prosperity, it might be wise to also use the potential of sport for collaboration between countries, for example, by a joint bid with its neighbours for a future Summer Olympic Games as part of a historic regional peace-making process.

Maintaining an Independent Foreign Policy

A further opportunity and challenge facing Qatar leading up to, and beyond, the 2022 World Cup lies in the state's maintenance of an independent foreign policy. Crucial in this regard will be Qatar's relationships with its neighbours, and the direction the state seeks to pursue post-2022. As mentioned in Chap. 2, in recent years, the major political issue within the Gulf has been the blockade of Qatar by its neighbours. The blockade ended in January 2021, and relations with the two largest blockading countries normalized when Saudi Arabia and Egypt sent ambassadors to Qatar in June 2021, for the first time since 2017 (*Doha News*, 24 June 2021g). In August 2021, diplomatic ties between Doha and Riyadh were restored when Qatar also appointed an ambassador to Saudi Arabia (*Doha News*, 12 August 2021b). In the same month, the improving relations were also reflected in sports when the Saudi Arabian Football Federation appointed two Qatari referees for the 2021–2022 season of the Saudi professional men's football league (*Doha News*, 9 August 2021k).

Through its ability to show a great deal of innovation and resiliency, in many ways, it is Qatar which has arguably emerged from the blockade symbolically victorious. An example of this is the increase in domestic food production and the restructuring of trade routes that Qatar forged during the blockade, with Iran and Turkey becoming key partners for Qatar's food security. Before the blockade, nearly 90% per cent of Qatar's food supply was imported, primarily by trucks via the Saudi-Qatari border, Qatar's only land border, or via ports in the UAE (Ulrichsen, 2020). Three years after the blockade started, Al Jazeera reported that the blockade 'presented a unique opportunity for the government to rely less on food imports and more on local production' (*Al Jazeera*, 9 June 2020b). As a result, Qatar became 'one of the highest-ranking countries in food security in the region', and managed to produce enough dairy and poultry products to meet domestic demand and increased local production of fruits and vegetables from 10 to 30% of domestic consumption (ibid.). Qatar also launched a 'Made in Qatar' campaign that was highly successful. In March 2019, Qatar not only become self-sufficient in dairy production, but also made its first export to another country, Afghanistan (Ulrichsen, 2020, p. 152).

Ulrichsen (2020) concludes that the blockade also left Qatar in a stronger position than before in national security terms. The blockade was supposed to isolate Qatar. However, only 13 days after the blockade started, Qatar's ally Turkey established a military base in Qatar and sent its first contingent of military personnel. After two years, the base was completed and stationed with approximately 5000 soldiers who, according to Turkey's president, Recep Erdogan, symbolize 'brotherhood' and 'regional security' (*Al Jazeera*, 25 November 2019). Alongside the 11,000 U.S. soldiers at the Al Udeid Air Base, the largest overseas airbase of the United States, the Turkish military base adds another essential feature to Qatar's short- and long-term national security. The Turkish newspaper *Hürriyet Daily News*, for instance, commented that the base contributes to regional peace and 'also became a counterbalancing power concerning Iran and Saudi Arabia' (*Hürriyet Daily News*, 14 August 2019).

Ulrichsen further argues in his book titled *Qatar and the Gulf Crisis* that the blockade on Qatar failed because of the maximalist demands of the blockading countries, their unwillingness to negotiate and a lack of international support. Moreover, Qatar's successful approach 'to win international hearts and minds' (Ulrichsen, 2020, p. 6) by 'adopting a rights-based approach to tackling the blockade at the level of international institutions' (ibid., p. 104) and by avoiding the temptation to retaliate against the blockading quartet further augmented the blockade's failure. For example, Qatar continued to supply Dubai with gas through the Dolphin pipeline, the GCC's first cross-border gas project, which provides around 40% of the city's consumption (ibid., p. 164). If Qatar had stopped the supply in the middle of the summer 2017, that is, during a time of the year when people in the Gulf heavily depend on the use of air conditioning, this would have been a human tragedy for Dubai's population. Moreover, since the other GCC countries are oil countries and lack sufficient gas resources, they are not in the position to replace Qatari gas with their own gas reserves.

However, Qatar's leaving of the Organization of the Petroleum Exporting Countries (OPEC) in January 2019, after 57 years of membership, could be seen as a mild form of retaliation for the blockade, given Saudi Arabia dominates the organization. Nevertheless, Qatar denied in official statements that the decision was related to the blockade. The country's energy minister said that the move represented a 'technical and strategic' change to focus on natural gas and was not politically motivated (*CNBC*, 3 December 2018). While leaving OPEC, Qatar at the same time intensified its bilateral energy relations with a number of countries. For example, in July 2021, Qatar signed a 20-year LNG deal with South Korea, becoming the largest exporter of LNG to the East Asian country, and a 15-year deal with Taiwan (*Doha News*, 12 July 2021c). According to Ulrichsen (2020, p. 168), 'energy partnerships created interdependencies that gave external actors a direct stake in the maintenance of domestic stability in Qatar and regional security in the Gulf.' Not only does the energy security of several countries, including the United Kingdom and Poland, depend on Qatar, but Qatar Petroleum has also invested in several new assets and joint-venture partnerships on different continents in countries such as Argentina, Brazil, China, Cyprus, Mexico, Mozambique, Morocco and, most significantly, the United States, amongst others. For Ulrichsen (2020, p. 171), 'new energy partnerships around the world sent a very clear message to the four blockading states that Doha remained open for business and had no shortage of willing partners.'

Furthermore, during the blockade, Qatar authorities announced their intention to expand their LNG production capacity by 40% from 77 million tonnes per annum (mtpa) to 110 mtpa by 2025 (*Doha News*, 14 June 2021d). The Qatari energy minister said that Qatar Petroleum would be ready to develop the North Field (the state's largest gas field) for the first phase of its LNG expansion project without any support from foreign companies (*Reuters*, 8 February 2021a). However, in the end, the government decided to launch a bidding process for international oil firms to take up to a 30% stake, a clear sign of using the project for diplomatic purposes and strengthening its relations with countries that host major international oil companies such as France, the United Kingdom and the United States. On 24 May 2021, the six Western energy giants, Chevron, ExxonMobil and ConocoPhillips (all American), Eni (Italy), Royal Dutch Shell (British-Dutch) and TotalEnergies (French), submitted bids for the expansion project (*Doha News*, 14 June 2021d). In a second phase (called the North Field South Project), Qatar's LNG production capacity will be further expanded to 126 mtpa by 2027 (*Reuters*, 8 February 2021a).

Qatar not only used its energy sector to maintain an independent foreign policy during the blockade, but also continued as a valued mediator of conflicts, thus showcasing its ability to be a vital actor within the international community, despite regional political tensions. The country sees itself as an 'impartial mediator' (*Deutsche Welle*, 31 August 2021). Qatar mediated political disputes in Lebanon (2008) and Palestine (2012) and resolved the Sudan-Eritrea dispute in 2011 (*Geopolitical Monitor*, 31 August 2021). Furthermore, it hosted intra-Afghan talks and negotiations between the Trump Administration and the Taliban, which led to the Doha Agreement in February 2020 (*Foreign Policy*, 5 October 2021). The parties agreed on U.S. troops' withdrawal in exchange for the Taliban's parting with terrorism. When the Taliban took control of Afghanistan on 15 August 2021, Qatar became 'indispensable as a venue for international mediation' (*Reuters*, 8 September 2021c):

- The country helped evacuate foreigners and Afghan nationals from Kabul to Doha.
- Facilities built for the World Cup 2022 housed Afghan refugees.
- The Afghan embassies of the United States and major European countries relocated from Kabul to Doha.
- Qatar delivered food and aid to Afghanistan and served as an intermediary between the Taliban and Western governments.

For the *New York Times*, the developments in Afghanistan were ''the latest evidence of the small but gas-rich country punching above its weight on the world stage (*The New York Times*, 7 September 2021).

In May 2021, in cooperation with Egypt, Qatar facilitated a ceasefire between Israel and Hamas after two weeks of deadly violence between the two parties. Qatar's role was recognized by the UN Secretary General, António Guterres, who said, 'I commend Egypt and Qatar for the efforts carried out, in close coordination with the UN, to help restore calm to Gaza and Israel' (*Doha News*, 21 May 2021f).

Furthermore, in the realm of sports, Qatar showed during the global Covid-19 pandemic its value to the international community by hosting several global events in different sports, including qualification events for the postponed Tokyo Olympic Games (moved from 2020 to the summer of 2021). Qatar also hosted the IOC Refugee Team for a training camp in Doha and served as one of the pre-Games vaccination hubs for all Olympic and Paralympic Games athletes that did not receive Covid-19 vaccines in their home countries (*Doha News*, 11 July 2021a). Doha was also a tournament hub for Asian football Champions League matches in 2020 and for the Asian qualifiers for the 2022 World Cup and 2023 AFC Asian Cup. 'The country was able to set a new benchmark for the safe return of the hosting of major international sport events', commented Kamilla Swart from Hamad bin Khalifa University in a media article. She said, 'Qatar is one of the first countries that have implemented the expanded bubble system by including large number of teams competitors for several sport events' (*The Peninsula*, 28 March 2021b). The diversity in Qatar's international (sporting) relations could also be seen when it hosted the African Super Cup final in men's football between Al-Ahly from Egypt and Moroccan RS Berkane in Doha in May 2021 (*Doha News*, 5 May 2021i).

In April 2021, major European football clubs including UAE-funded Manchester City announced plans to launch an exclusive European Super League as a rival competition to the UEFA Champions League. After protests from fans, football clubs, national federations and UEFA, the idea collapsed within a week (see: Brannagan et al., 2022). Qatar-owned Paris Saint-Germain had declined the offer to join the league. The Qatari PSG chairman Nasser Al-Khelaifi was praised in the international media for his decision to not join the Super League—a proposal which largely ignored the sentiment of a vast majority of European fans who reject the idea to Americanize European sports by eliminating meritocracy with closed leagues and no relegation and promotion. Rejecting the Super League enhanced PSG's international prestige which was, in the past, mainly associated with buying success through Qatari fossil fuel rents. For Manchester City owner UAE, this was another failure after its blockade of Qatar totally failed and not one of the 13 demands placed on Qatar in June 2017 was met, including the demand to shut down Al Jazeera, a news network that has set new standards for critical reporting in the Middle East. UEFA president Ceferin was quoted in the media by praising the PSG president: 'Thank you from the bottom of my heart to Nasser. You have shown that you are a great man and that you respect football and its values' (beIN, 20 April 2021).

The World Cup might have also helped Qatar to overcome the blockade. Ulrichsen (2021) commented in a blog article 'that the reopening of borders means that football fans from Saudi Arabia, Bahrain, the UAE, and Egypt will be able to attend games in Qatar in 2022'. Almost unimaginable would have been that one of the quartet's national teams qualified for the 2022 World Cup, only for their government not to allow their national team to participate and travel to one of the world's largest sporting event—a decision that could lead to social unrest in the concerned countries. Regardless of qualification, the Supreme Committee for Delivery and Legacy published during the blockade figures that out of nearly 175,000 people who applied to be volunteers at the 2022 World Cup nearly 1000 were nationals from the blockading countries of Saudi Arabia, the UAE and Bahrain (*Agence France-Press*, 21 September 2018). In response, Khashan (2021) wrote in a commentary that 'it would be unfair to belittle the World Cup's importance because it solidly put Qatar on the World map and made it challenging to blockade the country with impunity'. How relations between Qatar and it neighbours manifest post-2022, and who wields relative degrees of regional hegemony, remains to be seen.

CONTINUING WITH DOMESTIC REFORMS

A final opportunity and challenge facing Qatar leading up to, and beyond, the 2022 World Cup centres on the extent to which the state seeks to continue with implimenting meaningful domestic change. While the 2022 World Cup has not turned Qatar into a democracy—and the authors believe that a development that fundamentally challenges the ruling family's power is not likely to happen anytime soon—the 2022 World Cup has undoubtedly led to some tangible changes in the country. Although, for some developments, there might one day be a dispute amongst historians as to which event changed Qatar more: the blockade by Saudi Arabia, the UAE, Bahrain and Egypt; or the World Cup and its associated global spotlight in the lead-up to the event. While some domestic changes can be attributed to the blockade, other developments happened in the context of the World Cup. Nevertheless, some changes are shaped by both events, as Fig. 5.1 illustrates.

As we saw in Chap. 4, under the pressure from various non-state actors—particularly INGOs and the media—Qatar has sought 'to position itself as a regional leader in workers' welfare' (Ulrichsen, 2020, p. 249). We believe that only the international spotlight of the World Cup made these reforms possible and that a boycott of the tournament would have been counterproductive. However, concerns have been expressed about whether all reforms are adequately implemented and whether the country will be committed to its reform agenda after 2022. James Lynch from the INGO FairSquare, for instance, asked in an op-ed about what will happen

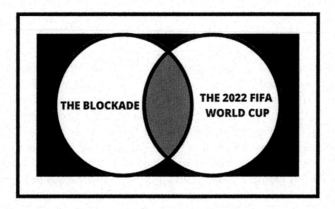

Fig. 5.1 Drivers for political changes in Qatar

'after December 18, 2022, when the football spotlight moves onto North America? The reality is that it will not be possible to simply 'solve' migrant labour abuse and move on. Those who want to see this through will need to remain engaged for the long haul' (Lynch, 2021). For scholar Andreas Krieg, 'At the heart of the struggle over the human and labour rights legacy in Qatar is the government's sensitive balancing act between international public pressure on the one hand, and domestic pressure from Qatar's powerful business elites on the other. Hence, to ensure that [labour] reforms in Qatar are sustainable, the way forward should be one of continued international engagement with Qatar's government' (Krieg, 2021). Nevertheless, a promising sign concerning the labour market reforms might be that, apart from the establishment of an ILO office in Doha, the Qatari legislation has also established a Minimum Wage Commission 'that will review the impact and application of the minimum wage, and propose adjustments, in consultation with different government bodies, experts, workers and employers' (ILO, 19 March 2021).

In some ways, changes to kafala have made Qatar somewhat of the exception when it comes to enforcing domestic reform on the back of a sports mega-event. Note, for example, how no significant social domestic changes have occurred in the states of China and Russia, despite their hosting of the Olympics and the World Cup, respectively. One might even argue that the situation for ethnic minorities (China) and critics of President Putin (Russia) have become even worse after the staging of these events. The 2022 World Cup, hosted in a rich but small and vulnerable state, differs from these examples. Indeed, the 2022 World Cup has impacted the host country in ways that might be unmatched in the global history of mega sporting events.

A promising sign that pressure on reform might continue post-2022 is that some local media networks have started to openly monitor the proper implementation of the labour market reforms, contributing to more open debates in the Qatari press. LaMay (2020) wrote in a commentary at the end of 2020 that media liberalization in Qatar is 'key to ensuring other social legacies of the tournament to which Qatar and FIFA have committed'. While state-controlled newspapers such as the *Gulf Times*, *The Peninsula* and *Qatar Tribune* mainly publish press releases from the government, *Doha News*, a private online news blog that was temporarily blocked by the Qatari government, and the website of *Al Jazeera*, the largest news network in the Middle East, have set new standards on critical discussions. For example, when the Shura Council recommended in February 2021 to undo some of the government's labour market reforms, *Doha News* published a popular op-ed titled 'Qatar has come too far to give in to pressure from business community'. The *Doha News* team wrote, 'For years, business owners in Qatar have been able to amass huge profits due to exploitation of labourers desperate to make a living.' It continued by demanding that 'Qatar's authorities cannot and should not be bullied into the demands of business owners that fail to see further than their profits.' The article concluded by stating, 'to put it bluntly, if a select number of Shura council members and business owners get their way, it's the state, Qatar's brand and its standing on the world stage that will pay the price. With much of the world ready to make its first trip to Qatar for the World Cup next year, any such blemishes can cause drastic impact' (*Doha News*, 25 February 2021h). Apart from this op-ed, several analytical articles were also published on the news blog that criticized the government. For example, in March 2021, *Doha News* reported on the 'unliveable conditions' in quarantine facilities for workers. It concluded that 'this episode seems to be yet another case of private companies failing people in Qatar, all of whom have been allowed to do so due to poor oversight from authorities' (*Doha News*, 17 March 2021e).

On the *Al Jazeera* website, which used to write on many issues in the region critically, but omitted Qatar from such reports, suddenly articles were published, such as the one in March 2021 asking 'Labour law changes: Are Qatar's migrant workers better off?'. The article presented cases of migrant workers who were, in violation of the new labour laws, not able to switch jobs: 'While a number of workers have been successful in switching jobs, the majority of those interviewed by *Al Jazeera* experienced delays in the process as well as threats, harassment, and exploitation by the sponsor, with some of the workers ending up in prison and eventually deported' (*Al Jazeera*, 21 March 2021). However, it should be noted that, according to Reporters Without Borders, there is a gap in the English and the Arabic reporting of the news network: 'The outspoken Qatari TV broadcaster Al Jazeera has transformed the media landscape in the rest of the Arab world, but the Arabic section ignores what happens in this small emirate, including conditions for the foreign workers who make up most of the population' (Reporters Without Borders, 2021).

One area where Qatar could add to its existing workers' welfare is on the issue of trade unions. Unions are generally banned in Qatar for most workers[1] (*The Economist*, 29 October 2015). The exception to this rule came in 2004, when the state passed a new law allowing Qatari workers the right to strike, to form various workers' committees, and join the country's only legal union, the General Union of Workers of Qatar. However, at present, those located in vital domestic sectors such as government, medicine and oil and gas are prohibited to strike, and all expatriate workers are forbidden to organize. This lack of union representation for the majority of Qatar's workforce has generated significant international criticism: the ITUC (2015, p. 28), for example, has argued on several occasions how the lack of union representation for expatriates places workers 'at even greater risk of being subjected to forced labour', while Amnesty International (21 May 2015) has previously argued how Qatar has made 'no significant advances in the protection of rights' on a number of fronts, one of which includes not allowing workers the 'freedom to form or join [a] trade union'. Nonetheless, as Winckler (1997, p. 485) locates, despite such scrutiny, for the majority of governments of the GCC, prohibiting foreign worker unions acts as a key and necessary mechanism through which to ensure continued national supremacy by further denying non-citizens any 'political force' domestically.

A further area of possible development in this aspect relates to if/when Qatar will introduce full democratic elections, something that has been promised by the state's hierarchy for some time. Alongside the state's human rights violations at home, Qatar firmly remains an authoritarian country (*Doha News*, 24 January 2013a). Kamrava, in his book *Small State, Big Politics*, assesses that 'political decision making in Qatar is a highly centralized process that involves no more than a handful of individuals' (2013, p. xi). Although published in 2013, Kamrava's assessment was still accurate in mid-2021, when the writing of this book was concluded. The only elections that have ever happened in Qatar are those for the Central Municipal Council (CMC). When the CMC was first elected in 1999, it seemed to be a promising sign for increased political participation in the country. Since then, the 29 members of the CMC are elected every four years, with one woman being a member since 2003 and two women being members since 2015. Zaccara positively attributes in his research on the CMS that this body contributed to a 'process of democratic training': 'The voting process, including the voter registration and identification process, the guarantees to the secrecy of the vote, and the vote counting procedures, as well as the campaign regulations, were fair, clean and transparent' (Zaccara, 2021, p. 56). However, voter turnout remained below 20% in the CMC elections. One of the main reasons might be the lack of power(s) of the Council: 'The CMC members are conscious of the lack of attributions and they have been struggling with the Ministry of Municipalities in order to become a more executive or controlling institution, rather than a mere advisory body' (ibid., p. 54).

In November 2020, Sheikh Tamim announced that elections for the Shura Council would be held for the first time in October 2021. 'This is an important step towards strengthening Qatari advisory traditions and developing the legislative process with wider citizen participation', Tamim was quoted saying in the media (*Al Jazeera*, 3 November 2020a). Unlike the elected CMC members, the 45 members of the Shura Council, established in 1972 after the country became independent, were historically appointed by the Emir. According to the constitution, which was approved by a referendum in 2003, two-thirds of its members (30) were to be elected by direct, general secret ballot and 15 were to be appointed by the Emir. Those Shura Council elections were announced several times by both Tamim and his father, Hamad, the previous Emir, but always postponed (Zaccara, 2021, p. 43). According to an article on the *Al Jazeera* website, following the planned 2021 elections, 'the council's power is expected to be expanded to include the ability to dismiss ministers, approve the national budget and propose legislation' (*Al Jazeera*, 3 November 2020a). The elections on 2 October 2021 saw a voter turnout of almost 64%. Although there were many female candidates, all 30 elected members were men. However, when the Emir nominated the 15 members he could choose after the elections, he also appointed two women (*Reuters*, 14 October 2021b).

Another challenge for Qatar is on women's rights. While some reforms in Qatar, particularly those in the labour market, have been far-reaching, progress in women's rights, another crucial societal domain, have been much slower. Qatar is an academically oriented society, and it has become common for women to pursue higher education. Qatar Foundation operates Education City, which is home to satellite campuses from leading international universities. The students study in a mixed-gender environment in English, different from Qatar University, which has sex-segregated classes taught in Arabic. In the academic year 2019–2020, 75% of students in Education City universities were women (*Doha News*, 7 March 2021j). In line with this data, Georgetown University in Qatar published a press release at the end of the academic year 2021 that stated that 53 of its 71 graduating students were women (Georgetown University Qatar, 9 May 2021). There are even more female graduates than males in a globally male-dominated discipline, engineering, at Education City's Texas A&M University (*Doha News*, 7 March 2021j). Mashael Muftah, who graduated from Georgetown University in Education City with an honours thesis on 'The Paradox of Qatari Females' Education', wrote in a blog post that 'Educated Qatari females are being used to help create an illusion of a "modern" Qatar'. She argues that 'despite more Qatari women graduating with Bachelors, Masters, and Ph.D.'s, the hurdles they face daily and the legal and socio-political challenges raise questions regarding the contradictions between their education and their assigned roles' (Muftah, 2021).

Human Rights Watch (HRW) recognizes that 'women in Qatar have broken barriers and achieved significant progress, including in education where there are now more female than male graduates, and as doctors, lawyers, and entrepreneurs' (Human Rights Watch, 2021, p. 1). However, the large numbers of Qatari female students at Qatar-based universities reflect the state's legal and cultural discriminations. There are, according to HRW, double the number of Qatari male students than Qatari female students at universities abroad on government scholarships (ibid., p. 5). The lower number of Qatari female students at universities abroad can also be explained by the country's guardianship rules and practices. For example, unmarried Qatari women under the age of 25 cannot travel outside Qatar without permission from their male guardian. HRW summarizes the discriminatory guardianship policies by stating that 'Women must obtain permission from their male guardians—who may be fathers, brothers, uncles, grandfathers, and, when married, their husbands—to exercise many of their basic rights, including to marry, obtain a government scholarship to pursue higher education, work in many government jobs, and obtain some reproductive health care' (ibid., p. 1).

Other discriminations are that women cannot be guardians of their children, and it is much more difficult for them to divorce than it is for men. However, progress has been made in at least one domain in the years before the 2022 World Cup: Since January 2020, Qatari women no longer need a male guardian's permission to obtain a driving license (Human Rights Watch, 2021, p. 1). The slow progress on women's rights in Qatar is also reflected in sports. In 2012, female athletes were a part of Qatar's Olympic delegation for the first time. At the 2016 Summer Olympic Games, only 2 out of 37 Qatari Olympic athletes were women (Reiche & Tinaz, 2019). While the Qatari men's national football team won the AFC Asian Cup in 2019 for the first time, the national women's football team has not been listed in the FIFA rankings since 2015 due to lack of sufficient activity (Lysa, 2020). Harkness (2021) criticizes the Qatari government and argues that 'by painting an overly positive picture of female athleticism, narratives of empowered sportswomen can reinforce the very inequalities they aim to reduce'.

It is noteworthy that the Qatari government tremendously supports sport for both girls and boys, and women and men at all levels (i.e. the introduction of a national sports holiday, new state of the art facilities and the establishment of the Qatar Women Sports Committee). Moreover, obstacles for Qatari women to practise a sport of their choice are often cultural rather than legal, which shows that a country can modernize its entire infrastructure and domains such as the education and health sectors in a brief time, as Qatar did. However, changes in society need more time as they require not only top-down action but also a willingness to change on the bottom-up level. How much further Qatar seeks to push on improvements to women's' rights in Qatar, as well as other domestic reforms, will act as both an opportunity and a challenge in the years following the 2022 World Cup.

CONCLUSION: FUTURE RESEARCH

As mentioned in Chap. 1, this text is the first full-dedicated academic book on Qatar and the 2022 World Cup. It has (we hope) thus contributed greatly to readers' understandings of the motives, strategies and consequences underpinning Qatar's forthcoming hosting of the World Cup. In this final chapter, we have identified several opportunities and challenges that we believe Qatar will face leading up to, and beyond, 2022: namely, *delivering a successful World Cup; maintaining an independent foreign policy; and continuing with domestic reforms.* In doing so, we hope we have motivated other researchers to build on our work by continuing the study of the politics, power relations and controversies surrounding Qatar, global sport and the 2022 World Cup in the years to come. In looking to the future, we wish to close by charting some avenues for potential future research. On the domestic level, research on Qatar should investigate whether the reform process in the labour market and on sustainability issues continues after 2022, and if/in what ways the promises made *prior* to the World Cup (such as donating World Cup stadium infrastructure to developing countries, providing a fully electric public transportation system by 2030 etc.) are indeed implemented *after* the tournament. The possible effect the World Cup will have on social progress (such as democratization, women's rights) is also one significant area that will require further monitoring/research. On the international level, an interesting area of research would be to look at how Qatar's standing in the world changes and how different populations (in democratic and non-democratic, developing and developed countries, small and large states) perceive Qatar after is has staged the World Cup.

Given the main focus of the soft power literature on liberal democracies (the inventor of the concept, Nye, focuses on the United States and other major powers), one further area of potential scholarship would be to compare Qatar's soft power endeavourers with policies for attraction by other, non-democratic, countries. Those countries could be small states such as Qatar: for example, Formula 1 host Singapore would be an interesting case to compare. However, such comparative research could also include larger authoritarian countries. Of particular interest might be to look at similarities and differences with Qatar's neighbour Saudi Arabia, given how the latter now appears to be following in Qatar's sporting footsteps— indeed, Saudi has in recent years hosted Italian (2018) and Spanish (2019) football cup finals, as well as events in boxing, motor racing and golf, amongst other sporting competitions, and, of course, the country's sovereign wealth fund became the majority shareholder of Newcastle United FC in 2021. Azerbaijan, which organized, for instance, the 2015 European Games and hosted in its capital Baku the 2019 UEFA Europa League final and 2021 European Football Championship matches, would be another candidate for a comparative analysis. Such research could look at the strategies of the respective countries to use sport for soft power purposes and the general and contextually specific outcomes of those endeavours. With its wealth and ambitions, the authors strongly believe Qatar remains an interesting case to study. Although not being democratic, Qatar's accessibility is remarkable: the presence of international universities and think tanks gives foreign researchers many contact points in the country; with its liberal visa policies (entering neighbouring country Saudi Arabia, for example, is much more difficult), it is comparatively easy for researchers to do field work in the country. Although government officials are not always welcoming and supporting foreign researchers (and particularly sceptical towards Western journalists), it is not difficult to move around Qatar, apart from some restricted areas such as workers' accommodations (but there are other venues to easily meet workers, e.g. community sports facilities). How this openness affects Qatar's development would itself be an interesting topic to study.

NOTE

1. This lack of union representation in Qatar generated significant scrutiny from the International Transport Workers' Federation (ITF) after it secured a Qatar Airways standard employment contract which it found to include 'clauses prohibiting staff from getting married or falling pregnant'. Such scrutiny eventually lead to the airlines' amending of such a policy in 2015 (*The Economist*, 29 October 2015).

REFERENCES

Agence France-Press. (2018, September 21). FIFA World Cup 2022: 1000 nationals from Saudi Arabia, Bahrain, UAE apply to be volunteers despite Qatar embargo [online]. Retrieved November 10, 2021, from https://www.firstpost.com/sports/fifa-world-cup-2022-1000-nationals-from-saudi-arabia-bahrain-uae-apply-to-be-volunteers-despite-qatar-embargo-5235731.html

Al Jazeera. (2019, November 25). Erdogan: Turkey-Qatar military base serves regional 'stability' [online]. Retrieved September 02, 2021, from https://www.aljazeera.com/news/2019/11/25/erdogan-turkey-qatar-military-base-serves-regional-stability

Al Jazeera. (2020a, November 03). Qatar to hold Shura Council elections next year: Emir [online]. Retrieved May 06, 2021, from https://www.aljazeera.com/news/2020/11/3/qatar-to-hold-shura-council-elections-next-year-emir

Al Jazeera. (2020b, June 09). Qatar's food security boost post-blocade [online]. Retrieved March 19, 2021, from https://www.aljazeera.com/program/newsfeed/2020/6/9/qatars-food-security-boost-post-blockade

Al Jazeera. (2021, March 21). Labour law changes: Are Qatar's migrant workers better off? [online]. Retrieved November 10, 2021, from https://www.firstpost.com/sports/fifa-world-cup-2022-1000-nationals-from-saudi-arabia-bahrain-uae-apply-to-be-volunteers-despite-qatar-embargo-5235731.html

beIN. (2021, April 20). European Super League: Ceferin thanks 'great man' Al-Khelaifi at PSG and other breakaway opponents [online]. Retrieved November 10, 2021, from https://www.beinsports.com/en/football/news/european-super-league-ceferin-thanks-great-1/1673401

Beyer, B., & Schulze-Marmeling, D. (2021). *Boykottiert Katar 2022! Warum wir die FIFA stoppen müssen*. Verlag Die Werkstatt.

Brannagan, P. M., Scelles, N., Valenti, M., Inoue, Y., Grix, J., & Perkin, S. J. (2022). The 2021 European Super League attempt: Motivation, outcome, and the future of football. *International Journal of Sport Policy and Politics*, 1–8.

CNBC. (2018, December 03). Qatar quitting OPEC means the oil cartel is now just a 'two-member organization', oil analysts say [online]. Retrieved June 09, 2021, from https://www.cnbc.com/2018/12/03/qatar-quitting-opec-leaves-oil-cartel-a-two-member-organization.html

CNN. (2011, February 03). Five things we've learnt from Qatar's Asian Cup [online]. Retrieved April 05, 2021, from http://edition.cnn.com/2011/SPORT/football/01/27/qatar.2022.asian.cup/

Designverse. (2020, September 25). First 37 stations completed on the Doha Metro Network [online]. Retrieved November 10, 2021, from https://designverse.com.cn/content/recommend/article/first-37-stations-completed-on-the-doha-metro-network-unstudio-en

Deutsche Welle. (2021, August 31). Why Qatar fosters close contact with the Taliban [online]. Retrieved November 10, 2021, from https://www.dw.com/en/why-qatar-fosters-close-contact-with-the-taliban/a-59030146

Doha News. (2013a, January 24). Report: Most nationals believe Qatar is facing 'demographic problem' [online]. Retrieved July 19, 2015, from https://dohanews.co/government-report-finds-most-nationals-believe-qatar-is/

Doha News. (2013b, May 18). Ticket-holders lament lockout at Emir Cup as Al Rayyan defeats Al Sadd [online]. Retrieved August 16, 2015, from https://dohanews.co/ticket-holding-football-fans-lament-being-locked-out-of/

Doha News. (2014, May 18). Blatter ruffles feathers after calling Qatar's 'World Cup a 'mistake' [online]. Retrieved May 12, 2015, from https://dohanews.co/blatter-ruffles-feathers-calling-qatars-world-cup-mistake/

Doha News. (2015, January 28). Qatar advances to handball semis; some fans left out in the cold [online]. Retrieved September 26, 2021, from https://dohanews.co/qatar-advances-handball-semis-fans-left-cold/

Doha News. (2021a, July 11). Qatar Olympic body to host refugee olympians at camp [online]. Retrieved July 11, 2021, from https://www.dohanews.co/qatar-olympic-body-to-host-refugee-olympians-at-camp/

Doha News. (2021b, August 12). Doha-Riyadh diplomatic ties restored as Qatar appoints first ambassador to Saudi Arabia [online]. Retrieved August 12, 2021, from https://www.dohanews.co/doha-riyadh-diplomatic-ties-restored-as-qatar-appoints-first-ambassador-to-saudi-arabia/

Doha News. (2021c, July 12). Qatar, South Korea sign 20-year LNG deal [online]. Retrieved July 12, 2021, from https://www.dohanews.co/qatar-south-korea-sign-20-year-lng-deal/

Doha News. (2021d, June 14). Top energy firms bid for stake in Qatar's LNG projects [online]. Retrieved June 14, 2021, from https://www.dohanews.co/top-energy-firms-bid-for-stake-in-qatars-lng-projects/

Doha News. (2021e, March 17). 'Unliveable conditions' unmasked at Qatar budget quarantine facilities [online]. Retrieved March 17, 2021, from https://www.dohanews.co/unliveable-conditions-unmasked-at-qatar-budget-quarantine-facilities/

Doha News. (2021f, May 21). UN, EU thank Qatar for facilitating ceasefire in Gaza Strip [online]. Retrieved May 21, 2021, from https://www.dohanews.co/un-eu-thank-qatar-for-facilitating-ceasefire-in-gaza-strip/

Doha News. (2021g, June 24). Qatar receives first Egypt ambassador since 2017 blockade [online]. Retrieved June 24, 2021, from https://www.dohanews.co/qatar-receives-first-egypt-ambassador-since-2017-blockade/

Doha News. (2021h, February 25). Qatar has come too far to give in to pressure from business community [online]. Retrieved February 25, 2021, from https://www.dohanews.co/qatar-has-come-too-far-to-give-in-to-pressure-from-business-community/

Doha News. (2021i, May 05). Egypt's Al Ahly to take on Morocco's RS Berkane at African Super Cup final in Qatar [online]. Retrieved May 05, 2021, from https://www.dohanews.co/egypts-al-ahly-to-take-on-moroccos-rs-berkane-at-african-super-cup-final-in-qatar/

Doha News. (2021j, March 07). Qatari women 'outnumber men' at local universities [online]. Retrieved March 08, 2021, from https://www.dohanews.co/qatari-women-outnumber-men-at-local-universities/

Doha News. (2021k, August 09). Two Qatari referees to lead Saudi league matches [online]. Retrieved August 09, 2021, from https://www.dohanews.co/two-qatari-referees-to-lead-saudi-league-matches/

Doha News. (2021l, June 09). Qatar's public transport to go 100% electric by 2030 [online]. Retrieved June 09, 2021, from https://www.dohanews.co/qatars-public-transport-to-go-100-electric-by-2030/

Doha News. (2021m, September 09). Sweden cancels annual football training camp in Qatar [online]. Retrieved September 09, 2021, from https://www.dohanews.co/sweden-cancels-annual-football-training-camp-in-qatar/
Foreign Policy. (2021, October 05). Qatari diplomat: 'there's a serious need for engagement' with the Taliban [online]. Retrieved November 01, 2021, from https://foreignpolicy.com/2021/10/05/qatar-diplomat-lolwah-rashid-al-khater/
Geopolitical Monitor. (2021, August 31). Qatar emerges as power broker in new Afghanistan [online]. Retrieved November 10, 2021, from https://www.geopoliticalmonitor.com/qatar-emerges-as-power-broker-in-new-afghanistan/
Georgetown University Qatar. (2021, May 09). Virtual 2021 commencement ceremony celebrates 71 Seniors [online]. Retrieved May 10, 2021, from https://www.qatar.georgetown.edu/georgetown-virtual-2021-commencement-ceremony-celebrates-71-seniors-at-qf/
Giffard, C. A., & Rivenburgh, N. K. (2000). News agencies, national images, and global media events. *Journalism & Mass Communication Quarterly, 77*(1), 8–21.
Global Destinations City Index. (2019) [online]. Available at: https://www.mastercard.com/news/insights/2019/globaldestination-cities-index-2019/ (Accessed 12.06.20)
Global Health Observatory. (2017). Qatar [online]. Retrieved September 12, 2021, from https://apps.who.int/iris/rest/bitstreams/1139345/retrieve
Goal. (2021, April 27). Sustainability at the forefront as Qatar plots a carbon-neutral 2022 World Cup [online]. Retrieved November 10, 2021, from https://www.goal.com/en-us/news/sustainability-at-the-forefront-qatar-world-cup-2022-carbon/b9kyx2gzgbas1wfbzeyn58g5u
Grix, J. (2016). *Sport politics: An introduction.* Palgrave Macmillan.
Gulf News. (2020, October 06). World Cup in Qatar to set standards for future editions: UK football author [online]. Retrieved October 07, 2020, from https://m.gulf-times.com/story/674681/World-Cup-in-Qatar-to-set-standards-for-future-edi
Harkness, G. (2021). Review of changing Qatar: Culture, citizenship, and rapid modernization. *Social Forces, 99*(4), 11.
Human Rights Watch. (2021, March 29). 'Everything I have to do is tied to a men': Women and Qatar's Male Guardianship Rules [online]. Retrieved August 07, 2021, from https://www.hrw.org/report/2021/03/29/everything-i-have-do-tied-man/women-and-qatars-male-guardianship-rules
Hürriyet Daily News. (2019). New military base in Qatar to inaugurate in autumn, 14 August, [online]. Available at: https://www.hurriyetdailynews.com/new-military-base-in-qatar-to-inaugurate-in-autumn-145760 (Accessed 09.01.21)
ILO. (2021, March 19). Qatar's new minimum wage enters into force [online]. Retrieved November 10, 2021, from https://www.ilo.org/beirut/projects/

qatar-office/WCMS_775981/lang%2D%2Den/index.htm?_sm_au_=iVV7VS
rgFWgMV5tPvMFckK0232C0F

ITUC. (2015). Frontlines Report: Qatar: Profit and loss [online]. Retrieved
   February 12, 2021, from https://www.ituc-csi.org/IMG/pdf/qatar_
   en_web.pdf

Kamrava, M. (2013). *Qatar: Small state, big politics.* Cornell University Press.

Khashan, H. (2021, January 31). Not the 2022 World Cup, Joe Biden Paved
   the way for ending the Qatar Blockade [online]. Retrieved February 01,
   2021, from https://cirs.qatar.georgetown.edu/not-the-world-cup-joe-biden-
   paved-the-way-for-ending-the-blockade/

Krieg, A. (2021, March 17). Qatar: From activism to pragmatism [online].
   Retrieved October 12, 2021, from https://static1.squarespace.com/
   static/5eeb7ecb8c133f2d5ead8f9c/t/6049ee73ec446c62bcec174c/
   1615457908157/Qatar.pdf

LaMay, C. (2020, December 16). Why media liberalization in Qatar would
   serve an important 2022 Legacy [online]. Retrieved February 12, 2021,
   from https://cirs.qatar.georgetown.edu/why-media-liberalization-in-qatar-
   would-serve-an-important-2022-legacy/

Lynch, J. (2021, February 21). Qatar's 2022 World Cup has put the spotlight on
   migrant workers, but what legacy will it deliver? [online]. Retrieved February
   22, 2021, from https://cirs.qatar.georgetown.edu/qatars-2022-world-cup-
   has-put-the-spotlight-on-migrant-workers-but-what-legacy-will-it-deliver/

Lysa, C. (2020). Fighting for the right to play: Women's football and regime-loyal
   resistance in Saudi Arabia. *Third World Quarterly, 41*(5), 842–859.

Muftah, M. (2021). *The paradox of Qatari females' education* (Doctoral dissertation, Georgetown University in Qatar, GU-Q).

Oxford Business Group. (2015). Qatar [online]. Retrieved February 02, 2021,
   from https://oxfordbusinessgroup.com/qatar-2015

Qatar Olympic Committee. (2011). Sports sector strategy [online]. Retrieved
   February 05, 2021, from http://www.aspire.qa/Document/Sports_sector_
   strategy_final-English.pdf

Qatar Social and Economic Survey Research Institute. (2015). A survey of the
   views of Qataris and expatriates vis-à-vis the hosting of the 2022 FIFA World
   Cup [online]. Retrieved September 19, 2021, from http://sesri.qu.edu.qa/
   web/publications/

Reiche, D. (2021, March 18). Why the FIFA World Cup 2022 in Qatar Should not be
   Boycotted [online]. Retrieved March 18, 2021, from https://cirs.qatar.george-
   town.edu/why-the-fifa-world-cup-2022-in-qatar-should-be-not-boycotted/

Reiche, D., & Tinaz, C. (2019). Policies for naturalisation of foreign-born athletes: Qatar and Turkey in comparison. *International Journal of Sport Policy
   and Politics, 11*(1), 153–171.

Reporters Without Borders. (2021). Qatar media caught in information warfare [online]. Retrieved October 17, 2021, from https://rsf.org/en/qatar

Reuters. (2021a, February 08). Qatar petroleum signs deal for mega-LNG expansion [online]. Retrieved August 02, 2021, from https://www.reuters.com/article/qatar-petroleum-lng-int-idUSKBN2A81ST

Reuters. (2021b, October 14). Qatar emir appoints two women to advisory council after men sweep polls [online]. Retrieved October 14, 2021, from https://www.reuters.com/world/middle-east/qatar-emir-appoints-two-women-advisory-council-after-men-sweep-polls-2021-10-14/

Reuters. (2021c, September 08). Analysis: The west owes Qatar a favor over Afghanistan. That was the point [online]. Retrieved October 14, 2021, from https://www.reuters.com/world/west-owes-qatar-favour-over-afghanistan-that-was-point-2021-09-08/

State of Qatar Ministry of Planning Delivery and Statistics. (2017, June). Sports in Qatari society [online]. Retrieved Spetember 17, 2020, from https://www.psa.gov.qa/en/statistics/Statistical%20Releases/Social/Sport/2016/Sport_In_Qatar_2016_En.pdf

The Economist. (2015, October 29). Qatar Airways begrudgingly moves with the times [online]. Retrieved November 02, 2021, from http://www.economist.com/blogs/gulliver/2015/10/qatar-heroes

The Independent. (2021a, August 10). Singapore dethroned as world's best airport after eight years on top [online]. Retrieved October 12, 2021, from https://www.independent.co.uk/travel/news-and-advice/best-airport-doha-qatar-singapore-changi-b1900045.html

The Independent. (2021b, March 25). Qatar builds entire new city in preperation for World Cup [online]. Retrieved October 13, 2021, from https://www.independent.co.uk/travel/news-and-advice/qatar-lusail-new-city-world-cup-2022-tourists-b1822413.html

The New York Times. (2021, September 07). From Afghanistan to the World Cup, tiny, wealthy Qatar steps up [online]. Retrieved October 14, 2021, from https://www.nytimes.com/2021/09/07/world/middleeast/afghanistan-qatar-airlift.html

The Peninsula. (2021a, April 25). 1,100 electric buses to ferry FIFA World Cup 2022 fans [online]. Retrieved August 18, 2021, from https://thepeninsulaqatar.com/article/25/04/2021/1,100-electric-buses-to-ferry-FIFA-World-Cup-2022-fans

The Peninsula. (2021b, March 28). Qatar among first countries to implement expanded bubble system for sport events [online]. Retrieved April 18, 2021, from https://thepeninsulaqatar.com/article/28/03/2021/Qatar-among-first-countries-to-implement-expanded-bubble-system-for-sport-events

Ulrichsen, K. C. (2020). *Qatar and the gulf crisis: A study of resilience.* Oxford University Press.

Ulrichsen, K. C. (2021). The Impact of the Lifting of the Blockade on the Qatar World Cup, 24 Janurary, Centre for International and Regional Studies [online]. Available at: https://cirs.qatar.georgetown.edu/the-impact-of-the-lifting-of-the-blockade-on-the-qatar-world-cup/ (Accessed 24.08.21).

Winckler, O. (1997). The immigration policy of the Gulf Cooperation Council (GCC) states. *Middle Eastern Studies, 33*, 481–493.

World Health Organization. (2017). Qatar [online]. Available at: https://apps.who.int/iris/rest/bitstreams/1139345/retrieve (Accessed 13.04.20)

Zaccara, L. (2021). Political participation in Qatar: The Central Municipal Council Elections (1999–2019). In *Contemporary Qatar* (pp. 39–57). Springer.

APPENDIX 1: MAJOR DEVELOPMENTS IN QATAR SINCE THE AWARDING OF THE 2022 WORLD CUP IN DECEMBER 2010

Event	Date
International Centre for Sports Security (ICSS) launched.	March 2011
Qatar was pivotal in rallying Arab backing for the NATO-led campaign to oust Libyan leader, Colonel Muammar Gaddafi.	March-August 2011
Paris Saint Germain added to the list of Qatar's Sport Investment (QSI) assets.	June 2011 (sole shareholder starting March 2012)
Qatar initiated Darfur Peace Agreement, signed between the Sudanese government and rebel group, the Liberation and Justice Movement.	July 2011
Qatari Diar purchases the London 2012 Olympic Village for a fee of £557 million.	August 2011
Qatar's support of the Muslim Brotherhood in Egypt during the 2011 Arab Spring.	2011
Qatar held the United Nations Conference on Trade and Development, during which time 155 World Trade Organization members agreed to sign the 'Doha Development Agenda.'	April 2012
Female athletes were a part of Qatar's Olympic delegation for the first time.	July 2012
Sheikh Hamad bin Khalifa Al Thani voluntarily abdicated power and Sheikh Tamim took over.	June 2013

(*continued*)

P. M. Brannagan, D. Reiche, *Qatar and the 2022 FIFA World Cup*, https://doi.org/10.1007/978-3-030-96822-9

151

continued

Event	Date
Qatar has consistently remained in the top 30 of the FutureBrand Country Brand Index list, a marked improvement on its position of 72 in 2010. 2020 rank: 18.	November 2014–present
Coalition of Saudi Arabia, Bahrain, the UAE and Egypt withdrew their ambassadors from Doha in protest of Qatar's support of the Muslim Brotherhood.	March 2014
Qatar was central in securing the release of U.S. Army Sergeant, Bowe Bergdahl, who was being held in Afghanistan by Taliban forces.	May 2014
A slump in oil prices forced the tightening of domestic fiscal spend.	June-December 2014
Qatar negotiated the release and return of U.S. journalist, Peter Curtis, who was held hostage for two years in Syria by Al-Nusra Front.	August 2014
After intense pressure from the GCC, Qatar finally asked senior Muslim Brotherhood leaders to leave the country.	September 2014
Qatar Red Crescent sent staff to Nepal to treat more than 300 patients after the Kathmandu earthquake; Qatar donated around $1.6 billion worth of food, clothing, and medical supplies to help those caught up in the Syrian civil war.	April 2015
beIN (then known as 'Al Jazeera Sport') secured the Middle East and North African broadcasting rights to the 2018 and 2022 FIFA World Cups.	July 2015
beIN won the Middle East and North African rights to broadcast the 2018 and 2022 Winter Olympic Games, and the 2020 and 2024 Summer Olympic Games.	August 2015
Al Jazeera America, closed, leading to the loss of over 700 jobs.	April 2016
KSA, Bahrain, UAE, Egypt cut all diplomatic and trade links, as well as suspending all shipping and air routes with Qatar.	June 2017
Qatar's ally Turkey established a military base in Qatar and sent its first contingent of military personnel.	June 2017
QSI's acquisition of Brazilian star, Neymar Jr, for a world record fee of €222 million.	August 2017
Qatari government announced to waive entry visa requirements for citizens of 80 countries	August 2017
ILO's Project Office for the State of Qatar was established in Doha.	April 2018
QSI's purchase of French forward, Kylian Mbappé, for a fee of €180 million.	July 2018
Qatar has become 'the most open country in the Middle East in terms of visa facilitation'	September 2018
Qatar left the Organization of the Petroleum Exporting Countries (OPEC).	January 2019
The Qatari men's national football team won the AFC Asian Cup.	February 2019
Qatar became self-sufficient in dairy production.	March 2019

(*continued*)

continued

Event	Date
IAAF World Championships held in Doha.	September 2019–October 2019
beIN acquired the Middle East and North Africa rights to the 2019 and 2020 FIFA Club World Cups.	November 2019
Qatari women no longer need a male guardian's permission to obtain a driving license.	January 2020
Kafala system dismantled: Qatar introduced new laws that marked, according to the ILO, 'a new era' for the Qatari labour market. The requirement of an exit permit to leave the country was abolished. Furthermore, workers no longer need to obtain a No Objection Certificate (NOC) from their employers to change jobs.	August 2020
Taliban and Afghan government negotiators began meeting in Doha for peace talks to end decades of war.	September 2020
Three metro lines (Red, Green and Gold) with 37 stations were completed in Doha.	September 2020
The blockade is resolved after Kuwait and the U.S. forces helped broker a deal between Qatar and its regional neighbours.	January 2021
The minimum wage, which became mandatory for all newly signed contracts from August 30, 2020, extended to existing employment agreements.	March 2021
Qatar plans to convert 25% of public transport to electric energy in 2022 and set the goal for 100% by 2030.	April 2021
Opening of real estate ownership offices for non-Qatari people in the new city of Lusail as well as on the artificial island, the Pearl, which will enable the buyer and their family to receive long-term residence 'in less than one hour'.	April 2021
The Qatari cabinet approved a draft law that would allow foreign investors to own up to 100 per cent of companies listed on the Qatar Stock Exchange.	April 2021
Qatar pledged to pay $500 million for the reconstruction of the Gaza strip.	May 2021
The six Western energy giants Chevron, ExxonMobil, and ConocoPhillips, Eni, Royal Dutch Shell, and TotalEnergies submitted bids for the expansion project.	May 2021
Qatar facilitated a ceasefire between Israel and Hamas after two weeks of deadly violence between the two parties.	May 2021
Doha hosted the African Super Cup final in men's football.	May 2021
Qatari government introduced new rules that immediately became effective to better protect workers from heat stress. The new measures also introduced requirements for annual health checks for workers.	May 2021

(*continued*)

continued

Event	Date
Qatar authorities announced plans to expand its LNG production capacity by 40 per cent from 77 million tonnes per annum (mtpa) to 110 mtpa by 2025.	June 2021
Qatar ranked most peaceful country in the Arab World.	June 2021
Qatar ranked third safest country in the world	July 2021
Diplomatic ties restored as Qatar appoints ambassador to Saudi Arabia.	August 2021
Hamad International Airport named world's best airport for 2021.	August 2021
Lionel Messi transferred to PSG from Barcelona.	August 2021
Qatar won two gold medals at Olympics.	July/August 2021
Qatar helped evacuate foreigners and nationals from Afghanistan; Western embassies relocated from Kabul to Doha.	August 2021
Shura Council elections	October 2021
First ever Formula 1 Grand Prix in Qatar	November 2021

References

Abbot, S. (2018). *The away game: The Epic search for Soccer's next superstar*. Norton.

ABC News. (2011, March 21). Clinton: Al Jazeera is 'real news' [online]. Retrieved September 16, 2021, from https://abcnews.go.com/Politics/video/hillary-clinton-al-jazeera-real-news-13042310

Abdullah, J., & Al-Nasiri, N. (2014). *Qatari foreign policy: Carryover or redirection?*. AlJazeera Centre for Studies. Retrieved September 12, 2021, from https://studies.aljazeera.net/sites/default/files/migration/ResourceGallery/media/Documents/2014/7/10/201471011483120573 4 Qatari%20Foreign%20Policy%20Carryover%20or%20Redirection.pdf

Agence France-Press. (2018, September 21). FIFA World Cup 2022: 1000 nationals from Saudi Arabia, Bahrain, UAE apply to be volunteers despite Qatar embargo [online]. Retrieved November 10, 2021, from https://www.firstpost.com/sports/fifa-world-cup-2022-1000-nationals-from-saudi-arabia-bahrain-uae-apply-to-be-volunteers-despite-qatar-embargo-5235731.html

Al Jazeera. (2016, December 14). Qatar introduces changes to labour laws [online]. Retrieved April 12, 2021, from https://www.aljazeera.com/economy/2016/12/14/qatar-introduces-changes-to-labour-law

Al Jazeera. (2019, November 25). Erdogan: Turkey-Qatar military base serves regional 'stability' [online]. Retrieved September 02, 2021, from https://www.aljazeera.com/news/2019/11/25/erdogan-turkey-qatar-military-base-serves-regional-stability

Al Jazeera. (2020a, November 03). Qatar to hold Shura Council elections next year: Emir [online]. Retrieved May 06, 2021, from https://www.aljazeera.com/news/2020/11/3/qatar-to-hold-shura-council-elections-next-year-emir

Al Jazeera. (2020b, June 09). Qatar's food security boost post-blocade [online]. Retrieved March 19, 2021, from https://www.aljazeera.com/program/newsfeed/2020/6/9/qatars-food-security-boost-post-blockade

Al Jazeera. (2021a, March 21). Labour law changes: Are Qatar's migrant workers better off? [online]. Retrieved November 10, 2021, from https://www.firstpost.com/sports/fifa-world-cup-2022-1000-nationals-from-saudi-arabia-bahrain-uae-apply-to-be-volunteers-despite-qatar-embargo-5235731.html

Al Jazeera. (2021b, May 26). Qatar pledges $500 m for Gaza reconstruction [online]. Retrieved July 12, 2021, from https://www.aljazeera.com/news/2021/5/26/qatar-pledges-500-million-to-gaza-reconstruction

Al-Hammadi, M. I. (2018). Presentation of Qatari identity at National Museum of Qatar: Between imagination and reality. *Journal of Conservation and Museum Studies, 16*(1), 3.

Andersen, R. (2006). *A century of media, a century of war.* Peter Lang.

Antwi-Boateng, O. (2013). The rise of Qatar as a soft power and the challenges. *European Scientific Journal, 2*(1), 39–51.

Arabian Business. (2016, May 22). Qatar's World Cup stadiums to cost $10bn, official says. Retrieved June 17, 2021, from https://www.arabianbusiness.com/qatar-s-world-cup-stadiums-cost-10bn-official-says-632410.html

Armstrong, H., & Read, R. (2006). Geographical 'handicaps' and small states: Some implications for the Pacific from a global perspective. *Asia Pacific Viewpoint, 47*(1), 79–92.

Aspetar. (n.d.) About Aspetar [online]. Available at: https://www.aspetar.com/about.aspx?lang=en (Accessed 17.09.21)

Aspire. (2019, December 11). Aspire Football dreams graduate Wague in solid CL debut for Barca, 11 December [online]. Retrieved January 18, 2021, from https://www.aspire.qa/Media/News/aspire-football-dreams-graduate-wague-in-solid-cl-debut-for-barca

Aspire. (2021). Football Dreams [online]. Retrieved April 12, 2021, from https://www.aspire.qa/football/football-dreams

Avraham, E. (2020). Nation branding and marketing strategies for combatting tourism crises and stereotypes toward destinations. *Journal of Business Research, 116*, 711–720.

Bachrach, P., & Baratz, M. S. (1975). Power and its two faces revisited: A reply to Geoffrey Debnam. *American Political Science Review, 69*(3), 900–904.

Bahgat, G. (2015). Geopolitics of energy: Iran, Turkey, and Europe. *Mediterranean Quarterly, 26*(3), 49–66.

Bajracharya, R., & Sijapati, B. (2012). *The Kafala system and its implications for Nepali domestic workers.* Center for the Study of Labour Mobility [online].

Retrieved February 09, 2021, from http://www.ceslam.org/files/Policy%20 Brief%201_The%20Kafala%20System%20and%20Its%20Implications%20 for%20Nepali%20Domestic%20Workers.pdf

Ball, T. (1992). New faces of power, in T.E. Waternberg (ed.), *Rethinking Power*. Albany: State University of New York Press.

Barnett, M. (2005). Social constructivism. In J. Baylis (Ed.), *The globalization of world politics: An introduction to international relations*. Oxford University Press.

Barnett, M., & Finnemore, M. (2004). *Rules for the World: International Organizations in Global Politics*. Cornell University Press.

Barney, D. (2004). *The network society*. Polity.

Bátora, J. (2005). *Public diplomacy in small and medium-sized states: Norway and Canada*. Netherlands Institute of International Relations.

Baumann, R., & Matheson, V. (2018). Mega-events and tourism: The case of Brazil. *Contemporary Economic Policy, 36*(2), 292–301.

Baylis, J., & Smith, S. (2005). *The globalization of world politics: An introduction to international relations*. Oxford University Press.

Bayoumy, Y. (2017, June 23). UAE says will not back down in dispute if Qatar declines to cooperate [online]. Retrieved March 13, 2021, from https://www. reuters.com/article/uk-gulf-qatar-emirates-idAFKBN19E29B

BBC. (2011, July 11). Qatar 2022 World Cup bid 'did nothing wrong' [online]. Retrieved March 17, 2021, from http://www.bbc.co.uk/sport/ football/14112036

BBC. (2013, June 25). Qatari emir Sheikh Hamad hands power to son Tamim [online]. Retrieved June 17, 2021, from https://www.bbc.co.uk/news/ world-middle-east-23026870

BBC. (2014a, June 14). Qatar 2022 World Cup a 'high security risk', report claimed [online]. Retrieved February 18, 2021, from https://www.bbc.co.uk/ sport/football/27852582

BBC. (2014b, June 09). World Cup 2014 sponsors face whole new ball game [online]. Retrieved September 12, 2021, from https://www.bbc.co.uk/news/ business-27667473

BBC. (2015a, June 11). British Champions Series secures record sponsorship deal [online]. Retrieved September 12, 2021, from http://beta.bbc.co.uk/ sport/0/horse-racing/33090512?print=true

BBC. (2015b, December 21). Fifa corruption crisis: Key questions answered [online]. Retrieved March 13, 2021, from https://www.bbc.co.uk/news/ world-europe-32897066

BBC. (2015c, April 08). How will Qatar build a good team for the 2022 World Cup? [online]. Retrieved July 23, 2021, from http://www.bbc.co.uk/sport/ football/32147203

BBC. (2016, December 13). Qatar abolished controversial 'kafala' labour system [online]. Retrieved February 15, 2021, from http://www.bbc.co.uk/news/ world-middle-east-38298393

BBC. (2018a, February 19). Arsenal and Emirates in £200m shirt sponsorship extension [online]. Retrieved March 12, 2021, from https://www.bbc.co.uk/news/business-43113951

BBC. (2018b, November 21). Qatar World Cup 2022: Four years out, what do we know sao far? [online]. Retrieved February 11, 2021, from https://www.bbc.co.uk/sport/football/46294929

BBC. (2021, March 29). Lebanon 'could sink like Titanic' without new government. Retrieved April 11, 2021, from https://www.bbc.co.uk/news/world-middle-east-56570407

Beck, U. (2006). Living in the world risk society: A hobhouse memorial public lecture given on Wednesday 15 February 2006 at the London school of economics. *Economy and Society, 35*(3), 329–345.

beIN. (2019, November 28). beIN Sports agrees exclusive broadcast rights deal [online]. Retrieved May 05, 2021, from https://www.beinmediagroup.com/article/bein-sports-agrees-exclusive-broadcast-rights-deal-for-the-next-two-editions-of-fifa-club-world-cup/

beIN. (2021, April 20). European Super League: Ceferin thanks 'great man' Al-Khelaifi at PSG and other breakaway opponents [online]. Retrieved November 10, 2021, from https://www.beinsports.com/en/football/news/european-super-league-ceferin-thanks-great-1/1673401

Bell, D. (1973). *The coming of post-industrial society: A venture in social forecasting.* Basic Books.

Beyer, B., & Schulze-Marmeling, D. (2021). *Boykottiert Katar 2022! Warum wir die FIFA stoppen müssen.* Verlag Die Werkstatt.

Bilton, T., Bonnet, K., Jones, P., Lawson, T., Skinner, D., Stanworth, M., & Webster, A. (2002). *Introductory sociology.* Palgrave.

Black, D. R. (2017). Managing the mega-event 'habit': Canada as serial user. *International Journal of Sport Policy and Politics, 9*(2), 219–235.

Boussaa, D. (2021). The past as a catalyst for cultural sustainability in historic cities; the case of Doha, Qatar. *International Journal of Heritage Studies, 27*(5), 470–486.

Brand Finance. (2021). Global soft power index [online]. Retrieved March 07, 2021, from https://brandfinance.com/press-releases/global-soft-power-index-2021-15-nations-from-mena-feature

Brannagan, P. M. (2017). *The state of Qatar and global sport: A case study of globalization, the nation-state and soft power* (Doctoral dissertation, Loughborough University).

Brannagan, P. M., & Giulianotti, R. (2014). Qatar, global sport and the 2022 FIFA world cup. In *Leveraging legacies from sports mega-events: Concepts and cases* (pp. 154–165). Palgrave Pivot.

Brannagan, P. M., & Giulianotti, R. (2015). Soft power and soft disempowerment: Qatar, global sport and football's 2022 World Cup finals. *Leisure Studies, 34*(6), 703–719.

Brannagan, P. M., & Giulianotti, R. (2018). The soft power–soft disempowerment nexus: The case of Qatar. *International Affairs, 94*(5), 1139–1157.

Brannagan, P. M., & Grix, J. (2014). Qatar's soft power gamble: The FIFA World Cup 2022. *E-International Relations.* Retrieved February 09, 2021, from https://www.e-ir.info/2014/01/18/qatars-soft-power-gamble-the-fifa-world-cup-2022/

Brannagan, P. M., & Rookwood, J. (2016). Sports mega-events, soft power and soft disempowerment: International supporters' perspectives on Qatar's acquisition of the 2022 FIFA World Cup finals. *International Journal of Sport Policy and Politics, 8*(2), 173–188.

Brannagan, P. M., Scelles, N., Valenti, M., Inoue, Y., Grix, J., & Perkin, S. J. (2022). The 2021 European Super League attempt: Motivation, outcome, and the future of football. *International Journal of Sport Policy and Politics,* 1–8.

Braveboy-Wagner, J. (2010). Opportunities and limitations of the exercise of foreign policy power by a very small state: The case of Trinidad and Tobago. *Cambridge Review of International Affairs, 23*(3), 407–427.

Breton, G., & Lambert, M. (2003). *Universities and globalization: Private linkages, public trust.* UNESCO/Université Laval/Economica.

Castells, M. (1996). *The rise of the network society, the information age: Economy, society and culture* (Vol. I). Blackwell.

Castells, M. (2007). Communication, power and counter-power in the network society. *International journal of Communication, 1*(1), 29.

Castells, M. (2013). *Communication Power* (2nd ed.). Oxford University Press.

Cerny, P. G. (1997). Paradoxes of the competition state: The dynamics of political globalization. *Government and Opposition, 32*(2), 251–274.

Chadwick, S., Widdop, P., & Burton, N. (2020). Soft power sports sponsorship–A social network analysis of a new sponsorship form. *Journal of Political Marketing,* 1–22.

Chong, A. (2010). Small state soft power strategies: Virtual enlargement in the cases of the Vatican City State and Singapore. *Cambridge Review of International Affairs, 23*(3), 383–405.

CNBC. (2018, December 03). Qatar quitting OPEC means the oil cartel is now just a 'two-member organization', oil analysts say [online]. Retrieved June 09, 2021, from https://www.cnbc.com/2018/12/03/qatar-quitting-opec-leaves-oil-cartel-a-two-member-organization.html

CNN. (2011, February 03). Five things we've learnt from Qatar's Asian Cup [online]. Retrieved April 05, 2021, from http://edition.cnn.com/2011/SPORT/football/01/27/qatar.2022.asian.cup/

CNN. (2013, June 06). Should soccer boycott Israel's European Championship? [online]. Retrieved July 10, 2021, from https://edition.cnn.com/2013/06/06/sport/football/israel-sarsak-uefa-u21-football/index.html

CNN. (2015, May 27). FIFA in crisis: The men who have been charged [online]. Retrieved July 25, 2021, from http://edition.cnn.com/2015/05/27/football/fifa-arrests-webb-warner-marin/

CNN. (2016, March 27). Al Jazeera announces 500 job cuts [online]. Retrieved February 24, 2021, from https://money.cnn.com/2016/03/27/media/al-jazeera-qatar-layoffs/index.html

CNN. (2019, October 01). Where are the crowds at the World Athletics Championships? [online]. Retrieved September 07, 2021, from https://edition.cnn.com/2019/10/01/sport/world-athletics-championships-low-crowds-doha-spt-intl/index.html

Cooper, A. F. (2008). Beyond one image fits all: Bono and the complexity of celebrity diplomacy. *Global Governance, 14*, 265.

Cooper, A. F., & Momani, B. (2011). Qatar and expanded contours of small state diplomacy. *The International Spectator, 46*(3), 113–128.

Cooper, A. F., & Shaw, T. (2009). *The diplomacies of small states*. Palgrave Macmillan.

Cull, N. J. (2008). The public diplomacy of the modern olympic games and China's soft power strategy. In M. E. Price & D. Dayan (Eds.), *Owning the olympics: Narratives of the New China*. University of Michigan Press.

Daher, R. (Ed.). (2007). *Tourism in the Middle East: Continuity, change, and transformation*. Channel View.

Dahl, R. A. (1957). The concept of power. *Behavioral Science, 2*(3), 201–215.

De Boer, K., & Turner, J. (2007). Beyond oil: Reappraising the Gulf states. *McKinsey Quarterly, 13*(1), 7–17.

De Genova, N., & Nathalie, P. (2010). *The deportation regime: Sovereignty, space, and the freedom of movement*. Duke University Press.

Deloitte Football Money League. (2021). Retrieved September 09, 2021, from https://www2.deloitte.com/uk/en/pages/sports-business-group/articles/deloitte-football-money-league.html

Department of Justice. (2015, May 27). Nine FIFA officials and five corporate exectutives indicated for racketeering conspiracy and corruption [online]. Retrieved March 06, 2021, from https://www.justice.gov/opa/pr/nine-fifa-officials-and-five-corporate-executives-indicted-racketeering-conspiracy-and

Designverse. (2020, September 25). First 37 stations completed on the Doha Metro Network [online]. Retrieved November 10, 2021, from https://designverse.com.cn/content/recommend/article/first-37-stations-completed-on-the-doha-metro-network-unstudio-en

Deutsche Welle. (2021, August 31). Why Qatar fosters close contact with the Taliban [online]. Retrieved November 10, 2021, from https://www.dw.com/en/why-qatar-fosters-close-contact-with-the-taliban/a-59030146

Doha Goals (n.d.) 2013 [online]. Available at: https://www.qfa.qa/doha-goals-2013-in-december/ (Accessed 19.03.21)

Doha News. (2013a, January 24). Report: Most nationals believe Qatar is facing 'demographic problem' [online]. Retrieved July 19, 2015, from https://dohanews.co/government-report-finds-most-nationals-believe-qatar-is/

Doha News. (2013b, May 18). Ticket-holders lament lockout at Emir Cup as Al Rayyan defeats Al Sadd [online]. Retrieved August 16, 2015, from https://dohanews.co/ticket-holding-football-fans-lament-being-locked-out-of/

Doha News. (2013c, April 26). To tackle labor rights violations, QF, 2022 Supreme Committee ratify workers' charters [online]. Retrieved July 12, 2015, from https://dohanews.co/to-tackle-labor-rights-violations-qf-2022-supreme/

Doha News. (2013d, April 26). To tackle labor rights violations, QF, 2022 Supreme Committee ratify workers' charters [online]. Retrieved July 12, 2021, from https://dohanews.co/to-tackle-labor-rights-violations-qf-2022-supreme/

Doha News. (2014, May 18). Blatter ruffles feathers after calling Qatar's 'World Cup a 'mistake' [online]. Retrieved May 12, 2015, from https://dohanews.co/blatter-ruffles-feathers-calling-qatars-world-cup-mistake/

Doha News. (2015a, November 16). How safe is Qatar from an ISIS attack? Experts weigh in [online]. Retrieved May 06, 2021, from https://dohanews.co/how-safe-is-qatar-from-an-isis-attack-experts-weigh-in/

Doha News. (2015b, January 28). Qatar advances to handball semis; some fans left out in the cold [online]. Retrieved September 26, 2021, from https://dohanews.co/qatar-advances-handball-semis-fans-left-cold/

Doha News. (2015c, June 13). Qatar launches legal offensive against some critics [online]. Retrieved August 26, 2016, from https://dohanews.co/qatar-launches-legal-offensive-against-some-critics/

Doha News. (2015d, July 05). Qatar launches legal offensive against some critics [online]. Retrieved August 26, 2016, from https://dohanews.co/qatar-launches-legal-offensive-against-some-critics/

Doha News. (2015e, June 13). Qatar launches legal offensive against some critics [online]. Retrieved August 26, 2021, from https://dohanews.co/qatar-launches-legal-offensive-against-some-critics/

Doha News. (2015f, May 07). Qatar relief workers arrive Nepal, extend mission to three months [online]. Retrieved February 14, 2021, from https://dohanews.co/qatar-relief-workers-arrive-in-nepal-extend-mission-to-three-months/

Doha News. (2016, May 22). Kafala reforms in Qatar still expected to take effect in December [online]. Retrieved September 15, 2021, from https://dohanews.co/kafala-reforms-in-qatar-still-expected-to-take-effect-in-december/

Doha News. (2021a, July 11). Qatar Olympic body to host refugee olympians at camp [online]. Retrieved July 11, 2021, from https://www.dohanews.co/qatar-olympic-body-to-host-refugee-olympians-at-camp/

Doha News. (2021b, August 12). Doha-Riyadh diplomatic ties restored as Qatar appoints first ambassador to Saudi Arabia [online]. Retrieved August 12, 2021, from https://www.dohanews.co/doha-riyadh-diplomatic-ties-restored-as-qatar-appoints-first-ambassador-to-saudi-arabia/

Doha News. (2021c, July 12). Qatar, South Korea sign 20-year LNG deal [online]. Retrieved July 12, 2021, from https://www.dohanews.co/qatar-south-korea-sign-20-year-lng-deal/

Doha News. (2021d, June 14). Top energy firms bid for stake in Qatar's LNG projects [online]. Retrieved June 14, 2021, from https://www.dohanews.co/top-energy-firms-bid-for-stake-in-qatars-lng-projects/

Doha News. (2021e, March 17). 'Unliveable conditions' unmasked at Qatar budget quarantine facilities [online]. Retrieved March 17, 2021, from https://www.dohanews.co/unliveable-conditions-unmasked-at-qatar-budget-quarantine-facilities/

Doha News. (2021f, May 21). UN, EU thank Qatar for facilitating ceasefire in Gaza Strip [online]. Retrieved May 21, 2021, from https://www.dohanews.co/un-eu-thank-qatar-for-facilitating-ceasefire-in-gaza-strip/

Doha News. (2021g, June 22). Spanish football star Javi Martinez set to join Qatar SC [online]. Retrieved June 22, 2021, from https://www.dohanews.co/spanish-football-star-javi-martinez-set-to-join-qatar-sc/

Doha News. (2021h, June 24). Qatar receives first Egypt ambassador since 2017 blockade [online]. Retrieved June 24, 2021, from https://www.dohanews.co/qatar-receives-first-egypt-ambassador-since-2017-blockade/

Doha News. (2021i, February 25). Qatar has come too far to give in to pressure from business community [online]. Retrieved February 25, 2021, from https://www.dohanews.co/qatar-has-come-too-far-to-give-in-to-pressure-from-business-community/

Doha News. (2021j, May 05). Egypt's Al Ahly to take on Morocco's RS Berkane at African Super Cup final in Qatar [online]. Retrieved May 05, 2021, from https://www.dohanews.co/egypts-al-ahly-to-take-on-moroccos-rs-berkane-at-african-super-cup-final-in-qatar/

Doha News. (2021k, March 07). Qatari women 'outnumber men' at local universities [online]. Retrieved March 08, 2021, from https://www.dohanews.co/qatari-women-outnumber-men-at-local-universities/

Doha News. (2021l, August 09). Two Qatari referees to lead Saudi league matches [online]. Retrieved August 09, 2021, from https://www.dohanews.co/two-qatari-referees-to-lead-saudi-league-matches/

Doha News. (2021m, June 09). Qatar's public transport to go 100% electric by 2030 [online]. Retrieved June 09, 2021, from https://www.dohanews.co/qatars-public-transport-to-go-100-electric-by-2030/

Doha News. (2021n, September 09). Sweden cancels annual football training camp in Qatar [online]. Retrieved September 09, 2021, from https://www.dohanews.co/sweden-cancels-annual-football-training-camp-in-qatar/

Dourian, K. (2020, July 20). Looming peak oil demand triggers Gulf race for natural gas [online]. Retrieved July 16, 2021, from https://agsiw.org/wp-content/uploads/2020/07/KateGasPaperONLINE.pdf

Dubinsky, I. (2021). China's stadium diplomacy in Africa. *Journal of Global Sport Management, 1–19.* https://doi.org/10.1080/24704067.2021.1885101

Dunne, T., Kurki, M., & Smith, S. (2013). *International relations theories: Discipline and diversity* (3rd ed.). Oxford University Press.

DW. (2015). Qatar: Buying their way to sporting success, 4 February, 2015 [online]. Available at: https://www.dw.com/en/qatar-buying-theirway-to-sporting-success/a-18233576 (Accessed 17.02.21)

El Mallakh, R. (2014). *The economic development of the United Arab Emirates (RLE Economy of Middle East).* Routledge.

Emirates. (2020, February 06). Emirates and Olympique Lyonnais announce new partnership [online]. Retrieved March 19, 2021, from https://www.emirates.com/media-centre/emirates-and-olympique-lyonnais-announce-new-partnership/

Exell, K., & Rico, T. (2013). 'There is no heritage in Qatar': Orientalism, colonialism and other problematic histories. *World Archaeology, 45*(4), 670–685.

FC Bayern. (2020, January 03). Bayern head to Doha training camp with 26-man squad [online]. Retrieved November 10, 2021, from https://fcbayern.com/en/news/2020/01/doha/bayern-travel-to-doha-training-camp-with-26-man-squad

FIFA. (2008, May 30). Joint decision on 2018 and 2022 [online]. Retrieved May 06, 2021, from http://www.fifa.com/worldcup/news/y=2008/m=5/news=joint-decision-2018-and-2022-783630.html

FIFA. (2017, May 7). Qatar Airways announced as official partner of FIFA until 2022. Retrieved September 16, 2021, from https://www.fifa.com/tournaments/mens/worldcup/qatar2022/media-releases/qatar-airways-official-partner-airline-fifa-2882728

FIFA. (2018, December 21). More than half the world watched record-breaking 2018 World Cup [online]. Retrieved Decmeber 03, 2020, from https://www.fifa.com/tournaments/mens/worldcup/2018russia/media-releases/more-than-half-the-world-watched-record-breaking-2018-world-cup

Financial Times. (2008, September 02). Qatari connection casts long shadow over Barclays [online]. Retrieved February 11, 2015, from https://www.ft.com/content/dadda8fa-0d58-11e7-a88c-50ba212dce4d

Financial Times. (2013, October 20). Doha's Education City is a boost for locals [online]. Retrieved September 12, 2015, from https://www.ft.com/content/b2fff52c-1711-11e3-9ec2-00144feabdc0

Financial Times. (2014, June 16). Royal Ascot breaks tradition with Qatari sponsorship [online]. Retrieved May 17, 2015, from https://www.ft.com/content/c18faca4-f55a-11e3-afd3-00144feabdc0

Financial Times. (2017, December 08). Manchester City and the 'Disneyfication' of football [online]. Retrieved May 13, 2021, from https://www.ft.com/content/e1961ea2-d6c5-11e7-a303-9060cb1e5f44

Financial Times. (2020, April 22). Qatar's beIN demands Premier League block Saudi takeover of Newcastle [online]. Retrieved May 14, 2021, from https://www.ft.com/content/bfcd005c-4506-432c-8535-57402407b486.

Finnemore, M., & Sikkink, K. (1998). International norm dynamics and political change. *International Organization, 52*(04), 887–917.

Forbes. (2015, June 02). Sepp Blatter resigning from FIFA will boost value of World Cup [online]. Retrieved February 15, 2021, from https://www.forbes.com/sites/mikeozanian/2015/06/02/sepp-blatter-resigning-from-fifa-will-boost-value-of-world-cup/?sh=5b8cba8f5970

Forbes. (2017, Decmeber 22). Belt and Road: China's strategy to capture supply chains from Guangzhou to Greece [online]. Retrieved January 09, 2021, from https://www.forbes.com/sites/riskmap/2017/12/21/belt-and-road-chinas-strategy-to-capture-supply-chains-from-guangzhou-to-greece/?sh=55bf292c6237

Forbes. (2019, February 06). Qatar's Asian Cup win was a fairy tale; now it faces the reality of 2022 [online]. Retrieved March 12, 2021, from https://www.forbes.com/sites/steveprice/2019/02/06/qatars-asian-cup-win-was-a-fairytale-now-it-faces-the-reality-of-2022/?sh=429065b13150

Forbes. (2021). Paris Saint Germain [online]. Retrieved September 17, 2021, from https://www.forbes.com/teams/paris-saint-germain/?sh=621dcbfe51f4

Foreign Affairs. (2016, April 18). Why Putin took Crimea [online]. Retrieved February 23, 2021, from https://www.foreignaffairs.com/articles/ukraine/2016-04-18/why-russian-president-putin-took-crimea-from-ukraine

Foreign Policy. (2014, September 30). The Case against Qatar [online]. Retrieved June 18, 2021, from http://foreignpolicy.com/2014/09/30/the-case-against-qatar/

Foreign Policy. (2021, October 05). Qatari diplomat: 'there's a serious need for engagement' with the Taliban [online]. Retrieved November 01, 2021, from https://foreignpolicy.com/2021/10/05/qatar-diplomat-lolwah-rashid-al-khater/

Fromherz, A. J. (2012). *Qatar: A modern history.* Georgetown University Press.

Fuentes-Julio, C. (2020). Norm entrepreneurs in foreign policy: How Chile became an international human rights promoter. *Journal of Human Rights, 19*(2), 256–274.

FutureBrand Country Brand Index. (2012–2013). [online] Retrieved March 17, 2021, from https://www.futurebrand.com/uploads/CBI_2012-Final.pdf

FutureBrand Country Brand Index. (2019). [online]. Retrieved March 10, 2021, from https://www.futurebrand.com/uploads/FCI/FutureBrand-Country-Index-2019.pdf

Gans, H. J. (1980). *Deciding what's news.* Vintage Books.

Gardner, A. M. (2011). Gulf migration and the family. *Journal of Arabian Studies,* *1*(1), 3–25.

Geopolitical Monitor. (2021, August 31). Qatar emerges as power broker in new Afghanistan [online]. Retrieved November 10, 2021, from https://www.geopoliticalmonitor.com/qatar-emerges-as-power-broker-in-new-afghanistan/

Georgetown University Qatar. (2021, May 09). Virtual 2021 commencement ceremony celebrates 71 Seniors [online]. Retrieved May 10, 2021, from https://www.qatar.georgetown.edu/georgetown-virtual-2021-commencement-ceremony-celebrates-71-seniors-at-qf/

Giddens, A., & Sutton, P. W. (2013). *Sociology* (7th ed.). Polity.

Giffard, C. A., & Rivenburgh, N. K. (2000). News agencies, national images, and global media events. *Journalism & Mass Communication Quarterly,* *77*(1), 8–21.

Global Destinations City Index. (2019) [online]. Available at: https://www.mastercard.com/news/insights/2019/globaldestination-cities-index-2019/ (Accessed 12.06.20)

Global Financial Centres Index. (2020). The Global Financial Centres Index [online]. Retrieved November 10, 2021, from https://www.longfinance.net/programmes/financial-centre-futures/global-financial-centres-index/

Global Health Observatory. (2017). Qatar [online]. Retrieved September 12, 2021, from https://apps.who.int/iris/rest/bitstreams/1139345/retrieve

Global Peace Index. (2021). [online]. Retrieved July 11, 2021, from https://www.visionofhumanity.org/wp-content/uploads/2021/06/GPI-2021-web-1.pdf

Goal. (2021, April 27). Sustainability at the forefront as Qatar plots a carbon-neutral 2022 World Cup [online]. Retrieved November 10, 2021, from https://www.goal.com/en-us/news/sustainability-at-the-forefront-qatar-world-cup-2022-carbon/b9kyx2gzgbas1wfbzeyn58g5u

Golan, G., & Wanta, W. (2003). International elections on US network news: An examination of factors affecting newsworthiness. *Gazette (Leiden, Netherlands),* *65*(1), 25–39.

Goldblatt, J., & Hu, C. (2005). Tourism, terrorism, and the new world for event leaders. *E-review of Tourism Research,* *3*(6), 139–144.

Grix, J. (2016). *Sport politics: An introduction.* Palgrave Macmillan.

Grix, J., Brannagan, P. M., Grimes, H., & Neville, R. (2021). The impact of Covid-19 on sport. *International Journal of Sport Policy and Politics,* *13*(1), 1–12.

Grix, J., Brannagan, P. M., & Lee, D. (2019a). *Entering the global arena: Emerging states, soft power strategies and sports mega-events.* Palgrave Macmillan.

Grix, J., Brannagan, P. M., & Lee, D. (2019b). Russia's unique soft power strategy. In *Entering the global arena: Emerging states, soft power strategies and sports mega-events.* Palgrave Macmillan.

Grix, J., Brannagan, P. M., & Lee, D. (2019c). South Africa and the 2010 FIFA World Cup. In *Entering the global arena: Emerging states, soft power strategies and sports mega-events.* Palgrave Macmillan.

Guiltinan, J. P. (1987). The price bundling of services: A normative framework. *Journal of Marketing, 51*(2), 74–85.

Gulf News. (2014a, April 25). Brotherhood leaders leave Qatar for Libya: Report [online]. Retrieved April 12, 2021, from https://gulfnews.com/world/gulf/qatar/brotherhood-leaders-leave-qatar-for-libya-report-1.1324196

Gulf News. (2014b, June 26). Al Sadd part ways with Raul [online]. Retrieved February 06, 2021, from https://www.gulf-times.com/story/398076/Al-Sadd-part-ways-with-Raul

Gulf News. (2020, October 06). World Cup in Qatar to set standards for future editions: UK football author [online]. Retrieved October 07, 2020, from https://m.gulf-times.com/story/674681/World-Cup-in-Qatar-to-set-standards-for-future-edi

Gulf News. (2021, November 06). Xavi faces 'biggest challenge of career' as Barcelona coach [online]. Retrieved April 12, 2021, from https://www.gulf-times.com/story/703952

Guzzini, S. (2000). A reconstruction of constructivism in international relations. *European Journal of International Relations, 6*(2), 147–182.

Handler, S. P. (2013). *International Politics: Classic and Contemporary Readings.* CQ Press.

Harkness, G. (2021). Review of changing Qatar: Culture, citizenship, and rapid modernization. *Social Forces, 99*(4), 11.

Hassan Al-Thawadi. (2013). Interview at Doha GOALS Forum, December 11.

Hassan Al-Thawadi. (2018). Interview at Sports Diplomacy: A vision for the future, November 30.

Hay, C. (1997). State of the art: Divided by a common language: Political theory and the concept of power. *Politics, 17*(1), 45–52.

Hay, C. (2002). *Political analysis: A critical introduction.* Palgrave Macmillan.

Herman, E., & Chomsky, N. (1988). *Manufacturing consent: The political economy of mass media.* New York: Pantheon.

Herman, E. S., & Chomsky, N. (2010). *Manufacturing consent: The political economy of the mass media.* Random House.

Heywood, A. (2014). *Global Politics.* Basingstoke: Palgrave Macmillan.

Ho, G., & Bairner, A. (2013). One country, two systems, three flags: Imagining Olympic nationalism in Hong Kong and Macao. *International Review for the Sociology of Sport, 48*(3), 349–365.

Hocking, B. (2005). Rethinking the 'New' public diplomacy. In J. Melissen (Ed.), *The new public diplomacy: Soft power in international relations.* Palgrave Macmillan.

Homayounpour. (2021). Labor market reforms and the World Cup 2022 [online]. Retrieved May 25, 2021, from https://soundcloud.com/cirsguq/episode-9-houtan-homayounpour

Horne, J. D., & Manzenreiter, W. (2004). Accounting for megaevents: forecast and actual impacts of the 2002 Football World Cup Finals on the host countries Japan/Korea. *International review for the sociology of sport, 39*(2), 187–203.

Hopf, T. (2013). The promise of constructivism in international relations theory. In S. P. Handler (Ed.), *International Politics: Classic and contemporary readings.* Sage.

Houlihan, B. (2015). Political science, sociology and the study of sport. In R. Giulianotti (Ed.), *Routledge handbook of the sociology of sport.* Routledge.

Houlihan, B., & Zheng, J. (2015). Small states: Sport and politics at the margin. *International Journal of Sport Policy and Politics, 7*(3), 329–344.

Huffington Post. (2013, June 26). London Mayor should get his facts straight on Qatar [online]. Retrieved May 25, 2021, from http://www.huffingtonpost.co.uk/nicholas-mcgeehan/london-mayor-should-get-h_b_3163127.html

Huffington Post. (2014a, July 09). Islamic State urges FIFA to deprive Qatar of the World Cup [online]. Retrieved February 15, 2021, from http://www.huffingtonpost.com/james-dorsey/islamic-state-urges-fifa_b_5569524.html

Huffington Post. (2014b, August 24). Shedding light on the threat of terrorism at Qatar's 2022 World Cup [online]. Retrieved June 29, 2021, from http://www.huffingtonpost.co.uk/quintan-wiktorowicz/qatar-world-cup-terrorism_b_5522455.html

Huffington Post. (2015, June 03). Qatar's World Cup death toll claim leaves migrant worker rights campaigners unimpressed [online]. Retrieved September 19, 2021, from http://www.huffingtonpost.co.uk/2015/06/03/qatar-world-cup-deaths_n_7500920.html

Human Freedom Index. (2020). [online]. Retrieved February 08, 2021, from https://www.cato.org/human-freedom-index/2020

Human Rights Watch. (2017, January 12). Qatar: Labour reforms leave abusive system intact [online]. Retrieved February 07, 2021, from https://www.hrw.org/news/2017/01/12/qatar-labor-reforms-leave-abusive-system-intact#

Human Rights Watch. (2019, August 14). New military base in Qatar to inaugurate in autumn [online]. Retrieved March 01, 2021, from https://www.hurriyetdailynews.com/new-military-base-in-qatar-to-inaugurate-in-autumn-145760

Human Rights Watch. (2021, March 29). 'Everything I have to do is tied to a men': Women and Qatar's Male Guardianship Rules [online]. Retrieved August 07, 2021, from https://www.hrw.org/report/2021/03/29/everything-i-have-do-tied-man/women-and-qatars-male-guardianship-rules

Human Rights Watch, World Report. (2020). [online]. Retrieved February 14, 2021, from https://www.hrw.org/world-report/2020#

Hürriyet Daily News. (2019). New military base in Qatar to inaugurate in autumn, 14 August, [online]. Available at: https://www.hurriyetdailynews.com/new-military-base-in-qatar-to-inaugurate-in-autumn-145760 (Accessed 09.01.21)

ICSS. (2012, June 18). The International Centre for Sport Security joins the United Nations Global Compact [online]. Retrieved September 23, 2021, from http://www.theicss.org/wp-content/uploads/2012/06/ICSS033.12-ICSS-joins-UN-Global-Compact-English-Press-Release.pdf?lbisphpreq=1

ICSS. (n.d.). Securing Sport Report [online]. Retrieved May 02, 2021, from https://webcache.googleusercontent.com/search?q=cache:UfauEHr6XXIJ:h ttps://members.ehf.eu/community/activities/download.ashx%3Freason%3D ehfcanFile%26id%3D1834+&cd=15&hl=en&ct=clnk&gl=uk

ILO. (2020, August 30). Dismantling the kafala system and introducing a minimum wage mark new era for Qatar labour market [online]. Retrieved November 11, 2021, from https://www.ilo.org/beirut/projects/qatar-office/WCMS_754391/lang%2D%2Den/index.htm

ILO. (2021a, March 19). Qatar's new minimum wage enters into force [online]. Retrieved November 10, 2021, from https://www.ilo.org/beirut/projects/qatar-office/WCMS_775981/lang%2D%2Den/index.htm?_sm_au_=iVV7VS rgFWgMV5tPvMFckK0232C0F

ILO. (2021b, May 27). New legislation in Qatar provides greater protection to workers from heat stress [online]. Retrieved November 10, 2021, from https://www.ilo.org/beirut/projects/qatar-office/WCMS_794475/lang%2D%2Den/index.htm

IMS. (2018, June 14). The World Cup effect: Requirements and costs of infrastructure [online]. Retrieved March 07, 2021, from https://resources.investormanagementservices.com/the-world-cup-effect/

Ingebritsen, C. (Ed.). (2006). *Small states in international relations*. University of Washington Press.

Ingebritsen, C., Neumann, I., & Gsthl, S. (Eds.). (2012). *Small states in international relations*. Washington: University of Washington Press.

International Institute for Strategic Studies' Military Balance Report. (2020). [online]. Retrieved February 03, 2021, from https://www.iiss.org/publications/the-military-balance/military-balance-2020-book

International Monetary Fund. (2021). GDP per capita [online]. Retrieved July 07, 2021, from https://www.imf.org/external/datamapper/NGDPDPC@ WEO/OEMDC/ADVEC/WEOWORLD

Interpol. (2015). *Summary of Activities [online]*. Available at: https://www.interpol.int/content/download/10994/file/Summary%20of%20activities% 20-%202014-2016.pdf

IOC. (2015, July 27). IOC awards 2018–2024 broadcast rights in Middle East and North Africa [online]. Retrieved July 26, 2021, from https://www.olympic.org/ news/ioc-awards-2018-2024-broadcast-rights-in-middle-east-and-north-africa

ITUC. (2014, February 11). Qatar World Cup workers' standards: No legal enforcement, no worker rights [online]. Retrieved March 05, 2021, from https://www.ituc-csi.org/qatar-world-cup-workers-standards

ITUC. (2015). Frontlines Report: Qatar: Profit and loss [online]. Retrieved February 12, 2021, from https://www.ituc-csi.org/IMG/pdf/qatar_en_web.pdf

Jackson, P. T., & Stanfield, J. R. (2004). The role of the press in a democracy: Heterodox economics and the propaganda model. *Journal of Economic Issues, 38*(2), 475–482.

Josselin, D., & Wallace, W. (2001). Non-state actors in world politics: A framework. In *Non-state actors in world politics* (pp. 1–20). Palgrave Macmillan.

Kaid, L. L. (Ed.). (2004). *Handbook of political communication research.* Routledge.

Kamrava, M. (2013). *Qatar: Small state, big politics.* Cornell University Press.

Karns, M. P., & Mingst, K. A. (2004). *International organizations: The politics and processes of global governance.* Lynne Reinner Publishers.

Keohane, R. O., & Nye, J. S. (2003). The concept of accountability in world politics and the use of force. *Michigan Journal of International Law, 24*(4), 1–21.

Khashan, H. (2021, January 31). Not the 2022 World Cup, Joe Biden Paved the way for ending the Qatar Blockade [online]. Retrieved February 01, 2021, from https://cirs.qatar.georgetown.edu/not-the-world-cup-joe-biden-paved-the-way-for-ending-the-blockade/

Khatib, L. (2013). Qatar's foreign policy: The limits of pragmatism. *International Affairs, 89*(2), 417–431.

Khatib, L. (2014). Qatar and the Recalibration of Power in the Gulf [online]. Available at: https://www.jstor.org/stable/pdf/resrep12983.pdf?acceptTC=true&coverpage=false&addFooter=false (Accessed 03.02.21)

Khodr, H. (2011). The dynamics of international education in Qatar: Exploring the policy drivers behind the development of Education City. *Journal of Emerging Trends in Educational Research and Policy Studies, 2*(6), 514–525.

Krane, J. (2019). *Energy kingdoms.* Columbia University Press.

Krieg, A. (2021, March 17). Qatar: From activism to pragmatism [online]. Retrieved October 12, 2021, from https://static1.squarespace.com/static/5eeb7ecb8c133f2d5ead8f9c/t/6049ee73ec446c62bcec174c/1615457908157/Qatar.pdf

Krug, M. (2019). *Journeys on a football carpet: An inside look at Qatar's football story and its transformation into the 2022 FIFA World Cup host.* Hamad bin Khalifa University Press.

Kurşun, Z. (2002). *The Ottomans in Qatar: A history of Anglo-Ottoman conflicts in the Persian Gulf.* Isis Press.

Lakatos, I. (2017). The potential role of small states and their Niche diplomacy at the UN and in the field of human rights, with special attention to Montenegro. *Pécs Journal of International and European Law, 97*, 58.

LaMay, C. (2020, December 16). Why media liberalization in Qatar would serve an important 2022 Legacy [online]. Retrieved February 12, 2021, from https://cirs.qatar.georgetown.edu/why-media-liberalization-in-qatar-would-serve-an-important-2022-legacy/

Lee, D. (2012). Global trade governance and the challenges of African activism in the Doha Development Agenda negotiations. *Global Society, 26*(1), 83–101.

Lee, D., & Smith, N. J. (2010). Small state discourses in the international political economy. *Third World Quarterly, 31*(7), 1091–1105.

Leifer, M. (2000). *Singapore's foreign policy: Coping with vulnerability.* Routledge.

Lendon, B. (2017, June 06). Qatar hosts largest US military base in Mideast [online]. Retrieved May 12, 2021, from https://edition.cnn.com/2017/06/05/middleeast/qatar-us-largest-base-in-mideast/index.html

Leonard, M., & Small, A. (2003). *Norwegian public diplomacy.* The Foreign Policy Centre.

Lukes, S. (2004). *Power: A radical view.* Macmillan International Higher Education.

Lukes, S. (2005). Power and the battle for hearts and minds, *Millennium-Journal of. International Studies, 33*(3), 477–493.

Lynch, J. (2021, February 21). Qatar's 2022 World Cup has put the spotlight on migrant workers, but what legacy will it deliver? [online]. Retrieved February 22, 2021, from https://cirs.qatar.georgetown.edu/qatars-2022-world-cup-has-put-the-spotlight-on-migrant-workers-but-what-legacy-will-it-deliver/

Lynch, M. (2006). *Voices of the new Arab public: Iraq, Al-Jazeera, and Middle East politics today.* Columbia University Press.

Lysa, C. (2020). Fighting for the right to play: Women's football and regime-loyal resistance in Saudi Arabia. *Third World Quarterly, 41*(5), 842–859.

Lysa, C. (2021, November 02). FIFA World Cup 2022: Increased opportunities for Qatar's women footballers? [online]. Retrieved November 15, 2020, from https://cirs.qatar.georgetown.edu/fifa-world-cup-2022-increased-opportunities-qatars-women-footballers/

Mahmood, S., & Earley, M. (2019). Oil and gas regulation in Qatar: Overview [online]. Retrieved July 15, 2021, from https://uk.practicallaw.thomsonreuters.com/5-525-5499?transitionType=Default&contextData=(sc.Default)&firstPage=true

MasterCard Global Destinations Cities Index. (2019). [online]. Retrieved February 15, 2021, from https://newsroom.mastercard.com/wp-content/uploads/2019/09/GDCI-Global-Report-FINAL-1.pdf

Mazzucato, M. (2011). The entrepreneurial state. *Soundings, 49*(49), 131–142.

McCombs, M., & Reynolds, A. (2009). How the news shapes our civic agenda. In J. Bryant & M. B. Oliver (Eds.), *Media effects: Advances in theory and research.* Routledge.

Mearsheimer, J. J. (2007). Structural realism. *International Relations Theories: Discipline and Diversity, 83*, 77–94.

Mills, C. W. (1959). *The sociological imagination.* Pelican.

Millward, P. (2017). World Cup 2022 and Qatar's construction projects: Relational power in networks and relational responsibilities to migrant workers. *Current Sociology, 65*(5), 756–776.

Mirincheva, V., Wiedmann, F., & Salama, A. M. (2013). The spatial development potentials of business districts in Doha: The case of the West Bay. *Open House International* [online]. Retrieved July 17, 2021, from https://www.emerald.com/insight/content/doi/10.1108/OHI-04-2013-B0003/full/html

Muftah, M. (2021). *The paradox of Qatari females' education* (Doctoral dissertation, Georgetown University in Qatar, GU-Q).

Nassif, N. (2020, December 01). How powerful has Qatar become in Elite Sport? [online]. Retrieved December 15, 2020, from https://cirs.qatar.georgetown.edu/how-powerful-has-qatar-become-elite-sport/

National Tourism Sector Strategy. (2014). [online]. Retrieved June 15, 2021, from https://www.visitqatar.qa/corporate/planning/strategy-2030

National Tourism Sector Strategy Q&A. (n.d.). [online]. Retrieved June 15, 2016, from https://www.visitqatar.qa/corporate/planning/strategy-2030

Neumann, I. B., & Gstöhl, S. (2004). *Lilliputians in Gulliver's World?: Small states in international relations.* Centre for Small State Studies, Institute for International Affairs, University of Iceland.

New York Times. (2012, August 30). Al Jazeera, seeking US viewers, bets on sport [online]. Retrieved May 18, 2021, from http://www.nytimes.com/2012/08/31/sports/soccer/al-jazeera-bets-heavily-on-soccer-on-us-tv.html

Nuruzzaman, M. (2015). Qatar and the Arab Spring: Down the foreign policy slope. *Contemporary Arab Affairs, 8*(2), 226–238.

Nye, J. S. (1990). Soft power. *Foreign Policy, 80*, 153–171.

Nye, J. S. (2002). The information revolution and American soft power. *Asia Pacific Review, 9*(1), 60–76.

Nye, J. S. (2004). *Soft Power: The means to success in world politics.* Public Affairs.

Nye, J. S. (2008). Public diplomacy and soft power. *The ANNALS of the American Academy of Political and Social Sciences, 616*(1), 94–109.

Nye, J. S. (2011). *The future of power.* Public Affairs.

Nye, J. S. (2014). *The information revolution and soft power.* Current History.

Onuf, N. G. (1989). *World of Our Making: Rules and Rule in Social Theory and International Relations.* Columbia: University of South Carolina Press.

Onuf, N., & Klink, F. F. (1989). Anarchy, authority, rule. *International Studies Quarterly, 33*(2), 149–173.

Ooredoo. (n.d.) Lionel Messi [online]. Retrieved March 26, 2021, from https://www.ooredoo.com/en/who_we_are/sponsorship/our-brand-ambassador/

Orttung, R., & Kazakov, V. (2018). Winter Olympics/World Cup. *Russian Analytical Digest (RAD), 216*, 1–9.

Oxford Business Group. (2015). Qatar [online]. Retrieved February 02, 2021, from https://oxfordbusinessgroup.com/qatar-2015

Pande, A. (2013). "The paper that you have in your hand is my freedom": Migrant domestic work and the sponsorship (Kafala) system in Lebanon. *International Migration Review, 47*(2), 414–441.

Parreñas, R. S. (2010). The indentured mobility of migrant women: How gendered protectionist laws lead Filipina hostesses to forced sexual labour. *Journal of Workplace Rights, 15*(3), 327–344.

Peterson, J. E. (2006). Qatar and the world: Branding for a micro-state. *The Middle East Journal, 60*(4), 732–748.

PSG.fr. (n.d.). Partners [online]. Retrieved July 14, 2021, from https://en.psg.fr/club/sponsors

Punnett, B. J., & Morrison, A. (2006). Niche markets and small Caribbean producers: A match made in heaven? *Journal of Small Business & Entrepreneurship, 19*(4), 341–353.

Qatar 2022. (n.d.). Stadiums [online]. Retrieved June 17, 2021, from https://www.qatar2022.qa/en/stadiums

Qatar Airways. (2019, September 18). Annual report highlights [online]. Retrieved February 13, 2021, from https://www.qatarairways.com/en/pressreleases/2019/September/2019AnnualReport.html

Qatar Airways Annual Report. (2019). [online]. Retrieved March 17, 2021, from https://www.qatarairways.com/content/dam/documents/annualreports/2019/ENG_Annual_Report_2019_V2.pdf

Qatar Foundation. (2013, April 24). Qatar foundation implements welfare standards to guarantee workers' rights [online]. Retrieved June 10, 2021, from http://www.qf.org.qa/news/240

Qatar Foundation. (2014, April 30). QF supports workers recreation initiative [online]. Retrieved June 17, 2021, from http://www.qf.org.qa/content/thefoundation/issue-64/qf-supports-workers-recreation-initiative

Qatar Foundation. (n.d.). Education city [online]. Retrieved March 14, 2021, from https://www.qf.org.qa/education/education-city

Qatar Ministry of Development Planning and Statistics. (2018). Total population [online]. Retrieved June 14, 2021, from http://www.mdps.gov.qa/en/statistics1/StatisticsSite/LatestStatistics/Pages/PopulationStats.aspx

Qatar Ministry of Planning and Statistics. (2020). Qatar Cenusus 2020 [online]. Available at: https://www.psa.gov.qa/en/statistics1/StatisticsSite/Census/Census2020/Pages/default.aspx (Accessed 13.03.2022)

Qatar Ministry of Development Planning and Statistics. (2021). Total population [online]. Retrieved June 14, 2021, from http://www.mdps.gov.qa/en/statistics1/StatisticsSite/LatestStatistics/Pages/PopulationStats.aspx

Qatar National Development Strategy 2011–2016. (2011). [online]. Retrieved May 11, 2021, from http://www.mdps.gov.qa/en/knowledge/HomePagePublications/Qatar_NDS_reprint_complete_lowres_16May.pdf

Qatar National Vision 2030. (2008). [online]. Retrieved May 12, 2021, from http://www.mdps.gov.qa/en/qnv1/Pages/default.aspx

Qatar Olympic Committee. (2011). Sports sector strategy [online]. Retreived February 05, 2021, from http://www.aspire.qa/Document/Sports_sector_strategy_final-English.pdf

Qatar Social and Economic Survey Research Institute. (2014). Qatari attitudes towards foreign workers report [online]. Retrieved February 06, 2021, from http://sesri.qu.edu.qa/web/publications/

Qatar Social and Economic Survey Research Institute. (2015). A survey of the views of Qataris and expatriates vis-à-vis the hosting of the 2022 FIFA World Cup [online]. Retrieved September 19, 2021, from http://sesri.qu.edu.qa/web/publications/

Qatar Sports Sector Strategy 2011–2016. (n.d.). [online]. Retrieved February 05, 2021, from http://www.aspire.qa/Document/Sports_sector_strategy_final-English.pdf

Qatar's Second National Development Strategy 2018–2022. (2018). [online]. Retrieved March 06, 2021, from https://www.psa.gov.qa/en/knowledge/Documents/NDS2Final.pdf

Qatari Diar. (n.d.) East Village [online]. Retrieved March 09, 2021, from https://www.qataridiar.com/English/OurProjects/Pages/East-Village.aspx

Rahman, H. (2005). *The emergence of Qatar: The turbulent years, 1627–1916*. Routledge.

Rathmell, A., & Schulze, K. (2006). Political reform in the Gulf: The case of Qatar. *Middle Eastern Studies, 36*(4), 47–62.

Reiche, D. (2015). Investing in sporting success as a domestic and foreign policy tool: The case of Qatar. *International Journal of Sport Policy and Politics, 7*(4), 489–504.

Reiche, D. (2021, March 18). Why the FIFA World Cup 2022 in Qatar Should not be Boycotted [online]. Retrieved March 18, 2021, from https://cirs.qatar.georgetown.edu/why-the-fifa-world-cup-2022-in-qatar-should-be-not-boycotted/

Reiche, D., & Tinaz, C. (2019). Policies for naturalisation of foreign-born athletes: Qatar and Turkey in comparison. *International Journal of Sport Policy and Politics, 11*(1), 153–171.

Reporters Without Borders. (2021). Qatar media caught in information warfare [online]. Retrieved October 17, 2021, from https://rsf.org/en/qatar

Reuters. (2012, March 06). Qataris buy remaining 30 pct of Paris St Germain [online]. Retrieved January 03, 2021, from https://www.reuters.com/article/france-psg-qatar-idUSL5E8E69CP20120306

Reuters. (2014a, August 28). American released by Syrian militants thanks Qatar, U.S. officials [online]. Retrieved August 01, 2021, from http://uk.reuters.com/article/us-syria-crisis-usa-curtis-idUKKBN0GQ1GP20140828

Reuters. (2014b, August 01). Kerry seeks Qatari, Turkish help to find Israeli soldier [online]. Retrieved October 12, 2021, from http://uk.reuters.com/article/us-mideast-gaza-kerry-soldier-idUKKBN0G14KV20140801

Reuters. (2014c, March 05). UPDATE 5-Three Gulf Arab states recall envoys in rift with Qatar [online]. Retrieved June 12, 2021, from http://uk.reuters.com/article/gulf-qatar-ambassadors-idUKL6N0M21P420140305

Reuters. (2018, April 23). AS Roma, Qatar Airway multi-year shirt sponsorship worth 40 mln euros [online]. Retrieved January 17, 2021, from https://www.reuters.com/article/soccer-italy-as-roma-qatar-airways-idUSI6N1RO00W

Reuters. (2020a, October 14). Qatar investment authority bets big on private and public equity—CEO [online]. Retrieved July 09, 2021, from https://www.reuters.com/article/swf-qatar-markets-int-idUSKBN26Z2SX

Reuters. (2020b, January 27). India wants to delink Qatar gas supply deals from crude; Qatar says no [online]. Retrieved April 02, 2021, from https://www.reuters.com/article/us-india-gas-idUSKBN1ZQ0VA

Reuters. (2021a, February 08). Qatar petroleum signs deal for mega-LNG expansion [online]. Retrieved August 02, 2021, from https://www.reuters.com/article/qatar-petroleum-lng-int-idUSKBN2A81ST

Reuters. (2021b, October 14). Qatar emir appoints two women to advisory council after men sweep polls [online]. Retrieved October 14, 2021, from https://www.reuters.com/world/middle-east/qatar-emir-appoints-two-women-advisory-council-after-men-sweep-polls-2021-10-14/

Reuters. (2021c, September 08). Analysis: The west owes Qatar a favor over Afghanistan. That was the point [online]. Retrieved October 14, 2021, from https://www.reuters.com/world/west-owes-qatar-favour-over-afghanistan-that-was-point-2021-09-08/

Risse, T., & Sikkink, K. (1999). The socialization of international human rights norms into domestic practices: Introduction. *Cambridge Studies in International Relations, 66*, 1–38.

Ritzer, G. (2010). *Globalization: A basic text*. Wiley-Blackwell.

Rizzo, A. (2014). Rapid urban development and national master planning in Arab Gulf countries: Qatar as a case study. *Cities, 39*, 50–57.

Roberts, D. B. (2017). *Qatar: Securing the global ambitions of a city-state*. C Hurst & Co Publishers Ltd.

Robertson, A. (2015). *Media and politics in a globalizing world*. Polity Press.

Rowe, D. (2000). Global media events and the positioning of presence. *Media International Australia, 97*(1), 11–21.

S&P Global. (2021). Qatar signs 15-year deal to sell China 3.5 mil mt/yr LNG [online]. Retrieved October 11, 2021, from https://www.spglobal.com/platts/en/market-insights/latest-news/lng/092921-qatar-signs-15-year-deal-to-sell-china-35-mil-mtyr-lng

Samuel-Azran, T. (2013). Al-Jazeera, Qatar, and new tactics in state-sponsored media diplomacy. *American Behavioral Scientist, 57*(9), 1293–1311.

Scholte, J. A. (2005). *Globalization: A critical introduction*. Palgrave Macmillan.

SESRI (2014). Attitudes towards foriegn workers [online]. Available at: https://sesri.qu.edu.qa/static_file/qu/research/SESRI/documents/Publications/14/Qatari%20Attitudes%20Towards%20Foreign%20Workers.pdf (Accessed 17.09.21)

Sky News. (2014, November 03). Emirates ends FIFA World Cup sponsorship [online]. Retrieved March 09, 2021, from https://news.sky.com/story/emirates-ends-fifa-world-cup-sponsorship-10383904

Smith, A. D. (1999). Ethnic election and national destiny: Some religious origins of nationalist ideals. *Nations and Nationalism, 5*(3), 331–355.

Snoj, J. (2019). Population of Qatar by nationality [online]. Retrieved April 04, 2021, from http://priyadsouza.com/population-of-qatar-by-nationality-in-2017/

Snyder, R. S. (2005). Bridging the realist/constructivist divide: The case of the counterrevolution in Soviet foreign policy at the end of the Cold War. *Foreign Policy Analysis, 1*(1), 55–71.

Soft Power 30. (2019). [online]. Retrieved March 08, 2021, from https://softpower30.com/wp-content/uploads/2019/10/The-Soft-Power-30-Report-2019-1.pdf

Solberg, H. A., & Preuss, H. (2007). Major sport events and long-term tourism impacts. *Journal of sport Management, 21*(2), 213.

Sönmez, S. F. (1998). Tourism, terrorism, and political instability. *Annals of Tourism Research, 25*(2), 416–456.

State of Qatar Ministry of Planning Delivery and Statistics. (2017, June). Sports in Qatari society [online]. Retrieved Spetember 17, 2020, from https://www.psa.gov.qa/en/statistics/Statistical%20Releases/Social/Sport/2016/Sport_In_Qatar_2016_En.pdf

Steiner, C. (2007). Political instability, transnational tourist companies and destination recovery in the Middle East after 9/11. *Tourism and Hospitality Planning & Development, 4*(3), 169–190.

Steiner, C. (2010). An overestimated relationship? Violent political unrest and tourism foreign direct investment in the Middle East. *International Journal of Tourism Research, 12*(6), 726–738.

Sterling-Folker, J. (2001). Evolutionary tendencies in realist and liberal IR theory. In *Evolutionary Interpretations of World Politics* (pp. 62–109). Routledge.

Stevens, C. A. (2017). The Libyan debate: Coercive diplomacy reconsidered. *Diplomacy & Statecraft, 28*(2), 320–343.

Stoldt, G. C., Dittmore, S. W., & Branvold, S. E. (2012). *Sport public relations: Managing stakeholder communication*. Human kinetics.

Street, J. (2005). Politics lost, politics transformed, politics colonised? Theories of the impact of mass media. *Political Studies Review, 3*(1), 17–33.

Suorsa, O. (2017). Maintaining a small state's strategic space: Omnidirectional hedging, International Studies Association Hong Kong [online]. Retrieved September 12, 2021, from http://web.isanet.org/Web/Conferences/HKU2017-s/Archive/f40db849-cb90-4826-9b7a-e449b602f398.pdf

Supreme Committee for Delivery and Legacy. (n.d.). Workers' welfare standards [online]. Retrieved June 02, 2021, from https://www.qatar2022.qa/sites/default/files/docs/Workers'-Welfare-Standards.pdf

The Democracy Index. (2020). [online]. Retrieved March 12, 2021, from https://www.eiu.com/n/campaigns/democracy-index-2020/

The Economist. (2013, December 09). Doha delivers [online]. Retrieved August 13, 2021, from http://www.economist.com/blogs/freeexchange/2013/12/world-trade-organisation

The Economist. (2015, October 29). Qatar Airways begrudgingly moves with the times [online]. Retrieved November 02, 2021, from http://www.economist.com/blogs/gulliver/2015/10/qatar-heroes

The Economist. (2018, March 10). An epic search for football's next superstars [online]. Retrieved July 13, 2021, from https://www.economist.com/books-and-arts/2018/03/10/an-epic-search-for-footballs-next-superstars

The Guardian. (2010, December 03). Football crosses new frontier as Qatar wins World Cup vote for 2022 [online]. Retrieved January 11, 2021, from https://www.theguardian.com/football/2010/dec/03/qatar-world-cup-2022

The Guardian. (2011a, August 12). Olympic Village snapped up by Qatari ruling family for £557m [online]. Retrieved July 16, 2021, from https://www.theguardian.com/sport/2011/aug/12/olympic-village-qatari-ruling-family

The Guardian. (2011b, July 11). World Cup corruption claims fuelled by prejudice, says Qatar bid chief [online]. Retrieved May 12, 2021, from https://www.theguardian.com/football/2011/jul/11/world-cup-corruption-prejudice-qatar-bid

The Guardian. (2012, December 12). Qatar promises fans to take the heat out of 2022 World Cup [online]. Retrieved May 12, 2021, from https://www.theguardian.com/football/2012/dec/12/qatar-cool-2022-world-cup

The Guardian. (2013a, November 17). Qatar 2022 World Cup workers 'treated like cattle', Amnesty report finds [online]. Retrieved June 29, 2021, from https://www.theguardian.com/world/2013/nov/17/qatar-world-cup-worker-amnesty-report

The Guardian. (2013b, September 25). Revealed: Qatar's World Cup 'slaves' [online]. Retrieved September 03, 2021, from https://www.theguardian.com/world/2013/sep/25/revealed-qatars-world-cup-slaves

The Guardian. (2014a, November 03). Fifa confirms 2022 World Cup in Qatar is likely to be held in winter [online]. Retrieved June 12, 2021, from https://www.theguardian.com/football/2014/nov/03/fifa-qatar-2022-world-cup-winter

The Guardian. (2014b, June 20). Qatar had the strongest bid for the 2022 Fifa World Cup. Here's why [online]. Retrieved March 21, 2021, from https://www.theguardian.com/commentisfree/2014/jun/20/why-qatar-had-strongest-bid-for-2022-fifa-world-cup

The Guardian. (2014c, December 17). Qatar hires migrant workers as 'fake sports fans' to fill up empty arenas [online]. Retrieved December 12, 2021, from   https://www.theguardian.com/sport/2014/dec/17/qatar-migrant-workers-fake-sports-fans

The Guardian. (2014d, June 15). Qatar hits back at allegations of bribery over 2022 World Cup [online]. Retrieved November 16, 2015, from https://www.theguardian.com/football/2014/jun/15/qatar-world-cup-bid-2022

The Guardian. (2014e, July 29). Qatar World Cup stadium workers earn as little as 45p an hour [online]. Retrieved February 09, 2021, from https://www.theguardian.com/global-development/2014/jul/29/qatar-world-cup-stadium-workers-earn-45p-hour

The Guardian. (2014f, August 24). US denies paying ransom as Qatar secures release of journalist in Syria [online]. Retrieved February 02, 2021, from https://www.theguardian.com/world/2014/aug/24/us-denies-ransom-qatar-peter-theo-curtis-syria

The Guardian. (2014g, June 01). World Cup raising Qatar's profile for all the wrong reasons [online]. Retrieved June 17, 2021, from https://www.theguardian.com/football/2014/jun/01/2022-world-cup-qatar-fifa

The Guardian. (2015a, December 21). Sepp Blatter and Michel Platini banned from football for eight years by Fifa [onine]. Retrieved March 14, 2021, from https://www.theguardian.com/football/2015/dec/21/sepp-blatter-michel-platini-banned-from-football-fifa

The Guardian. (2015b, March 20). Fifa's Sepp Blatter says 2018 World Cup in Russia will stabilise region [online]. Retrieved May 19, 2021, from https://www.theguardian.com/football/2015/mar/20/fifa-sepp-blatter-2018-world-cup-russia-peace-region

The Guardian. (2015c, May 14). Qatar claims life improving for World Cup workers, but rights groups sceptical [online]. Retrieved August 11, 2021, from https://www.theguardian.com/world/2015/may/14/qatar-claims-life-improving-for-world-cup-workers-but-rights-groups-demur

The Guardian. (2016, December 13). Migrant workers in Qatar still at risk despite reforms, warns Amnesty [online]. Retrieved January 18, 2021, from https://www.theguardian.com/global-development/2016/dec/13/migrant-workers-in-qatar-still-at-risk-despite-reforms-warns-amnesty

The Guardian. (2017, February 07). Qatar spending $500m a week on World Cup projects [online]. Retrieved March 06, 2021, from https://www.theguardian.com/football/2017/feb/08/qatar-spending-500m-a-week-on-world-cup-projects-2022

The Guardian. (2019, March 10). Fifa facing urgent calls to investigate Qatar World Cup bid claims [online]. Retrieved February 17, 2021, from https://www.theguardian.com/football/2019/mar/10/qatar-fifa-world-cup-2022-damian-collins

The Guardian. (2020). New labour law ends Qatar's exploitative kafala system, 1st September [online]. Available at: https://www.theguardian.com/global-development/2020/sep/01/newemployment-law-effectively-ends-qatars-exploitative-kafala-system. (Accessed 09.05.21)

The Independent. (2010, December 02). Shock as Qatar win vote for 2022 World Cup [online]. Retrieved September 02, 2021, from http://www.independent.co.uk/sport/football/news-and-comment/shock-as-qatar-win-vote-for-2022-world-cup-2149429.html

The Independent. (2013, April 09). Largest shirt sponsorship deals [online]. Retrieved July 12, 2021, from https://www.independent.co.uk/sport/football/news/ps160m-aon-training-ground-deal-ensures-manchester-united-stretch-lead-over-city-global-branding-league-8565102.html

The Independent. (2018, December 19). Qatar 2022: A reputation irrovocably damged, what has a minor Gulf state to gain from hosting the World Cup? [online]. Retrieved March 09, 2021, from https://www.independent.co.uk/sport/football/world-cup/qatar-world-cup-2022-host-bid-reputation-cost-soft-power-a8690366.html

The Independent. (2021a, August 10). Singapore dethroned as world's best airport after eight years on top [online]. Retrieved October 12, 2021, from https://www.independent.co.uk/travel/news-and-advice/best-airport-doha-qatar-singapore-changi-b1900045.html

The Independent. (2021b, March 25). Qatar builds entire new city in preperation for World Cup [online]. Retrieved October 13, 2021, from https://www.independent.co.uk/travel/news-and-advice/qatar-lusail-new-city-world-cup-2022-tourists-b1822413.html

The Independent. (2021c, October 06). Newcastle: Saudi-backed takeoever nears completion after broadcast dispute settled [online]. Retrieved November 01, 2021, from https://www.independent.co.uk/sport/football/newcastle-takeover-saudi-arabia-broadcast-b1933612.html

The New York Times. (2003, April 28). US will move air operations to Qatar base [online]. Retrieved April 11, 2021, from https://www.nytimes.com/2003/04/28/world/aftereffects-bases-us-will-move-air-operations-to-qatar-base.html

The New York Times. (2008, April 30). Emir of Qatar tours New Orleans to see fruit of his £100 million donations [online]. Retrieved February 17, 2021, from http://www.nytimes.com/2008/04/30/us/nationalspecial/30emir.html

The New York Times. (2014, November 23). Sudan and Rebels in Darfur begin peace talks [online]. Retrieved February 02, 2021, from https://www.nytimes.

com/2014/11/24/world/africa/sudan-and-rebels-in-darfur-region-begin-peace-talks.html

The New York Times. (2015a, March 19). FIFA confirms winter World Cup for 2022 [online]. Retrieved September 05, 2021, from https://www.nytimes.com/2015/03/20/sports/soccer/fifa-confirms-winter-world-cup-for-2022.html

The New York Times. (2015b, June 02). Sepp Blatter decides to resign as FIFA President [online]. Retrieved February 14, 2021, from https://www.nytimes.com/2015/06/03/sports/soccer/sepp-blatter-to-resign-as-fifa-president.html

The New York Times. (2018, August 17). U.S. imposes sanctions on Myanmar military over Rohingya [online]. Retrieved July 07, 2021, from https://www.nytimes.com/2018/08/17/us/politics/myanmar-sanctions-rohingya.html

The New York Times. (2020, April 06). U.S. says FIFA officials were bribed to award World Cups [online]. Retrieved April 11, 2021, from https://www.nytimes.com/2020/04/06/sports/soccer/qatar-and-russia-bribery-world-cup-fifa.html

The New York Times. (2021, September 07). From Afghanistan to the World Cup, tiny, wealthy Qatar steps up [online]. Retrieved October 14, 2021, from https://www.nytimes.com/2021/09/07/world/middleeast/afghanistan-qatar-airlift.html

The Peninsula. (2019, December 22). Qatar presented one of most successful FIFA Club World Cup tournaments: SC [online]. Retrieved January 07, 2020, from https://thepeninsulaqatar.com/article/22/12/2019/Qatar-presented-one-of-most-successful-FIFA-Club-World-Cup-tournaments-SC

The Peninsula. (2020, July 20). Spanish star Cazorla hails Xavi as signs on at Qatar's Al-Sadd: Club [online]. Retrieved January 17, 2021, from https://thepeninsulaqatar.com/article/07/08/2020/Spanish-star-Cazorla-hails-Xavi-as-signs-on-at-Qatar-s-Al-Sadd-club

The Peninsula. (2021a, April 25). 1,100 electric buses to ferry FIFA World Cup 2022 fans [online]. Retrieved August 18, 2021, from https://thepeninsulaqatar.com/article/25/04/2021/1,100-electric-buses-to-ferry-FIFA-World-Cup-2022-fans

The Peninsula. (2021b, March 28). Qatar among first countries to implement expanded bubble system for sport events [online]. Retrieved April 18, 2021, from https://thepeninsulaqatar.com/article/28/03/2021/Qatar-among-first-countries-to-implement-expanded-bubble-system-for-sport-events

The Sun. (2011, July 22). Should Qatar host the 2022 World Cup? [online]. Retrieved April 18, 2021, from https://www.thesun.co.uk/archives/news/680064/should-qatar-host-the-2022-world-cup/

The Sunday Times. (2014a, November 24). England's secret file on 'Russia and Qatar World Cup vote fixing' [online]. Retrieved January 03, 2021, from https://www.thetimes.co.uk/article/englands-secret-file-on-russia-and-qatar-world-cup-vote-fixing-pwhxb9zn03v

The Sunday Times. (2014b, June 01). Plot to buy the World Cup [online]. Retrieved December 14, 2021, from https://www.thetimes.co.uk/article/plot-to-buy-the-world-cup-lvxdg2v7l7w

The Sunday Times. (2014c, June 15). Security expert's warning: Tiny Qatar is wide open to attack [online]. Retrieved Febrary 17, 2021, from https://www.thetimes.co.uk/article/security-experts-warning-tiny-qatar-is-wide-open-to-attack-q6hv35pddbj

The Sunday Times. (2015, April 19). Fifa admits fixer helped Qatar cup bid [online]. Retrieved August 06, 2021, from https://www.thetimes.co.uk/article/fifa-admits-fixer-helped-qatar-cup-bid-f9xl3nxfxrx

The Sunday Times. (2019, March 10). Take it or leave it: Qatar's lucrative World Cup offer to FIFA [online]. Retrieved February 04, 2021, from https://www.thetimes.co.uk/article/take-it-or-leave-it-qatars-lucrative-world-cup-offer-to-fifa-qdj5fkxxm

The Telegraph. (2014a, December 17). Fifa report into World Cup bid process 'misrepresented' says investigator Michael Garcia [online]. Retrieved May 13, 2021, from http://www.telegraph.co.uk/sport/football/world-cup/11228523/Fifa-has-misrepresented-my-report-says-investigator.html

The Telegraph. (2014b, September 20). How Qatar is funding the rise of Islamist extremists [online]. Retrieved October 11, 2021, from http://www.telegraph.co.uk/news/worldnews/middleeast/qatar/11110931/How-Qatar-is-funding-the-rise-of-Islamist-extremists.html

The Telegraph. (2015a, March 19). World Cup 2022 final in Qatar will be on December 18 [online]. Retrieved May 26, 2021, from https://www.telegraph.co.uk/sport/football/world-cup/11483629/World-Cup-2022-final-in-Qatar-will-be-on-December-18.html

The Telegraph. (2015b, February 24). Qatar 2022 World Cup—the logistical nightmare before Christmas that will make Die Hard 2 look tame [online]. Retrieved March 27, 2021, from https://www.telegraph.co.uk/sport/football/world-cup/11432515/Qatar-2022-World-Cup-the-logistical-nightmare-before-Christmas-that-will-make-Die-Hard-2-look-tame.html

The Telegraph. (2015c, February 10). Assad is an enemy of Isil, but not the West's ally [online]. Retrieved August 05, 2021, from http://www.telegraph.co.uk/news/worldnews/middleeast/syria/11403949/Assad-is-an-enemy-of-Isil-but-not-the-Wests-ally.html

The Times. (2021, March 30). Qatar 2022: FA caught in dilemma over Qatar as protests show World Cup scandal still unresolved [online]. Retrieved August 14, 2021, from https://www.thetimes.co.uk/article/qatar-2022-player-protests-show-world-cup-scandal-still-unresolved-3x5lj55wj

The Wall Street Journal. (2021, April 25). How Qatar Airways, with its Covid-19 playbook, dethroned Emirates as biggest long-haul airline [online]. Retrieved July 19, 2021, from https://www.wsj.com/articles/how-qatar-airways-with-its-pandemic-playbook-dethroned-emirates-as-biggest-long-haul-airline-11619348400

The Washington Post. (2015, May 27). (UPDATED) The toll of human casualities in Qatar [online]. Retrieved June 05, 2021, from https://www.washingtonpost.com/news/wonk/wp/2015/05/27/a-body-count-in-qatar-illustrates-the-consequences-of-fifa-corruption/?utm_term=.35a00a25b997

Timms, D. (2003). Dyke Attacks unquestioning US media, The Guardian, 24 April [online]. Available at: https://www.theguardian.com/media/2003/apr/24/bbc.communicationsact (Accessed 15.01.21)

Tsaliki, L., Huliaras, A., & Frangonikolopoulos, C. A. (Eds.). (2011). *Transnational celebrity activism in global politics changing the world?* Intellect.

Turner, E. A. (2010). Why has the number of international non-governmental organizations exploded since 1960?. *Cliodynamics, 1*(1).

UK Government. (2019). Trends in trade of Liquefied Natural Gas in the UK and Europe [onine]. Available at: https://assets.publishing.service.gov.uk/government/uploads/system/uploads/attachment_data/file/875383/Trends_in_trade_of_Liquefied_Natural_Gas_in_the_UK_and_Europe.pdf (Accessed 12.04.20)

U.S. Embassy in Qatar @USEmbassyDoha. (2021, March 10). The U.S. Embassy values its partnership with @ADLSAQa and supports Qatar's new minimum wage legislation, the first of its kind in the region [online]. Retrieved March 10, 2021, from https://twitter.com/USEmbassyDoha/status/1369546352762437633?s=20

U.S. Energy Information Database. (2019). Qatar [online]. Retrieved May 13, 2021, from https://www.eia.gov/international/overview/country/QAT

U.S. News. (2021). Overall Best Countries Ranking 2021 Rankings [online]. Retrieved October 15, 2021, from https://www.usnews.com/news/best-countries/overall-rankings

Ulrichsen, K. C. (2017). What's going on with Qatar?. *The Qatar Crisis* [online]. Retrieved July 13, 2021, from https://www.researchgate.net/profile/Youssef-Cherif-2/publication/340741312_Everyone_is_Taking_Sides_in_the_Qatar_Crisis_Here_is_Why_these_Four_North_African_States_Aren't/links/5ea01b284585150839f41ba7/Everyone-is-Taking-Sides-in-the-Qatar-Crisis-Here-is-Why-these-Four-North-African-States-Arent.pdf#page=7

Ulrichsen, K. C. (2020). *Qatar and the gulf crisis: A study of resilience.* Oxford University Press.

Ulrichsen, K. C. (2021). The Impact of the Lifting of the Blockade on the Qatar World Cup, 24 Janurary, Centre for International and Regional Studies [online]. Available at: https://cirs.qatar.georgetown.edu/the-impact-of-the-lifting-of-the-blockade-on-the-qatar-world-cup/ (Accessed 24.08.21).

UNDP Human Deveopment Index. (2019). Annual Report [online]. Available at: https://hdr.undp.org/sites/default/files/hdr2019.pdf (Accessed 12.03.20)

United Nations, World Tourism Barometer. (2019). [online]. Retrieved May 02, 2021, from https://www.unwto.org/world-tourism-barometer-2019-nov

Vincent, N. (2021, May 16). Qatar Airways' football sponsorships as a foreign policy strategy [online]. Retrieved May 27, 2021, from https://cirs.qatar.georgetown.edu/qatar-airways-football-sponsorships-as-a-foreign-policy-strategy/

Wanta, W., Golan, G., & Lee, C. (2004). Agenda setting and international news: Media influence on public perceptions of foreign nations. *Journalism & Mass Communication Quarterly, 81*(2), 364–377.

Webster, F. (2002). *Theories of the information society* (2nd ed.). Routledge.

West, M. D. (2008). *Secrets, sex, and spectacle*. Illionois: University of Chicago Press.

Winckler, O. (1997). The immigration policy of the Gulf Cooperation Council (GCC) states. *Middle Eastern Studies, 33*, 481–493.

Wood, J., & Meng, S. (2020). The economic impacts of the 2018 Winter Olympics. *Tourism Economics*. https://doi.org/10.1177/1354816620921577

World Bank. (2019). Land Area—Qatar [online]. Retrieved April 07, 2021, from https://data.worldbank.org/indicator/AG.LND.TOTL.K2?name_desc=true&locations=QA

World Health Organization. (2017). Qatar [online]. Available at: https://apps.who.int/iris/rest/bitstreams/1139345/retrieve (Accessed 17.01.20)

World Trade Organization. (2004). Income volatility in small and developing economies: Export concentration matters [online]. Retrieved February 03, 2021, from https://www.wto.org/english/res_e/booksp_e/discussion_papers3_e.pdf

World Travel and Tourism Council Report. (2017). Coping with success [online]. Retrieved March 08, 2021, from https://wttc.org/Portals/0/Documents/Reports/2017/Coping%20With%20Success%20-%20Managing%20Overcrowding%20in%20Tourism%20Destinations%202017.pdf?ver=2021-02-26-192645-677

Wright, S. (2011). Qatar. In C. M. Davidson (Ed.), *Power and politics in the Persian Gulf monarchies*. Columbia University Press.

Wright, S. (2012). Foreign policies with international reach: The case of Qatar. In D. Held & K. Ulrichsen (Eds.), *The transformation of the Gulf: Politics, economics and the global order*. Routledge.

Zaccara, L. (2021). Political participation in Qatar: The Central Municipal Council Elections (1999–2019). In *Contemporary Qatar* (pp. 39–57). Springer.

Zahlan, A. (1979). The Arab brain drain. *Population bulletin of the United Nations Economic Commission for Western Asia, 16*, 19–38.

Zahlan, R. S. (2016). *The creation of Qatar*. Routledge.

Zhang, C., & Meadows, C. W., III. (2012). International coverage, foreign policy, and national image: Exploring the complexities of media coverage, public opinion, and presidential agenda. *International Journal of Communication, 6*, 20.

Index[1]

---

[1] Note: Page numbers followed by 'n' refer to notes.

Printed by Printforce, United Kingdom